SOLVING
BEHAVIOR
PROBLEMS
— AT HOME & AT SCHOOL —

ELAINE A. BLECHMAN

Research Press
2612 North Mattis Avenue
Champaign, Illinois 61821

Advisory Editor, Frederick H. Kanfer

Research for this book has been supported in part by the NIMH fund (MH 31403).

Cover design by Ruth Downes

Composition by Graphix Group, Inc.

ISBN 0-87822-247-2

Library of Congress Catalog Card Number 85-61468

To
Wolf Atkins & Sara Atkins Rosenfield

Contents

List of Modules vii

Preface ix

Acknowledgments xi

1 Solutions to Child Behavior Problems 1

2 Family Competence and Child Behavior Problems 23

3 The Family Meeting 31

4 Solving Problems at Home 45

5 Solving Problems at School 195

Bibliography 269

About the Author 283

List of Modules

The Home-Problem Modules

Module 1: Assessment 49
Module 2: Putting Clothes and Toys Away 60
Module 3: Bedtime 66
Module 4: Toileting 76
Module 5: Temper Tantrums 88
Module 6: Fights Between Children 100
Module 7: Following Instructions 107
Module 8: Good Behavior Away from Home 116
Module 9: School Attendance 125
Module 10: Chores and Allowances 142
Module 11: Homework, Reading, and Television 150
Module 12: Loneliness, Unhappiness, Fearfulness, and
            Self-Injury 161
Module 13: Swearing, Lying, Cheating, Stealing,
            Fire Setting, and Violence 182

The School-Problem Modules

Module 1: Assembling a Home-School Team 201
Module 2: Assessment 212
Module 3: Improving Academic Performance 225
Module 4: Improving School Behavior 248

Preface

Children with behavior problems deserve more in the way of treatment than training to conform quietly to the demands of poorly functioning homes and schools. Contemporary behavior therapy aspires to reshape the social environment, so that family and classroom foster children's social, emotional, and intellectual competence. The solutions presented in this book aim to promote environmental change and foster competence by improving adults' and children's communication, problem solving, and behavior-management skills.

Women are usually the ones to seek help for child behavior problems. Even in the two-parent family, mothers are more likely to participate in treatment than fathers. As a result, behavioral family therapy has two obligations: to involve both mothers and fathers in the treatment process and to structure the treatment process so that it not only resolves child behavior problems, but also enhances parents' competence outside of the family, in the workplace, and in the community. This means that the success of the solutions presented in this book requires that the solutions do more than just resolve a child's problems. They should also teach couples to share childrearing and to be enriched by the experience.

Behavior therapists have typically approached the training of parents and teachers by explaining abstract behavior analysis and reinforcement principles and showing how these principles can resolve child behavior problems. The approach I have taken is different. I present problems of the sort that frequently perplex parents and teachers and then describe the steps involved in resolving these problems. In a manner consistent with contemporary behavior therapy, I show how the severity of problems can be assessed, how solutions can be tailored to suit the needs of home and school, and how the efficacy of solutions can be measured. Some parents will deduce abstract principles from the solutions I present; others will not. My experience leads me to believe that, even without such deductions, this book will provide most parents and teachers with useful responses to their most pressing questions about children's behavior.

Some parents and teachers who want to improve their skills and whose problems with children are minor will use this book for self-help. Since self-help books are fraught with dangers for the novice, readers are cautioned about how to evaluate the impact of their efforts and about when to seek professional advice. The book is also intended to be used by professionals in consultation with parents and teachers who face serious child behavior problems. The book can be put to a third use, structuring school-based prevention and intervention programs.

Although I have already conducted studies evaluating the solutions described in this book, further research on these solutions, and the development of solutions for the behavior problems of adolescents and of physically ill youth, are likely to keep my laboratory busy for a number of years to come.

This is a book that I have long needed for clinical work with children and parents, consultation with teachers and school administrators, supervision of mental-health, medical, and education professionals, and informal contacts with friends and neighbors about their families. In my eyes, the book has achieved its immediate purpose if it provides practical, concrete advice to parents, teachers, and therapists about the resolution of child behavior problems and at the same time sensitizes the reader to the need for treatments that enhance children's competence and their families' effectiveness.

Acknowledgments

I have left the writing of these acknowledgments for last, making it all the more delightful to recall the people who shaped my point of view about families and about behavior change. My family: Reva Blechman and Arthur Beck. My UCLA mentors: Chuck Nakamura, Lenore Love, and Gertrude Baker. My Middletown, CT colleagues: Steve Bank and Dave Audette. My NIMH colleagues: Teresa Levitin and Joy Schulterbrandt. My Wesleyan research team: Elaine Carella and Mike McEnroe. My friends on the shoreline of Connecticut: the Ehrenkranzes and Scholnicks and the TBT softball team and its MVPs. Fred Kanfer encouraged me to write this book. Ann Wendel at Research Press put up with my slow progress, and Mary Wolf did a marvelous job of editing. Cyril Franks, Jim Alexander, and Sheila Eyberg were kind enough to comment on portions of the manuscript.

1

Solutions to Child Behavior Problems

This book is written for therapists, parents, and teachers who want to prevent child behavior problems, resolve problems while they are still minor, and treat major problems in the child's own home and class-room. The approach to solving behavior problems presented in this book is called Family Skill Training. Family Skill Training is a form of behavioral family therapy and a modification of Parent Training, a well-established behavior therapy subspecialty. While Parent Training teaches new skills to parents and focuses on problems at home, Family Skill Training can involve the entire family and the child's teachers, and it can confront home and school problems. The aim of Family Skill Training is to help parents and teachers become self-sufficient experts at solving child behavior problems.

This training guides family members and teachers through the solution of common and less common child behavior problems. Partici-pants in Family Skill Training learn elementary principles of child development, behavior assessment, behavior change, and group prob-lem solving. Adults learn how to identify what child behaviors are associated with healthy psychological development, what to do about behavioral problems that pose real threats to child and family compe-tence, and how to remedy child behavior problems in a way that strengthens family cohesiveness.

Family Skill Training has a number of advantages for children, parents, teachers, and therapists over child psychotherapy. Traditional one-on-one child psychotherapy is lengthy, expensive, and its effects are often limited and fleeting. In contrast, behavioral approaches that train adults in the child's natural environment (either parents, teachers, or the whole family) are briefer, less expensive, and offer the possibility of more extensive and more enduring benefits.

1

Tharp and Wetzel, pioneer researchers in parent training, recognized that individual psychotherapy with children has only limited benefits, since children spend only a fraction of their time each week with a therapist. In their book, *Behavior Modification in the Natural Environment,* they discuss an experiment at an institution for delinquent children in which they trained adults to reward honest, cooperative behavior with attention, approval, and enjoyable activities. The result was diminished antisocial behavior. Gerald Patterson, in the books *Families* and *Living with Children,* developed methods of parent training that are especially suited to families of aggressive children and evaluated the effects of these procedures in a number of important studies. His results and those of others strongly suggest that when the most important adults in a child's life learn to promote desirable behavior, suppress undesirable behavior, and arrange the child's environment so that new skills are strengthened, traditional child psychotherapy often becomes unnecessary.

In the past, behavior modification approaches to child treatment have been criticized for treating problems out of context, for neglecting developmental goals, and for ignoring the way in which family and school systems encourage deviance. The solutions to child behavior problems in this book are designed not only to eliminate behavior problems but also to enhance children's happiness and psychological development. They are also designed to encourage adults to become more competent at managing their own lives. Solutions are presented in small steps that guide parents, teachers, and therapists as they assess and resolve a broad range of home and school problems. Rather than having children "sit still and be quiet," this approach focuses on the promotion of competent behavior and of solutions likely to contribute to a better functioning family and school. If this book's stepwise approach to problem solving is adopted, criticisms to behavior modification should be overcome, and satisfactory treatment of the whole child should result.

The following chapters present a brief rationale for this approach to solving child behavior problems; prepare parents, teachers, and therapists for problem solving; and provide two sets of modules, one containing solutions for problems at home, the second, for problems at school. Chapter 2 discusses how families of different skill levels may benefit from the solutions in this book. Chapter 3 presents information about the family meetings in which home problems are discussed by family members. Chapter 4 contains the Home-Problem Modules, written for parents who are confronting home problems with a therapist or on their own. Chapter 5 contains the School-Problem Modules, written for therapists, teachers, and parents who are concerned about children's problems at school. A bibliography of readings arranged by chapter follows Chapter 5.

This chapter begins with a few examples of common child behavior problems and considers how behavior problems might originate and some obstacles to their solution. How adults influence children to change and elementary principles of behavior change are then related to the solutions presented in this book.

Examples of Child Behavior Problems

In every family, important new problems emerge as family members grow older, as members join and leave the family, and as outside pressures on individuals and on the group grow and diminish. Every couple faces some childrearing problems, such as deciding which parent should feed the baby at night, toilet train the toddler, take care of a sick child, supervise homework, or discipline children. Every parent responsible for childrearing must decide what to do when an infant cries (pick her up or let her cry), how to toilet train a toddler (provide examples and praise or wait for her to figure out what to do herself), and how to care for a sick child (nurse the child or teach the child to be more and more responsible for her own health care). Child behavior problems are also a routine part of classroom teaching, just as they are a routine part of childrearing. Here are some examples of child behavior problems faced by parents and teachers that are considered in this book.

"My 8-year-old son wakes up with a stomachache every weekday morning, although the doctor says he is perfectly healthy. This week he simply refused to go to school. What should I do?"

"My 12-year-old son beats up my 10-year-old daughter every time I turn my back. I keep taking away my son's bike and his television privileges but that seems to have no effect."

"No one listens to me. I've told the children over and over that I expect them to keep their rooms clean, do their chores, and show me their homework each weekday, but they don't do a thing without being reminded. In fact, the children act just like my husband."

"Every time I ask for help, some expert gives my child a different label. But nobody tells me what to do to help him. I've been told that my 7-year-old son has a learning disability and Tourette's syndrome and attention-deficit disorder. All I know is that he doesn't mind me or his teachers, he yells and hits people whenever he pleases, and he uses gutter language."

"Since my husband and I split up, my children have gotten worse and worse grades at school. I'm really worried about my 11-year-old. She used to be a top student, and now she is failing math and science. On top of that, she's developed a real sullen, angry attitude toward me. I've asked her teacher for advice, but the teacher seems to feel that short of remarriage there is nothing I can do to help her. Can the teacher be right?"

"My 9-year-old son has been tested by the school because his teacher says he is slow catching on to new ideas and lazy. The school psychologist says he doesn't have a learning disability and doesn't qualify for extra help outside the classroom. Can't his classroom teacher do something to get him to work harder?"

"I've been married for 14 years and my relationship with my husband has gone from bad to worse in that time. He wants everything done his way and he doesn't hesitate to tell me I'm stupid if I disagree with him. Our 11-year-old never does what I ask and has had a lot of trouble with his teachers this year. They complain that he's got a surly attitude. I know that, but I don't know what to do about it."

"My wife walked out on me after 5 years of marriage, leaving me to raise our 3-year-old daughter. I think I've done a good job with her, but now that she's approaching adolescence, I want to be sure. Because my ex-wife is so moody and has attempted suicide a few times, I'm particularly concerned about my daughter's moods. How can I tell the difference between normal teenaged irritability and serious depression?"

"My son was diagnosed as hyperactive when he was 3 and treated with medication until he was 7. For the last 3 years, he's been in play therapy. His teachers complain that he is always restless and that he demands constant attention. He's a very sad boy with no friends. The school wants to place him in a residential treatment center, but I'm afraid he'll be even unhappier away from home than he is now."

"A lot of the children in my sixth-grade classroom just never do homework. I've tried talking to their parents, but they don't know how to get their children to do their homework either. What could I advise these parents to do?"

"I have one student in my fourth-grade class who worries me a lot. He is in the top reading and math groups, but he disrupts the class by clowning around just about every day. When I send him to the principal's office, he ends up kidding around with the principal's secretary. I've asked for him to be tested, but it will be months before the testing is completed. What can I do for him until he is tested?"

"A 7-year-old boy in my class is the son of recent immigrants who speak little English. The boy is often teased because of the way he talks and dresses. The only way he seems to be able to deal with teasing is through violence. Last week he broke another boy's arm. I'm not sure we'll be able to keep him in school unless he cools down.''

A child has a behavior problem when someone is dissatisfied with what the child does or doesn't do. There are two kinds of child behavior problems: behavior excesses and behavior deficits. Excesses or deficits can be in actions (too much fidgeting in class, too little smiling) or speech (too much complaining, too little problem solving) or in the permanent products of behavior (too many wet sheets, too many failing grades on math tests, too many pounds gained in 1 month, too few completed homework assignments, too few invitations to friends' houses).

Usually, a parent, a teacher, or a neighbor is dissatisfied with the child's behavior. Rarely do children, without any prompting, express dissatisfaction with their own behavior, although children who have been criticized by adults do talk about their own shortcomings. Among adolescents, self-criticism is very common, even more common than among adults, but adolescents are less aware of solutions for behavior problems than are adults and less likely to seek help on their own. As a result, complaints about the behavior problems of children and early adolescents come almost exclusively from adults.

The way children think or feel can also be problematic. Problems with the way they think or feel are evident in children's actions, speech, and permanent behavior products. When asked to draw a house, for example, a boy who isn't a creative thinker always looks for a picture of a house to copy. A girl who feels sad rarely talks about pleasant things she's done. A boy who feels unsure of himself tears his homework up and refuses to hand it in to the teacher.

Adults sometimes disagree about children's behavior problems. One couple considers their son well-behaved, while his teacher considers the boy a monster. A father worries about his daughter's fear of dogs—after interviewing and observing her, the psychologist he consults tells the father that his daughter is bright and outgoing and that her fear of dogs is a minor problem that she will soon outgrow. A school psychologist surprises a mother by telling her that her son performs far below his potential in reading and math.

Disagreements about child behavior problems often arise because different adults have different standards for child behavior (some adults are more tolerant of children's behavior than others), different information (some adults know more about normal child development and about methods of changing children's behavior than others), different opportunities to observe the child (some see the child in her home, others in the classroom, and others outside with her friends at play), and different past experiences with the child (some have known the child all her life, others have just met her).

Chapters 4 and 5 provide parents, teachers, and therapists with one approach they can all use to measure children's actions, speech, and the permanent products of their behavior. This common measurement approach makes it likely that all adults will agree about the presence of significant child behavior problems and about the success of solutions for these problems.

Origins of Child Behavior Problems

Child behavior problems can come about in several ways. Some child behavior problems are directly caused by actions of the family. One father teaches his son to lie, for example, by always punishing the boy when he volunteers information about mistakes he has made. Another father teaches his son to be honest by praising all of his voluntary admissions of errors and by reserving the most severe punishments for times when his son breaks important rules and doesn't own up to his misbehavior.

Other child behavior problems have their origin in events outside of the family's control, and the course that the behavior problem takes is influenced by the family's parenting procedures. From birth, babies' temperaments differ; some babies are fussier and more irritable than other babies. One mother teaches her fussy baby daughter to become a temperamental child by picking her up and comforting her every single time that she cries. In contrast, another mother teaches her fussy baby daughter to become a happy and outgoing child by picking her up and playing with her every time that she smiles and gurgles.

Some child behavior problems are caused by events outside the family's control, and the initial development of the problem is influenced very little by the family. Even in these cases, resolution of the problem requires the family's involvement. School-aged boys sometimes develop a problem called encopresis, in which they retain feces, become constipated, and intermittently soil. The tendency to develop this bowel dysfunction may be genetic, and it is usually brought on or exacerbated when teachers prevent boys from visiting the toilet on demand or when young boys are harassed by older boys while using the toilet. Neither of these causes of dysfunction can be blamed on parents. Nevertheless, a good resolution of the problem does require considerable effort on the parents' part, including advocacy for the child at school.

Obstacles to Solving Child Behavior Problems

Each solution for a child behavior problem proposed in this book is a two-part task. The first part of the task involves convincing parents, teachers, and children themselves that child behavior problems can be solved. The second part of the task involves instructing parents, teachers, and children in the specifics of the solutions and helping them make these solutions work.

Belief that children can't change or learn

Many people believe that children's behavior problems are inherited, and therefore can't be helped. If a 12-year-old boy wets his bed at night just like his father did as a boy or if a 6-year-old girl is as shy as her mother is, people tend to conclude that bad genes are at fault.

Although it is difficult to decide how much influence heredity has on behavior, it is safe to say that all human behavior is affected by heredity and environment. This book focuses on ways of changing the environment to resolve child behavior problems, including problems resulting from heredity, trauma, accident, or illness.

There are differences between children in how fast they can learn, in how many new skills they can learn, and in their best method of learning. For example, a few children are natural athletes who can learn many sports-related activities very quickly. A few children are natural students who can learn many school-related activities very quickly. Some children are learning disabled; they must work very hard to master school-related tasks. Some children have delayed social development; they must work very hard to learn to deal with other people. Fortunately, children with a weakness in one area often have a strength in another. It is not at all unusual to find a learning-disabled boy who is a natural athlete or a girl who has trouble making friends who is a natural student.

Despite differences in learning potential and learning style, each child is capable of behavior change. Each child can learn new behaviors and new skills (chains of behaviors) in order to accomplish important tasks. For example, holding a two-wheel bicycle steady before mounting may be a new behavior, bicycle riding, a new skill, and delivering newspapers from the bicycle, an important task.

Despite the cause of the problem, every childhood behavior problem can be remedied, to some extent, by helping the child to learn new skills that compete with the problem behavior. The problems of an angry, unhappy boy with few interests or friends might be remedied by his learning to ride and maintain a bicycle, getting a job delivering newspapers, dealing with customers, and managing the money earned from the job.

New skills can be helpful even with problems that are rooted in family history or parental inadequacy. A 12-year-old boy might learn to wake up when his bladder is full rather than wet his bed, even if his dad used to wet the bed. A 6-year-old girl might learn to approach and talk to other 6-year-old girls and to take part in their game of tag, even if her mom is very shy.

Many of the solutions presented in this book focus on skill training, not by directly teaching the child new skills, but by arranging conditions in such a way that the learning of these skills is very likely. For example, the module on putting clothes and toys away in Chapter 4 arranges conditions in the home in such a way that children are encouraged to learn to care for their belongings without reminders, and parents learn to focus on child-created household clutter only once during the day.

Preoccupation with the past

One of the biggest obstacles to remedying child behavior problems is a preoccupation with historical causes and a belief that encouraging children to remember significant past events is necessary for resolution of behavior problems.

Children rarely do understand the origin of their difficulties, although with subtle persuasion they will often say what adults want to hear, confirming adults' psychological theories. There is no evidence to confirm the idea that when children recall supposedly significant past events in their lives their behavior problems move swiftly to resolution.

Some causes of child behavior problems cannot be altered. Nothing can be done to alter a divorce that has contributed to a boy's overdependence upon his mother, although his mother can learn to encourage increasingly self-sufficient behavior. Also, the historical causes of behavior problems can never be known for sure. No one can ever prove that an 8-year-old boy's speech disorder was caused by the births of his three younger brothers and early demands upon him for self-reliance. His parents can learn, though, to encourage more effective communication.

As Chapter 3 indicates, a therapist should gather a reasonable amount of historical information about the child and the family, yet this information rarely is necessary for the success of the solutions proposed in this book. In fact, lengthy deliberation about past events and about current subjective reactions to these events often wastes time that could be spent implementing solutions. Significant past events tend to leave traces in the child's current environment; when behavior problems are successfully resolved by changing the environment, the impact of the historical cause of the problem often dims. Parents whose son drowned at age 3 and who overprotected their daughter from birth may still overprotect that daughter when she is 6 and fears leaving home for school. When these parents learn to encourage their daughter to take reasonable risks and see that she survives, they may realize that they were not to blame for their son's death.

Guilt and worry
Since problems in childrearing and education are widespread, guilt, except on the part of parents or teachers who have acted out of bad intentions, is irrational and hinders solution of behavior problems. Since solutions for childhood behavior problems are more available now than ever, worry is equally unreasonable until all the available, relevant solutions have been given a fair trial.

Wise adults who feel excessive guilt and worry do not communicate these concerns to children. When children learn that adults are extremely worried about them, they lose confidence in their ability to change.

Adults who are worried and guilty may profit from realizing that in a complex society such as ours successful child development is not automatic. Difficulties in childrearing and in education are inevitable and the successful resolution of these difficulties and of mild to severe child behavior problems demands from parents and from teachers considerable knowledge, judgment, experience, effort, and love, as well as social and physical resources.

In an ideal world, children would be raised so that as adults they can love and care for children. When adults decided to be parents or teachers, they would be provided with the knowledge needed for resolving behavior problems at home and at school. As novices, they would be guided by expert parents and teachers, until they acquired the necessary judgment and experience. They would have the strength to work hard at childrearing and to feel love for their children because in times of trouble, without embarrassment, they could depend upon family, educators, friends, and neighbors for the social and physical support they need.

In the real world, few children are reared under ideal conditions; many children are prepared to be abusive, indifferent, or overindulgent caretakers. Few adults are encouraged to delay having or caring for children until they are psychologically ready. Neither parents nor teachers are adequately informed about human learning or about human growth and development. Novice parents and teachers are rarely provided with expert and supportive supervision. In times of trouble, most parents and teachers are on their own. Social and physical resources tend to be provided begrudgingly under conditions that shame the recipient.

When ignorance, misfortune, poor resources, and chronic stress conspire to produce child behavior problems, caretakers usually feel that they are to blame and that they are incapable of remedying the situation. They look to experts to fix the child up and, when the experts have failed, to remove the child from the home and from the classroom.

Most failures to resolve child behavior problems result not from children's inability to learn or from traumatic past events or from adults' bad intentions but from adults' ignorance about the way human behavior changes and from their lack of necessary resources. Chapter 2 discusses further how parents differ in their competence at childrearing because of lack of resources and other problems and how less competent parents and families can be helped to solve child behavior problems and raise happy, well-adjusted children.

How Adults Influence Children to Change

Parents' and teachers' responsibilities for the children in their care require them to use their influence, or social power, to rear and educate healthy, competent, problem-free children. The sources of social power are described in a classic article by French and Raven in the book *Group Dynamics*. An explanation of these sources of social power and how they contribute to the solution of child behavior problems or cause behavior problems follows.

Legitimate power
When a child does what an adult says just "because she said so," the adult has legitimate power. Legitimate power has little effect on children whose problem behavior derives from ignorance of alternative, skillful behavior, and it has little effect on older children and adolescents who have begun to question adults' rights to control their lives. This book is designed to help adults who now rely with little effect on appeals to legitimate power to shift to other more effective sources of social influence.

Reward power
When a child does what an adult says because the adult controls important social and tangible rewards, the adult has reward power. Adults with reward power are able to motivate children with behavior

problems to work hard in order to learn new skills or demonstrate skills they already possess. The influence of adults with reward power tends to dwindle as children mature and prefer the resources controlled by peers. Nonetheless, adults who have provided noncontingent love as well as contingent praise and attention tend to remain important to children even when the children are struggling for independence. This book is designed to help parents and teachers increase their reward power and to shift, when appropriate, from tangible to social rewards, consistent with the needs of growing children.

Coercive power
When a child does what an adult says because the adult uses threats and punishment, the adult has coercive power. Adults with coercive power tend to hurt, rather than help, children with behavior problems. As children mature they distance themselves as much as possible from adults with coercive power. This book is designed to help adults who now rely on coercion to shift to other modes of influence.

Referent power
When a child does what an adult says because the adult has a lot in common with the child, the adult has referent power. Peers tend to have much more referent power than adults. Adults often try to boost their referent power by trying to be a child's pal or by pointing out similarities between adult and child, but these efforts rarely provide the adult with much influence. Adults who fulfill their responsibilities as parents and teachers can look forward to having referent power when children are grown. This book is designed to help adults who now attempt to use referent power to shift to other modes of influence.

Expert power
When a child does what an adult says because the adult provides success-producing instructions and examples, the adult has expert power. Adults with expert power are able to influence children with behavior problems to learn new skills. Their influence tends to get more powerful as children mature. This book is designed to help parents and teachers increase their expert power so that they can compete successfully with "bad influences"—people who use their expertise to encourage unhealthy, incompetent, illegal, and unethical behavior.

Principles of Behavior Change

The best way to remedy child behavior problems is by encouraging skillful behavior that competes with problematic behavior. While few of the solutions proposed in this book involve direct teaching of new skills, most of the solutions provide the opportunity for learning new skills. For example, Patrick rarely owns up to his mistakes. He denies having done anything wrong even when his mother and sister see him take his sister's doll, drop it, and break it. Patrick's dishonesty will be remedied when he learns a competing response: to tell his mother when he has broken a rule and to make restitution for his rule breaking. (The discussion of lying in Chapter 4 shows parents how they can encourage honesty and restitution.) Principles of behavior change examined in this section include observation, instructions, positive reinforcement, and punishment.

Observation
One way that children learn new skills, especially simple familiar ones, is through observation of the people around them—their social environment. Children are most likely to learn new skills from the examples of people they like, who seem similar to them in some way, and whose behavior has good results. This is why it is so important for adults to demonstrate the attitudes and the skills they want children to learn. The very best teacher is one who is always learning new things and enjoys solving problems under difficult circumstances. The best place for children with behavior problems to learn new skills is in the regular classroom and at home, and the very best "therapy group" is the regular classroom and classmates who've mastered difficult childhood problems. Observational learning plays an important part in the solutions presented in this book.

Instructions
A second way that children learn new skills is by the instructions that they hear, read, or watch. Children often learn unfamiliar, complex skills in this way. They are most likely to benefit from instructions that specify in precise detail and proper order each action required to complete a task. This is why it is so important for caretakers to be expert at the skills they want children to master and to be aware of how they succeed at these skills.

Good instructions are exemplified by a recipe for baking bread that tells the baker what ingredients to buy, what utensils to use, how to prepare and blend the ingredients, and in what order to take each step. Good instructions are also exemplified by the directions the softball coach gives to the novice hitter, including how to hold the bat, where to place the hands and feet, where to look while hitting, and how and when to run the bases. The best recipes and the best coaches tell novices what to do when things go wrong, how to diagnose critical errors, and how to regain enthusiasm for trying again. A boy who is afraid of the dark, for example, may learn from good instructions to leave his reading lamp on until he is sleepy, to avoid reading monster comic books at night, to draw pictures of monsters and tear them up when he awakens after a nightmare, to not mind if he doesn't fall asleep, and to tell his parents in the morning how he acted brave the night before. In another example, a schoolyard bully may benefit from instructions on making friends.

> John was a bully, disliked by classmates and teachers. He wanted friends, but did not know what to do when children avoided him. He learned to approach other children from these instructions: "When a boy you want to play with looks at you, smile at him and say 'Hi.' Wait for him to say something. If he smiles and says 'Hi,' ask him if he ever plays basketball after school."

When a task is important to children, they try hard to learn relevant skills through instructions. A girl who has a storybook she wants to read will listen carefully as her teacher explains how to decode new words. A girl whose parents watch television all night and never read will gaze around the classroom with obvious disinterest during reading group.

Helpful instructions build on available behaviors and skills, slowly guide the child through the steps required for completion of the task, provide positive feedback each time the child is even slightly successful, and help the child correct mistakes. This is how good classroom teachers instruct children in complex academic subjects.

Some parents and educators give instructions but do not follow them up with actions. A parent who says, "Put on your seat belt as soon as we get into the car" and never puts on his provides a child with good instructions and a bad example. Perhaps because examples are more striking and easier to follow than instructions, the child will probably follow her father's example and leave her seat belt off. Giving good instructions and following them up with good examples is important to the solutions in this book.

Positive reinforcement

A third way that children learn new skills is from the effects their actions have on the environment. Actions that pay off tend to be repeated in the future. This process is called positive reinforcement.

> On Tuesday as children lined up after school to take the bus home, John walked up to Tony, smiled, and said, "Hi." Tony smiled in return and asked, "You playing ball after school?" On Wednesday, John again walked up to Tony, smiled, and said, "Hi."

In this example, Tony reinforced John for smiling and saying "Hi," encouraging John to act friendly again on Wednesday. If we didn't know what happened on Wednesday, or if on Wednesday John stayed away from Tony, we would have no evidence of positive reinforcement and no reason to call Tony's invitation to play ball a positive reinforcer. When positive reinforcement is provided, children often increase their performance of familiar skills.

> In the past, Anna knew how to get washed and dressed by herself, but hardly ever did. This month, Mother began putting a slice of homemade chocolate cake in Anna's lunch box on days when Anna got ready for school on her own. (Anna loves this cake, and Mother never provides it except as a reward for independent morning behavior.) In the last 2 weeks, Anna has washed and dressed on her own on 9 out of 10 school days.

Very soon, Anna's mother will be able to shift from chocolate cake to recognition of Anna's independence. In a while, Anna will be so used to being in charge of her morning routine, and she will feel so good about it, that Mother's praise will be pleasant but unnecessary. Positive reinforcement is an important part of the solutions presented in this book.

Positive reinforcement can be used to teach complex, unfamiliar new skills through shaping. To shape a new skill, a child is first rewarded for performing each behavioral component of a skill, beginning with the last component in the chain. Little by little, more and more components are required before the reward is delivered, until the child finally earns the reward only after performing the complex skill. Shaping requires as much knowledge and skill as does giving good instructions. In addition, shaping requires extraordinary patience and time. Shaping is often used by expert physical and speech therapists. Because of the difficulties involved in its use, shaping is not a major requirement of the solutions presented in this book.

Punishment

Punishment involves the application of a painful, unpleasant consequence, such as spanking, washing out the mouth with soap, criticism, and nagging. Child abuse is a severe form of punishment.

Punishment does suppress behavior. As a last resort, an expert behavior therapist may decide it is necessary to use punishment. But punishment is easily misused and it is often used long before it is needed. In this book, no solutions involving punishment are recommended. Moreover, parents and teachers who follow this book's recommendations will quickly abandon the methods of punishment they now use.

Punishment has several shortcomings. First, punishment makes the child dislike, fear, and mistrust the punisher. As a result, the child is unlikely to learn from the punitive adult's example, to listen carefully to the punitive adult's instructions, or to be reinforced by the punitive adult's attention and affection. Thus, punitive adults lose the ability to teach skillful, prosocial behavior to children they punish.

Second, punishment misleads the punisher. Since punishment suppresses problem behavior for a while, the punitive adult may feel very effective and may continue to use punishment even though the likelihood of future problem behavior really has not been altered.

Third, punishment teaches the child that aggression is permissible as long as the aggressor is bigger and stronger than the victim. Punitive adults provide the child with an opportunity to learn to be aggressive from a familiar example. Thus, children who are frequently punished often grow up to be abusive parents.

Gerald Patterson has pointed out in his book *A Social Learning Approach* (Vol. 3) a fourth problem with punishment. Unhappy families tend to get trapped into using more and more punishment with one another, in part because each member of the family ignores one another's low-level punishments and responds to one another's high-level noise and physical abuse. In this way, family members train one another to become more noisy, aggressive, and obnoxious.

Parents who use punishment a lot often complain that their children trap them into using more and more punishment by acting indifferent about mild punishment and provoking them into making punishment tougher. For example, a boy who is spanked holds back his tears, rather than letting his father see how much pain he feels. His father whacks him harder, as if this will make the punishment work. This book provides more effective solutions than punishment for children's behavior problems and encourages adults to choose solutions not because they hurt, but because they have observably good effects on children's future behavior.

Using Positive Reinforcement Correctly

Children's behavior problems are remedied by positive reinforcement only when the child earns rewards by skillful behavior and in no other way and only when the reward is given after the skillful behavior is demonstrated. Some people call this principle of contingent, positive reinforcement Grandma's Law: "First you eat your spinach, then you get your ice cream."

Every once in a while someone says, "I tried positive reinforcement and it didn't work." Careful examination usually reveals that failures to remedy child behavior problems with positive reinforcement stem from one of these errors:

1. Providing a reward that has no reinforcement value for the child.
2. Providing the reward noncontingently. (The child doesn't have to perform new, skillful behavior in order to earn the reward.)
3. Providing the child with a daily example of the distressing problem behavior.
4. Threatening the child with the loss of the reward before the child has a chance to perform skillful behavior. (The reward loses its positive reinforcement value and the child makes no effort to earn it.)
5. Attempting to teach a complex, unfamiliar skill without shaping and without opportunity for observational learning or learning through instructions.

Rewards are consequences that adults guess will reinforce children's behavior. To be certain, an adult must observe the effects of a reward on a child's behavior, since consequences that reward one child can punish or mean nothing to a second child.

Susan and Frank's fourth-grade teacher thinks that all children are motivated by gold stars on good papers. He is right about Susan. On Fridays, Susan reviews her spelling words very carefully, because she wants to add another gold-star spelling test to the schoolwork her mother displays on the refrigerator door. The teacher is wrong about Frank. Since Frank's parents never look at his schoolwork, Frank doesn't review his spelling words and usually fails the spelling test on Friday afternoon. For Susan, a gold star on a spelling test is reinforcing; for Frank, it is not. To reinforce Frank's review of spelling words, his teacher must find a more potent reward than a gold star.

Rewards useful in reinforcing children's behavior include attention, praise, physical affection, knowledge of results, favorite activities, money, food, and toys. An unhappy child, for example, could be rewarded for happy behavior in all of these ways. Her mother could reward her happy behavior with attention, for example, by chatting pleasantly with the child whenever she sees her smile. She could praise her when she smiles: "Your face looks so pretty when you smile." She could use physical affection, giving a big hug every time she sees the child smile. She could inform the child about the results of her smiling: "I see you are smiling. Each time you smile, I feel very good." And, she could make a favorite activity, food, or toy or money available to the child when she smiles: "Since you look so happy, let's take that bike ride you've been asking for."

Social rewards

Attention, praise, physical affection, knowledge of results, and favorite activities are social rewards. They should be used liberally to teach and strengthen skillful behavior. Extensive use of these rewards solves many behavior problems and increases children's liking for themselves and for other people. Attention and praise should be used whenever a child exhibits the least bit of a new and important skillful behavior. Once skillful behavior is so well established that it earns its own rewards, attention and praise will be needed only once in a while. Praise should be directed at the behavior or its products ("You are being very patient with your baby brother today. That's great!" "This is a very interesting story you've written. Where did you get the idea for it ?"), not at the child ("You are the most patient boy I've ever seen." "What a writer. A little Hemingway!"). When praise is too often directed at children rather than at their actions, they don't learn how and when to give themselves a pat on the back. Instead they become excessively dependent on other people's approval.

Good classroom teachers use knowledge of results to reinforce children's homework efforts. As soon as students turn in math homework assignments, an expert math teacher corrects the assignments, records the grade, and tells each child what problems he got right and wrong. At times, she also encourages the children to tell her how they managed to get correct answers to difficult problems. She spends little or no time asking children why they made errors.

The things children do when given a choice are their favorite activities; they will work hard to gain access to these activities. A girl who spends every evening talking on the telephone to friends will work hard for a chance to spend time on the telephone. A boy who spends every Saturday and Sunday afternoon watching sports on television will work hard for television time. Use of access to favorite activities to reinforce skillful behavior is called the Premack Principle.

Activity rewards have a number of obvious advantages, especially when a child's favorite activities are low in cost and involve enjoyable time spent with family or friends. Every once in a while, however, a child's favorite activities—fire setting is an example—are unhealthy and should not be used as a reinforcer.

Tangible rewards

Money, food, and toys are tangible, concrete rewards. These rewards need to be used more cautiously than social rewards.

When children seem indifferent to adult attention and praise and have few healthy favorite activities, tangible rewards must be used to teach and strengthen skillful behavior. Gradually, the people who dispense these rewards may become important to the child and capable of using praise and attention as reinforcers. Eventually, it may be possible to rely largely upon social rewards to maintain skillful behavior and to enhance the child's relationships with peers and adults. Whenever a child is responsive to social rewards, tangible rewards should be used sparingly and should be directed only at high-priority targets of behavior change.

Children who grow up in industrialized countries must learn to use money properly if they are to become independent, self-sufficient adults. They need to know how to earn, save, and spend money. They also need to know that while money is useful it is not as important as self-respect and concern for other people. It is easy to overuse money as a reward, because it is so often a potential reinforcer. Unfortunately, heavy reliance upon money rewards can backfire, promoting unethical behavior and interfering with the development of moral judgment.

Chapter 4 describes how to use a daily money allowance to reward children for doing chores without reminder. Money is a good reward for chores, because daily praise for chores might quickly lose its value. Also, school-aged children do need money to buy lunch at school, presents for friends' birthdays, and school supplies. An allowance linked to daily chores is a good way for children to earn this money.

When a child is responsive to social rewards, food rewards should be used sparingly and only for positive reinforcement. That is to say, the child should be allowed to earn special treats and snacks that are otherwise unavailable or rarely available. Examples are homemade favorite dishes, "junk" or "fast" food, and sweets.

Since children often favor foods that they have helped to prepare (the more involved they are in the preparations, the more they seem to enjoy the results) and food that is served under special conditions (by candlelight, for example), parents with limited budgets or parents of overweight or diabetic children can still use food rewards.

There is rarely a good reason for using food as a negative reinforcer. Depriving a child of nourishing, good-tasting meals after misbehavior by, for example, sending a boy to bed without dinner after he hits his sister is not recommended.

Some parents overemphasize food and are preoccupied with their children's diets. These parents often encourage children to eat when they are upset and to become charter members of the "clean-plate club." The results are usually unfortunate—children with limited capacity for direct communication of emotions, eating and weight problems, and a lot of anger towards parents. Parents who overemphasize food can begin to change their ways by making eating completely voluntary and by requiring children to earn preferred treats and snacks (but not by cleaning their plates). When children show little interest in eating, and when their behavior at the table leaves a lot to be desired, it is reasonable to excuse them from the table as soon as fidgeting begins.

After a while, children tire of tangible rewards. They get sick of chocolate ice cream and of miniature trucks. Once children's appetite for a reward is satiated, they no longer work hard for it. Children are less likely to be satiated when they can work for a choice from a large "reward menu" that lists favorite tangible rewards and activities. Chapter 4 explains how to construct reward menus and when to use them.

Withdrawal of positive reinforcement
Some child behavior problems have to be suppressed so that the child has a chance to learn skillful behavior. A child who frequently bangs his head has very little time to talk to people, and so head banging must be suppressed.

Many problem behaviors are maintained by positive reinforcement. Suppression of these problem behaviors requires "timeout," or withdrawal of positive reinforcement. Timeout for inappropriate behavior is most effective when combined with positive reinforcement for appropriate behavior. This combination is involved in several solutions proposed in this book.

Michael and Irene are sister and brother. They fight constantly. Each time they argue, their mother pleads with them to stop and lectures them to be kind to one another. Some days she spends an hour or more trying to decide who started the fight and why they were fighting. Michael and Irene have learned that all they need to do in order to get their mother's attention is to start a fight.

In order to suppress fighting so that Michael and Irene can learn to resolve their differences on their own, their mother will have to withdraw positive reinforcement, using a timeout procedure described in Chapter 4. Michael and Irene's mother probably doesn't realize how much she attends to her children's arguments. Nor does she realize that even when she scolds them her attention acts as a positive reinforcer for sibling rivalry. She is not unusual in this respect. Adults are rarely aware of how much they attend to inappropriate behavior and how little they attend to children's good behavior. Parents and teachers often fail to understand how much children crave adults' physical presence, their touch, and their speech.

When adults use timeout for good behavior (rather than for inappropriate behavior) and positive reinforcement for inappropriate behavior, they often shape serious child behavior problems.

At 8 years of age, Jane was left to babysit for her baby brother. She neglected the baby, and he suffocated. Since that time, Jane has become increasingly aggressive, hitting children and adults whenever she is upset. She eats food reserved for other family members and wets her bed most nights. Her problem behavior often makes Jane the center of unpleasant attention. Whenever her aunt (and guardian) visits with friends, she tells them about Jane's latest bad deed. Every once in a while, Jane has a good day, when she tries hard to please her aunt. Because her aunt thinks Jane is a "bad seed," she pays little attention to Jane on her good days, saying she is "just putting on an act." By discounting Jane's brief episodes of self-control and paying close attention to her bad days, Jane's aunt is ensuring that Jane will have fewer and fewer good days in the future.

Children who break familiar rules and seem to purposely get in trouble are probably responding to adults who reinforce rule breaking with attention and ignore rule-following behavior. How much time do children spend carefully planning to break a rule so that they can get in trouble and gain adult attention? Probably little or none. Most children with antisocial and aggressive behavior problems are so impulsive that they haven't thought much about the consequences of their actions. Many of them are so severely punished for their actions that it is hard to believe that a child with any options would choose to get in trouble.

Unfortunately, the majority of children with behavior problems have limited options; the only way they can get adult attention is through problematic behavior. The adults around them are hypersensitive to misbehavior and discount appropriate behavior. The children themselves are unskilled in the appropriate behaviors that earn positive reinforcement. The playground bully, for example, rarely knows how to get his teachers' and classmates' attention, except by inflicting pain on weaker children.

Rules and contracts

Children's behavior problems can be remedied by thoughtful provision of rewards to strengthen skillful behavior and by careful withdrawal of attention and other rewards to weaken and suppress problem behavior. A rule states the rewards earned for skillful behavior and the consequences for problem behavior in words or actions that a child can understand. When a family or a classroom negotiates the details of a set of rules and agrees upon these details together, a verbal or written contract is the result. Rules and contracts are involved in many solutions proposed in this book.

For behavior to change, children need only experience appropriate consequences. But children's behavior may change more quickly if they understand the rules and know when to expect which consequences. Explaining rules one time and giving children ample opportunity to ask questions about rules is a very good idea. All of the solutions proposed in this book describe how to provide appropriate explanations and how, after rules have been explained, to let the child learn the rule through personal experience of consequences.

Explanations of rules should not be repeated over and over; such repetition teaches the child not to listen the first (or the second or the third) time and seems like nagging to the child. After explaining the rules once, adults should simply provide agreed upon consequences when desirable or undesirable behavior occurs. All the solutions in this book discourage repeated explanations of rules and extended discussions of problem behavior.

Threats and bribes
Threats ("If you yell one more time, you're going into timeout") and bribes ("If you do your chores, you'll get your allowance") signal children that adults are impatient and unwilling to let children experience the consequences of their own behavior. Threats tempt children to misbehave and see what will happen. Exaggerated threats ("Speak back to me one more time, and I'll ground you for a year") signal children that the adult may not do anything about misbehavior. Exaggerated bribes ("Get an A in math, and I'll take you to Disneyland for a week") lack meaning for the same reason. This book discourages the use of threats and bribes.

Adults often justify threats and bribes by calling them reminders. Once reasonable rules are agreed upon for home and school, it is children's responsibility to remind themselves ("If I do this, what will happen is that"). Self-reminding is the first step toward self-control. So long as adults threaten, bribe, and repeatedly explain rules, children are unlikely to learn to remind themselves to stop problem behavior and to try skillful new behavior.

Adults often underestimate children's capacity to understand and remember rules. It is adults' responsibility to ensure that rules are easy enough for the child to understand, either through words or through experience. The best way to explain a rule to a child is by consistently providing the agreed upon consequence. Adults who want children to follow rules but who are lax about administering the rules are contributing to the problem, not to the solution.

2

Family Competence and Child Behavior Problems

Competent parents, who are good at managing their own lives, tend to raise competent children. Children can be considered competent when compared to their peers they are free from behavior problems, immaturity, anxiety, and depression and have high self-esteem, popularity with peers, and success at school. Both competent families and less competent families, though, do face child behavior problems. As noted in Chapter 1, child behavior problems have a variety of origins, including parents' lack of skill at childrearing and causes beyond the family's control. Competent families, because of their skills and resources, will probably have an easier time solving behavior problems and be easier for clinicians and educators to work with than less competent families.

One of the aims of this book is to help parents and children become more competent. They do this by working the Home-Problem and School-Problem Modules. The Home-Problem Modules use brief case histories of competent and less competent families to introduce problems and solutions and to demonstrate that the remedies for child behavior problems discussed apply equally to both kinds of children and families.

These case histories should reassure competent families that they are not inadequate just because of the child behavior problem in their midst. They should also reassure less competent families that, despite their difficulties in working together, they can succeed at resolving child behavior problems.

This chapter describes the relationship between child behavior problems, family competence, and change. It also considers how modern and traditional family styles affect child behavior problems.

Competent and Less Competent Families

There are a number of important differences between competent and less competent families, both in their normal day-to-day interactions and in how they confront child behavior problems. Descriptions of some of these differences follow.

Recognition of problems and willingness to change

Although there seem to be many types of competent families, all competent families recognize child behavior problems and are willing to change in order to solve these problems. This means that competent families are more likely than less competent families to identify child behavior problems, to seek help for these problems from trustworthy sources, and to take sensible actions to resolve these problems. Competent families are also likely to seek help early, when only a little effort is needed to resolve a minor problem and to prevent larger ones from erupting.

In a competent family, parents notice child behavior problems and work as hard as necessary to solve those problems to the satisfaction of the whole family and of trusted outsiders, such as teachers and therapists. In a less competent family, parents are either not fully aware of child behavior problems or they worry too much about commonplace child behavior. Less competent families don't work together effectively to solve child behavior problems; the solutions these families come up with do not completely satisfy all family members and trusted outsiders. Individual members of less competent families may work hard to resolve child behavior problems and be satisfied with the outcome, but the whole group works together less effectively than the competent family.

Competent families enjoy change and growth. In these families, parents accept differences between themselves and their children as healthy and expect that each of their children will have different strengths and weaknesses. These parents realize that their job is to prepare children for adult life in a world that will be very different from their own. They know that they can't supply their children with all the right answers, although they can prepare them to know what they value and to find solutions consistent with their values. This book is likely to be used by competent families who have recognized on their own emerging child behavior problems and by less competent families who have been told about serious problems by teachers or other people outside the family.

Problem-solving ability

A lot of unnecessary mystery surrounds childrearing. Some people think that rearing children requires a special skill not applied to any other task of daily life. For example, many men feel disenfranchised because they have so often heard that women have unique talents for childrearing.

In fact, adults who are good at solving life's problems tend to become competent parents. They may become competent parents with no outside help at all (this is very rare) or they may profit from informal teaching by friends and family members (this is very common) and by formal teaching by professionals (this is increasingly common).

A parent's ability to raise healthy children can be predicted by the parent's past solution of important problems (such as finishing school, getting and holding a job, resolving interpersonal conflicts). It is for this reason that parents who have little money, don't have a steady job, or are locked in conflict with a spouse or ex-spouse tend to be handicapped when it comes to childrearing.

Parents who have repeatedly demonstrated slow learning in other areas of their lives are likely to run into difficulties when they rear children. Note that these slow learners can become competent parents but they are likely to need some extra help. Unfortunately, slow learners often lack a network of family and friends capable of providing good informal teaching about childrearing as well as access to good formal teaching about childrearing by professionals. Competent parents are likely to have separated successfully from their families of origin, and, because they are independent adults, competent parents can have relaxed and friendly relationships with members of their own extended families and with other competent families. From these ties, competent parents get useful information about childrearing, physical help, and emotional support. Children benefit from these ties by learning how to make and keep friends and how to enjoy being with people. The childrearing of less competent families is often handicapped by a lack of social support and information.

Chapters 4 and 5 repeatedly lead families through the process of problem solving. This process of rehearsal may not only solve pressing child behavior problems, it may also contribute to the family's competence by teaching the group to recognize and resolve new problems as they arise.

Worry about children's problems
Competent parents do not worry constantly and needlessly about their children. Merely being worried about a child behavior problem doesn't make a family competent. Many parents who are dissatisfied with their jobs and their marriages worry unnecessarily about their children's development. Eventually the worry itself causes a behavior problem. Thus a parent who worries about a child's speech development causes a stuttering problem by paying attention each time the child's speech is

not fluent. Despite their parents' dissatisfactions, preschool-aged children of depressed parents often behave no differently than their peers. If these depressed parents worried less about their children's behavior and were more creative in remedying the causes of their personal unhappiness, their children's futures would be brighter.

Control and freedom

Competent families provide children with the right amounts of control and freedom. The family's job is to train or socialize the child for adult life while protecting the fragile, growing child from the dangers of the world outside the family. The two parental tasks of socialization and protection require a considerable amount of control over child behavior. Parents gain this control early in their children's lives by providing primary reinforcers such as food and warmth and pleasant touch and by removing punishing stimuli such as wet, dirty diapers. After a while, parents find that children enjoy their mere presence, their smiles, their approving words; these symbolic events become secondary reinforcers. It is only natural for parents to try to use their positive primary and secondary reinforcers to shape new skills. But parents exercise their most potent control over children without any effort, since children are so eager to imitate everything that parents with positive control say and do.

Competent parents are probably quite skillful in the art of control: at achieving secondary reinforcement value; at shaping, describing, and demonstrating desirable behavior; and at encouraging imitation of their behavior. In short, competent parents seem to know how to provide the structure and the limits that are prerequisites for the growth of self-control.

As good as competent parents are at the art of control, they seem to be equally skilled in the art of freedom, always providing children with safe, age-appropriate, developmentally appropriate opportunities to experiment with new forms of behavior and to experience the consequences of good and bad choices. At every age and developmental stage, these parents provide their children with opportunities to try out their problem-solving skills in settings that are reasonably free of adult control, advice, and supervision. By balancing control and freedom, competent parents help children learn to take risks, to trust themselves, and to master challenges. Chapters 4 and 5 are designed to help parents and other adults become more competent in the arts of control and freedom.

Less competent families provide children with too much control or too much freedom. While competent parents seem to know how to achieve the correct balance of control and freedom, less competent families tend to emphasize control and forget about freedom or emphasize freedom and forget about control.

Authoritarian parents are very concerned about control. Paradoxically, authoritarian parents have trouble achieving effective control over their children because they are heavy handed with punishment, because they provide an example of poorly controlled behavior, and because they are so unpleasant that children are unlikely to imitate their good qualities. A few authoritarian families are so concerned about control and so ignorant about normal child development that they physically abuse infants who cry or toddlers who wet their beds. Marital conflict, sometimes open, sometimes hidden, is common in authoritarian families. If the father uses punishment to excess with the children (sometimes subtly egged on by his wife), he is equally coercive with his wife. Wife and children become allies to protect one another against Father. The father's anger at being pushed out of the family encourages an escalation of family violence. Unfortunately, the authoritarian family that so values control generally produces aggressive children with little self-control.

Laissez-faire, permissive, or overly indulgent parents are very concerned about freedom and pleasure. They believe that "The child knows best"; that if all their needs are satisfied, children will naturally unfold into healthy adults. Laissez-faire parents establish primary reinforcement control by taking excellent care of their children's basic needs, but they never use their positive control to shape independent problem solving. Instead, by gratifying their children's every whim, they promote immaturity and dependency.

By refusing to set limits on child behavior, laissez-faire parents rob their children of the opportunity to experience frustration and to master challenges on their own. These laissez-faire parents overindulge themselves as much as they do their children. Although they often know that giving in to a whining child is bad for the child, they just can't tolerate the child's complaints. Rather than allowing children to fall down, scrape their knees, and console themselves, these parents do their best to prevent their children from taking risks and feeling pain. When their children do hurt themselves, these parents provide all the necessary consolation; their children never learn to cheer themselves up.

If the mother indulges the children to excess and ignores her husband (sometimes subtly egged on by her husband), the father eventually protests his inferior status in the family and directs his anger at the children. An alliance between Mother and the children often develops at this point to ensure that the children will continue to be indulged by Mother at Father's expense. Unfortunately, the laissez-faire family that so values freedom and personal gratification often produces dependent, unhappy, lazy children. The procedures in Chapters 4 and 5 can be tailored to suit the special needs of authoritarian and laissez-faire families.

Every once in a while, parents who have the deck stacked against them do a great job of childrearing. Every once in a while, competent children survive despite serious problems at home, at school, and in the community. Very little is known about the conditions that give rise to these unusual success stories.

Modern and Traditional Families

Many critics have questioned the role in children's lives played by the modern American family. American families have certainly changed a lot in the last 2 decades. The most noticeable changes have been dramatic increases in the numbers of working mothers and single-mother-headed families. These changes frighten people who believe that only the family headed by an employed father and a homemaker mother can prepare children for self-reliant adult life and full participation in a democratic society.

Delinquency, drug addiction, and school failure have each been blamed on one-parent families and on working mothers. According to some experts, a dominant father and a nurturant mother are needed if boys are to identify with adult men and girls with adult women. Moreover, these experts maintain that same-sex identification is critical to healthy adult psychological adjustment. They believe that a boy who plays with dolls or a girl who is a tomboy may be maladjusted as adults because of these unusual preferences.

In fact, these experts may be wrong. The best and most current evidence indicates that poverty, limited parental education, conflict between parents, and one or more parents with serious behavior problems encourage child behavior problems and obstruct adult adjustment. These seem to be the real culprits, not the mere absence of a father or the presence of a strong, capable mother. Parents who have not finished high school, who don't have steady employment, who have no friends, and who can't resolve conflicts with one another without physical violence or verbal cruelty have great difficulties rearing competent children.

Children reared by a capable single working mother may well have different strengths and weaknesses than children reared by an equally capable working father and homemaker mother, but on balance children from both family types are likely to be equally well-functioning adults. As for their different strengths, children reared by capable single mothers, particularly girls, will probably be very achievement oriented, and children reared by capable coupled parents, particularly boys, will probably value traditional family life.

Even if there are differences in the masculinity and femininity of children raised in modern and traditional families, children's competence in interpersonal relationships and in achievement depends more upon their problem-solving skills than upon their masculinity or femininity. The most competent children probably have a wide range of interests and abilities, some traditionally masculine and some traditionally feminine.

Competent two-parent families tend to have some common features. In these families, because the bond between parents is always stronger than the bond between either parent and any child, mothers never feel the need to protect their children from their husbands. If the mother is a homemaker with primary responsibility for childrearing, the father tends to concentrate on giving his wife emotional support and nurturance. If both parents work, both parents are likely to share in childrearing work and decision making. From these experiences, children in competent two-parent families may learn how to be lifetime marital partners.

Competent one-parent families tend to have some common features as well. In these families, the bond between single parent and children is much stronger than it is in the two-parent family. Because competent single parents know that they are very important to their children, their children rarely fear abandonment or rejection. Competent single parents have a small amount of time in which they do a lot: take care of their children, earn a living, and maintain adult relationships that provide social support, intimacy, and sexual gratification. As a result, children in these families have more early responsibility for household management and self-care, and they get used to rotating between adult caretakers and between custodial and noncustodial parents. From these experiences, children in competent single-parent families learn to be self-reliant and innovative and flexible in their relationships with people.

Single or part of a couple, many parents worry about the impact of their lifestyles on their children, even though their children are happy, popular with peers, and successful at school. Chapters 4 and 5 permit parents to determine whether their children are troubled by a variety of behavior problems and then tell them what to do when a problem is detected. Recognizing the relationship between family competence and successful childrearing, many of the recommended solutions require better problem solving and more flexibility rather than more conventional family behavior.

This book concerns child behavior problems common in modern and in traditional families. Whether they are headed by one or by two parents, whether one or both parents work outside the home, competent families, who are open to change, will find the solutions offered in this book easy to implement. In contrast, modern and traditional families who are ineffective at problem solving and resist change may need some professional assistance to use this book with success.

3

The Family Meeting

Meetings involving all family members are an important part of the Home-Problem Modules presented in Chapter 4. The leader of these meetings is usually a therapist or a clinician. When families are working through the book without the guidance of a therapist, parents can lead the family meetings.

This chapter presents the goals of family meetings, principles of behavior change used during family meetings, and guidelines on running the family meetings. It provides the context for the Home-Problem Modules. Parents running family meetings on their own and parents that therapists gradually want to encourage to take control of family meetings will find guidance in this chapter, particularly in the checklist at the end.

Goals of the Family Meeting

Few troubled families appear open to change. Rarely does a parent say, "Tell me what to do differently, and I'll do it." Instead, members of troubled families, when engaged in unstructured conversations, spend a lot of time describing past treatment failures, the target child's problems, the manner in which other people cause and promote these problems, how tired they are of these problems, and how these problems have drained the family's bank account and damaged their relationships with co-workers, neighbors, and friends.

Troubled families are not so much resistant to change as ignorant about how to change. These families do not know how to solve human problems; many of them believe that such problems cannot be remedied. If troubled families knew when change in family functioning was necessary and how to effect such change, they could have prevented or quickly resolved their current problems.

The goals of the family meetings are to help families realize when they need to change, how they can change, and how they can solve and prevent future problems. This is done by providing solutions for behavior problems that the family can succeed at and that will remedy their present problems. The family is also trained in communication and problem-solving skills that profoundly alter how family members treat each other and how they perceive themselves and that reduce the future probability of new behavior problems.

Communication

Communication is structured with the family and between family members so that family members provide and receive useful information with a minimum of bickering and blaming. Good communication helps parents understand how conditions in the home and in the school might have contributed to their problems and helps them learn how to resolve current problems and prevent future difficulties. Parents may sometimes feel uncomfortable discussing problems in front of their children. Unless parents have severe problems that do not relate to the children, the children should be included in meetings. As parents improve their communication skills, this uncomfortableness will pass.

Family members sometimes are not enthusiastic about following suggestions for change. People who don't know how to change often act as if they don't want to change or as if they fear change. The therapist or meeting leader encourages enthusiasm through good communication skills: knowing when and how to listen and say nothing; questioning and answering questions; sympathizing, paraphrasing, and reflecting; telling jokes, laughing at jokes, teasing, and being teased; and explaining, persuading, and exhorting the family to work hard. It is important throughout this communication process that the goals of the family meeting are always kept in mind.

Problem Solving

The therapist gathers information from family members and other sources before, during, and after treatment. This information is used to make decisions during treatment and to isolate significant and observable problems in family members and in the family group. It is also used to set priorities for resolution of problems and to generate solutions for top-priority problems. The therapist gradually proposes these solutions to the family and guides them as they carry these solutions through to success. Finally, after the family has repeatedly succeeded at carrying out solutions largely devised by others, the family members take increasing responsibility for problem solving until no major problems are left to be solved or the family is able to resolve remaining problems on their own.

Principles of Behavior Change Applied to Family Meetings

The processes of communication and problem solving are enhanced in family meetings through the principles of behavior change described in Chapter 1. Application of these principles as described in this book does not aim to change the structure of the family, the roles that family members play, or any other aspect of the family social system. Much too little is known at this time about the social systems of competent families for reorganization of the social system to be a goal.

Learning through observation

Therapists help families learn through observation in family meetings by showing them new skills and behaviors. This may involve role playing the parts of parents or children, asking them to copy what they have seen, and rewarding them for doing it accurately. Family members may be asked to rehearse the new skills and behaviors at home.

Learning through instructions

All of the modules in this book contain detailed instructions for bringing about behavior change. The therapist may summarize these instructions to a family in a meeting and have them read relevant portions at home. The therapist tries to alter instructions to suit a family's needs, accompany instructions with demonstrations, give feedback about instruction following, and reward rehearsal and mastery. The therapist may ask parents to keep a chart of how they follow instructions given in the meeting.

The modules are designed to put the burden of responsibility for following instructions on parents. Thus, all the important assignments are made to parents. Children's assignments consist of understanding, as best they can, the new conditions that will be put in place at home and at school and getting used to these changes. At first it will be important for them to understand and experience the consequences of their actions. Later, they may be ready to suggest creative, useful changes in home and school conditions.

Learning through positive reinforcement

Positive reinforcement, or rewarding, of new behaviors and skills is important for therapists to use in family meetings. This reinforcement, particularly through praise and attention, helps the family feel good about what they have accomplished and encourages them to continue working. The therapist informs family members about the effects of their instruction following, with emphasis upon success and the actions that produced success. For example, the therapist might say, "For this whole hour, you've ignored Sam's temper tantrums, just as I asked. Did you notice that as a result Sam's temper tantrums got shorter and shorter over the hour?"

Once the therapist knows what a family prefers to do during the family meetings, these favorite activities can be offered as rewards when the family demonstrates skillful behavior. For example, the therapist might offer a couple an opportunity to work on a child behavior problem that troubles them a lot (for example, lying) once they demonstrate effective instruction following. Material rewards, such as taxi fare home or a free babysitter for 3 hours following the session, are sometimes used with low-income families to reward prompt appearance at a family meeting, instruction following during the meeting, or evidence of rehearsal or instruction following between meetings. With middle-income families, therapists may draw a connection between instruction following within and between meetings and the cost of treatment by saying something like this: "You did a good job of following instructions this past week. Of course, the more instructions you follow, the more quickly you'll get rid of your problems, and the less time and money you'll spend here."

Withdrawal of positive reinforcement

Withdrawing positive reinforcement from problem behavior in the meetings accomplishes two purposes: It makes that behavior less likely to occur again and provides an example to family members of what to do about problem behavior. The therapist might withdraw attention from problem behavior as follows. During a meeting with the entire family, two boys and a girl are playing on the floor while the therapist and both parents are talking together. The girl approaches the therapist and says, "My brothers are taking all the toys away from me. Tell them to stop." The therapist continues talking to the parents. Later, after the girl has returned to playing on the floor, the therapist asks the parents to recall what the girl did and how he responded. When the parents answer, "She interrupted you when you were talking. You kept on talking and didn't answer her. She stopped interrupting and returned to play," the therapist asks the parents to think about situations in which they could withdraw attention from problem behavior and practice withdrawing attention from problem behavior while the meeting continues.

This withdrawal of attention is always used with positive reinforcement for desirable behavior in a process called selective attention. The therapist uses selective attention to shape skillful child and family behavior, and parents are encouraged to use selective attention with their children and to find some good in even the most troubled child.

Learning through punishment

Punishment is not used in family meetings for two reasons. First, it erodes the therapist's relationship with the family and leads them to drop out of treatment. Second, it encourages the use of punishment within the family.

Some parents and children are very sensitive to the reactions of others and they may experience punishment when this is not the intent. When this is the case, more work is needed on communication before problem solving will be possible. Therapists do this by carefully listening to what family members say and frequently paraphrasing what they have said to ensure that the meaning is really understood. Family members can follow the same steps to understand the therapist: When the therapist speaks, they paraphrase (one member at a time), and the therapist either says, "Yes, you got it right" or "No, what I really meant was..." When family members master this technique, they are ready to go on with problem solving.

Rules and contracts

Expectations between family members and the therapist should be made very clear. The therapist negotiates rules and contracts with the family that take into account both the therapist's and family's needs. For example, if an adolescent family member doesn't want to attend family meetings, a therapist might work out an attendance schedule whereby quick resolution of specific problems pays off with fewer meetings, shorter meetings, or more conveniently timed meetings.

Running the Family Meeting

The first meeting, and usually all subsequent meetings, between the therapist (or meeting leader) and family involves the entire family. Young children play with quiet toys while adults and older children join in discussion. Infants should be supervised by a babysitter or an assistant in another room. Adults will be more relaxed if coffee and tea are provided, and children will enjoy hot chocolate and juice.

Demonstrating parenting skills during the meeting

In many cases, children will engage in disruptive behavior from the moment they enter the meeting room. As soon as this happens, the therapist or meeting leader ignores the behavior or calls timeout. (See Chapter 4, Module 5 for more information on timeout.) If children are talking loudly and interrupting adult speech, the therapist ignores the children and says to the parents, "When children interrupt while we are talking, it is a good idea not to pay any attention to, talk to, or look at them. If we follow that rule—paying no attention to children while they are interrupting—there will be fewer and fewer interruptions." Since children will hear this explanation, they will learn the rule without receiving attention right after they have interrupted. The therapist or meeting leader then continues to model inattention to low-level disruptive behavior and praises parents' selective attention throughout this and future meetings.

Despite the example provided, some parents may tell their children to be quiet and stop interrupting. When this happens, repeating the earlier statement and role playing inattention with them is necessary. The parents play the role of children demanding attention inappropriately, and the therapist plays the role of the good parent who is silent and looks away when a child demands attention. After the demonstration, the therapist asks parents to tell her what she did. Their answer should be "Nothing." This demonstration is repeated as many times as necessary, until parents stop paying attention to children's interruptions.

When young children are out of control during the first or later meetings, a modified form of timeout is used. With a young child, a parent picks the child up and puts the child back on the floor with the toys, facing away from the parent, each time the child approaches the parent and demands attention. The parent does this repeatedly until the child stays seated on the floor and stops approaching the parent. This is done gently and silently. Young children who frequently have temper tantrums may have a temper tantrum on the floor. This temper tantrum is ignored. When children are playing quietly or are clearly waiting their turns to speak, they are praised, or if they are very young, they are patted. With some poorly controlled children, their temper tantrums and the demonstration of timeout may last an entire meeting. Teaching timeout in the family meetings is very important since this skill is necessary for later meetings and in the modules. If a child is so out of control as to prevent anything from being accomplished in the first meeting, a back-up meeting is scheduled or the problem child is supervised in another room.

Giving and Getting Information

What the family can expect in the first meeting needs to be explained early in the meeting. The therapist might simply tell the family that during most of the meeting she will be getting information from them about their problems and that toward the end of the meeting she will give them information about what she recommends as a way of solving their problems.

Although the family may have already been in treatment before or have been interviewed by others recently, the family will still need to provide information to the therapist at this first meeting. The therapist will want to request records from these other mental-health practitioners, physicians who care for the children, and any available test reports or academic records from the children's schools.

Throughout the meeting, the therapist takes notes. The first questions are aimed at getting to know the family: learning the names and ages of all family members, the school grades of all children, the occupations of all adults; finding out if there is any chronic illness in the family; getting a brief history of the family, including the length of time parents have been married, all the places the family has lived, and whether extended family members live close by.

After this period of getting acquainted, the therapist finds out what complaints parents have about all of the children and what complaints each child has about the parents and siblings. These complaints should be very specific about the exact nature of the problem behavior— when it happens, who does it, how often it occurs, when it was first observed. Thus, if a parent says, "John is lazy and sloppy," the therapist will say, "Be more specific. What does John do that tells you he is lazy? What does he do that tells you that he is sloppy?" Family members may try to interrupt each other in order to disagree with complaints levelled at them. The therapist redirects them by saying something such as, "Give her a chance. I want to hear everyone's point of view. Don't worry, I know that there are two sides to every story." It is necessary for every family member to have an opportunity to complain without interruptions.

Parents and children may have marked differences of opinion, including children who say they never fight while their parents say they fight several times a day. Parents may regard one of their children as the problem and the others as angels. If parents have made this point, the therapist will press them to be more objective with a statement such as, "You mean to say Charlie lies to you all the time, and Louis is an angel? I find that hard to believe." If parents continue to blame one child and protect the others, the child who is blamed will often speak up. The family needs to understand that the child who is blamed has problems but so do the child's siblings.

Children need permission to complain about parents. This permission should be given by parents and parents should stop themselves from interrupting their children's comments. If the therapist believes that a certain problem has not been mentioned, she will explain that there are problems that every family describes, and that she would like to know how often these problems come up in the family. Problems that tend to be omitted by children involve parents' out-of-control behavior (yelling, hitting, drinking), arguing between parents, and parental neglect.

After finding out what the family's problems are, the therapist will ask the family what they believe to be the cause of the problems. Quite often, parents believe that child behavior problems are caused by an inherited bad temperament, genes, or minimal brain dysfunction. Some parents will say, "He's got the devil in him." Many parents will mention that their problem child resembles a wayward family member "who came to no good." In some single-parent families, the problem child is viewed as a carbon copy of the absent, disliked spouse.

When the therapist learns that parents or children believe that child behavior problems are the result of an immutable cause, the therapist lets them know that, regardless of the original cause of the problem, as soon as parents change what they are doing, children's behavior changes as well. Parents will never know if the therapist is right unless they bring about real changes at home and observe the effects on the child.

When children seem to have problems only at school, parents may blame the school and wonder why they should be involved in intervention. Some children really do function poorly only at school. Other children function equally poorly at school and at home, but parents dismiss difficulties at home as minor. If children really are functioning very well at home, parents will cooperate when the therapist explains that it is a good idea to work through relevant Home-Problem Modules quickly and then to use the School-Problem Modules to help children at school. Resolving problems at home puts the family in a strong position vis-a-vis the school. Parents can say to school personnel, "We worked hard to clear up even minor difficulties at home, and now we feel it's time for school personnel to do the same." If children are not functioning well at home, but parents dismiss their difficulties as minor, the therapist will explain to them why their children's problems at home are significant and discuss how these problems affect children's current functioning at school and in the community and their future adjustment at home and away. The leverage they gain from clearing up problems at home before they address school problems can also be discussed.

In some families, the onset of child behavior problems coincided with a major crisis—a divorce, a death, a job loss, a move, a chronic illness. Whether or not the family noticed the temporal relationship between the crisis and the onset of behavior problems, the therapist will let them know that it is possible that the crisis had a bad effect on the child. Perhaps the child became more anxious. Perhaps the child reverted to younger behavior. Perhaps the parents provided less support for appropriate child behavior. Any of these circumstances could explain why problems suddenly emerged. No one will ever know exactly what caused the child's problems. Regardless of the true cause, changes in parenting tactics will improve child behavior.

Through observation of family members and by listening to their complaints about one another, the therapist will often be able to detect depression in adults or children. When parents say that a child mopes, is often discontented, has few friends, performs below potential at school, and is lazy and without goals, depression must be considered a possibility. Parents will often share their ideas about why the child might be depressed. For example, they may have noticed the onset of depression in their 10-year-old firstborn daughter when their 2-year-old son was born. Parents need to know that working through the Home-Problem Modules may improve the child's mood in two ways: by remedying potential causes of the depression and by teaching the child to act and feel more competent.

When a parent has many complaints about a child and when careful questioning reveals that the child's behavior at home is not exceptionally difficult (compared to other children of that age), depression in the parent is a possibility to be explored by further interviewing and testing of the parent. If evidence of parental depression is convincing (for example, if the parent is currently being treated for depression), parental unhappiness may be more of a problem than child behavior. Parents will often agree and explain that they realize that their difficulty managing normal child behavior is the real problem. For example, a mother may report that she realizes that her 2-year-old is no more contrary than most children his age, but that she has no patience for his noncompliance.

Preparing the Family for Treatment and Maintenance

The therapist explains treatment goals, taking into account the problems the family has described as well as what will be done to help the family achieve those goals. This includes agreement between therapist and family about the goals and about the methods of reaching these goals. The therapist will estimate the number of meetings required to achieve short-term goals and explain how to ensure that maintenance occurs. The importance of rapid communication about problems during the first few meetings will be explained and a mechanism for easy two-way contact will be set up. Here is an example of how one family was prepared to work through the Home-Problem Modules.

"Given the problems your family has just described, it seems to me that what we do together should have these results: less fighting, fewer temper tantrums, less noncompliance by children, less nagging and ineffective punishment by parents, and more self-controlled behavior by children at home and in public. I'll help you achieve these results by showing you in very specific ways how to handle the problems you are having at home. During our meetings, I'll demonstrate what to do, and you'll practice these new procedures at home until you are all experts at these new ways of doing things. My guess is that it will take us about 12 meetings in all to solve the problems you've got now. After those meetings, or as soon as we're successful in achieving our goals, I'll meet with you every once in a while (in 1 month, then in 2 months, then in 3 months, then in 6 months), to ensure that no new problems have come up. From now on, I expect you to call me right away if you are having difficulty doing anything I've explained to you. Now I need to know if we are all in agreement about these goals and about how we will reach them."

Format for Meetings After the First

The format for every meeting after the first includes the following elements:

1. Finding out what new things have happened to the family during the week,
2. Checking on assigned work by looking at charts and listening to everyone's reports about what was done,
3. Dealing with problems that emerged during the discussion of assignments, particularly failure to follow directions,
4. Explaining one new Home-Problem Module, or part of a module, verbally and using role playing for further demonstration, if the family was successful with the last meeting's assignment,
5. Checking for comprehension of the new module on the part of parents and children by asking "What if" questions and by role playing,
6. Checking for objections to the new module and countering these objections,
7. Giving a specific assignment to family members and checking that everyone knows what he is expected to do before the next meeting and what he is expected to bring to the next meeting.

In a given session, from one to two new modules or component procedures may be presented, repeating relevant steps as often as needed. The Checklist for Home-Problem Modules that follows can be copied for use as a guide during family meetings.

CHECKLIST FOR HOME-PROBLEM MODULES

Fill in this checklist each time you have a family meeting.

Before the meeting begins, fill in this information:

Leader's name _____ Meeting date_____

Family members at the meeting_____

_____

_____

Which module, or which parts of a module, do you hope to cover in this meeting? _____

_____

What problems do you anticipate during the meeting?_____

_____

_____

What can you do to avoid these problems? _____

_____

_____

At the beginning of the meeting, follow these steps:

1. Find out what new things have happened to the family during the week. List here any events, good or bad, that either you or the family considers important.

_____

_____

_____

2. Look at the assessment chart and listen to everyone's reports about what assigned work was done. Congratulate those who did their work. List their names here and what they did.

_____

_____

_____

3. Talk with the family about work that was not done. Decide if it still needs to be done. If so, develop a plan to ensure that the work will be finished this week. Take into account the problems that prevented the work from being done thus far. Describe your plan here.

_____

_____

_____

4. If the work has been done, review the assessment chart and consult the module to decide if the family is ready to move on to the next module or if it is best to continue working on the current module. What have you decided to do? Why?

_____

_____

_____

During the family meeting, make sure to:

1. Explain the reason for the new module, including what it is likely to achieve in the short run and in the long run.

2. Tell the family what they need to accomplish, why it is important, and how much time will be required for accomplishment of the task.

3. Read or explain one section of a module at a time, sharing the reading with family members whenever possible. Have family members take turns answering questions about that section. Use role playing for further demonstration, if necessary.

4. Check for comprehension of the new module on the part of the parents and children by asking "What if" questions and role playing.

5. Check for objections to the new module and counter these objections only after you have listened carefully to everyone's opinions, respected everyone's ideas, and let everyone know that his opinions are valued. Make sure that everyone knows what he is expected to do before the next meeting and what he is expected to bring to the next meeting.

6. Congratulate family members each time they help the group solve a difficult problem or show enthusiasm for the task.

After the family has finished going through the module and before the meeting ends, make sure to:

1. Remind the family about what they need to do, pointing out to each family member what new things he will be doing from now on. Describe what each family member needs to do.

   _____

   _____

   _____

2. Ask each family member to tell you, in his own words, about what he needs to do, making sure that all family members understand and agree to their responsibilities.

3. Ask family members to think of things that could go wrong with what each person is assigned to do, and together with the group modify the assignments to solve these problems. Describe potential problems in the assignments and how the group has agreed to solve these problems.

   _____

   _____

   _____

4. Make sure that someone will complete the assessment chart and attend every meeting of the family. Who will this be?

   _____

5. Set a time and place for the next family meeting and remind the family to bring evidence of the work they have done to the next meeting. When and where will this meeting be?

   _____

4

Solving Problems at Home

This chapter shows families how to solve problems at home by working through 13 Home-Problem Modules. Each module in this chapter concerns a child behavior problem or group of problems that often occur at home and describes procedures that will solve the problems.

Which Children Can Benefit from the Modules

The Home-Problem Modules are primarily designed for children from age 3 through the end of elementary school, or age 13. Some, but not all, of these modules are appropriate for teenaged children 14 or older. The modules teach parents to exercise considerable control over child behavior. This amount of behavior control interferes with teenaged children's struggle for independence and self-sufficiency and is impractical for parents whose teenagers are already self-sufficient. Moreover, many parents find it impossible to exercise this amount of control with their teenaged children.

Modules 1 (Assessment), 2 (Putting Clothes and Toys Away), 9 (School Attendance), 10 (Chores and Allowances), 11 (Homework, Reading, and Television), 12 (Loneliness, Unhappiness, Fearfulness, and Self-Injury), 13 (Swearing, Lying, Cheating, Stealing, Fire Setting, and Violence) are all appropriate for teenaged children through the senior year in high school (age 17).

Some children older than age 13 will benefit from all of the modules in this chapter. These children include those who are developmentally delayed; fearful, dependent children; school refusers; and children with frequent temper tantrums. Almost as soon as the Home-Problem Modules are applied to these older children with consistent success it is time to shift to procedures that encourage more self-control and less external control. For this reason, it is a good idea for

45

a family with older troubled children to seek professional guidance as they work through the modules.

If a family includes both poorly controlled elementary-school-aged and high-school-aged children, the family should begin by working through the modules and applying all of them to the problems that the elementary-school-aged children have. If the family is working through Modules 3 to 8 with the elementary-school-aged children, they must exercise care not to use the standards set in these modules for the children older than 13. As mentioned earlier, parents usually cannot enforce these standards and the standards make older children too dependent upon their parents' judgment. After the problems with the elementary-school-aged children have been successfully resolved, the next step would be to solve, with professional help, the outstanding problems with the high-school-aged children.

How Professionals Can Use the Modules

Mental-health professionals and paraprofessionals and educators can use the modules to organize parent training or behavioral-family therapy sessions. Since the modules in this chapter are written for parents, practitioners can adopt the modules' wording to explain new procedures, use the comprehension questions to guide client review of information and rehearsal of skills, and encourage parents to reread the modules at home in order to review new concepts.

All of the modules can also be used in most day schools and community residential placements. Many modules are also applicable in children's psychiatric hospitals and children's medical wards. A problem is more likely to be solved if it is dealt with in the same way at home and at school. Transition from a community placement back to the child's own home is easier if the parents and other responsible adults use these modules in all the settings where the child lives, studies, and plays.

How Parents Can Use the Modules

Most parents, either alone or guided by a professional, will be able to understand a module in an hour or less, answering all the questions attached to each section in the module. Each module provides procedures for behavior change. It is through these procedures that problems are resolved and goals achieved. Most families can successfully carry out a module's procedures in 1 to 2 weeks and be ready to move on to the next module. Allowing 2 weeks to gather baseline information during Module 1, families could work through the first 11 core modules in 12 weeks.

Motivated parents who want to improve their parenting skills and whose children do not have serious behavior problems will be able to follow these modules without professional help. Parents whose children have serious behavior problems will benefit from professional guidance as they work through the modules.

Families working with a professional meet with the professional once a week for an hour. Each weekly meeting includes all adults and children who live in the home. Young children play on the floor while the rest of the family talks. From time to time, even very young children make a useful contribution. Consult Chapter 3 for more information on arranging a family meeting.

When a family works with a professional, the professional leads the weekly family meeting. Some professionals, to encourage generalization to the home setting, prepare parents to lead family meetings themselves.

When a family works without professional guidance and when the family is headed by two parents, the couple decides whether one or both will lead these family meetings. Couples who have a hard time working together and would both like the responsibility of leadership can flip a coin to choose a leader for one or all meetings. Successful use of the modules requires that the meeting leader follow the steps listed in the Checklist for Home-Problem Modules in Chapter 3. It is a good idea to make copies of the checklist and to use it to keep track of progress through each module.

Makeup of the Modules

Some modules focus on easy problems, while others focus on harder ones. Modules that are easily accomplished by almost every family, no matter how troubled, come early in the series. These early modules present the problems most families are likely to encounter. Modules that build on procedures presented in other modules come later in the series.

Each module after the first targets a common family problem such as temper tantrums or a system for chores and allowances. Most modules begin by explaining how the problem might affect a reasonably well functioning, or competent, family and how the problem might affect a poorly functioning, or less competent, family. Modules are designed so that the solution to the problem can be tailored to fit the needs and preferences of all family members.

Questions follow most sections in the modules. The questions aim to help the family think about the section and suit the section to their values, problems, and life circumstances. When a family cannot answer questions attached to one section, they should review the section until they can answer the questions and then move on to the next section.

Families can move forward from one module to the next as quickly or as slowly as they wish. Best results are achieved by working carefully through a module, answering every question, and following behavior-change procedures. Some families will prefer to spend several weeks getting used to new procedures before moving on; other families will be eager to resolve new problems. Families can always move back to earlier modules when new problems arise or when old problems reoccur. Sections at the end of the modules help families decide when to move on to new modules or when it is a good idea to return to the beginning of a module.

Deciding Which Modules to Work Through

Parents should read and work through the modules in the order in which they are presented. All parents should work through Module 1, Assessment; Module 3, Bedtime; and Module 5, Temper Tantrums. Module 1 assesses the problems that exist in the family. The parents can use what they learn from this module to decide what other modules they need to work through. The nonmandatory modules begin with sections that help parents use their assessment data to decide if the family needs to work through the module. Modules 3 and 5 must be worked on by all families because they teach techniques vital to many of the rest of the modules.

Module 1: Assessment

Most parents want child behavior problems and family conflict to be resolved quickly with good short-term and long-term results. Deciding that a family problem is satisfactorily resolved can be difficult if your family relies only on opinions. Opinions about change may differ between family members; some may think the problem has cleared up, while others may disagree. Or, your family may think the problem has been resolved, while a professional may disagree. Some problems may disappear for a short time, only to crop up again later. Other problems may be resolved, but the solution itself may cause new problems.

Parents who gather evidence about all family problems before they confront any are in the best position to determine what problems to work on and if the problems have been resolved. These parents will be certain of which problems have been resolved and which have not. They will know for how long solutions have worked and what unexpected new problems have emerged.

This module shows you how to chart information useful in deciding what problems to work on and how to measure the success of your efforts as you work through modules 2 to 13. This is the only module that does not require children's involvement in a family meeting, although involvement of children even at this stage is a good idea.

1. Keeping an Assessment Chart

Make a copy of the Home-Problem Assessment Chart that follows. Enter daily dates (month, day, year) in the date column, beginning with tomorrow's date. Continue entering consecutive daily dates until you have filled the date column.

The columns after the date column are named for the modules in this chapter. You will fill in this chart for 7 to 14 days, watching for each of the things named in the column labels, to get a "baseline record." The baseline record will show how your family behaves before you use any of the modules that follow. By making a baseline record, you will be able to tell what problems your family needs to work on and, later, by comparing your baseline record with the assessment charts you will keep as you work on modules, you will know how well your family is doing. The long-term effects of modules on your family can also be shown by continuing to keep charts when you have finished the modules. One way to ensure continued success is to keep the assessment chart for 6 months after all modules have been successfully completed. After this time, collect a baseline record and return to the appropriate modules whenever you have reason to believe that an old problem has reoccurred or that a new problem has emerged.

Home-Problem Assessment Chart

1. DATE	2. Clothes, toys away		3. Bedtime problems		4. Toileting problems		5. Temper tantrums		6. Fights		7. Instructions followed
	YES	NO	Earned, owed bedtime for all modules	NO	Accidents, good behavior, rewards given	NO	Timeouts called, completed	NO	Timeouts called, completed	YES	Timeouts called, completed

8. Good behavior away from home		9. On time to school		10. Chores done		11. Homework done		12. Loneliness, unhappiness, fearfulness, self-injury		13. Swearing, lying, cheating, stealing, fire setting, violence	
YES	Timeouts called, completed	YES	Good behavior, rewards given	YES	Good behavior, rewards given	YES	Good behavior, rewards given	NO	Problems, good behavior, rewards given	NO	Timeouts called, completed. Problems, good behavior, rewards given

Work through the rest of this module to learn how to fill in your assessment chart. You will not be filling in all the boxes on your chart. Some of them are not needed to get a baseline but are used later as you work through the modules. Begin by keeping the baseline record for 7 days. If anything unusual happens during this baseline (such as relatives come to visit for several days or your family goes on vacation), extend the baseline until you've kept a record for at least 7 fairly typical days. If unusual events and crises are typical of your family, keep a baseline record for 14 days in a row. Figure 1, One Family's Home-Problem Assessment Chart, gives you an example of how a baseline record might look after 1 week.

During baseline, do nothing different other than charting. Do not remind family members that you are charting. Once you have completed your initial baseline record, begin working through Modules 2 to 13. Don't stop charting for the other modules when you begin working on a module. By continuing to keep a record for other modules as you go along, you will produce what is called a multiple-baseline design. This design helps you determine if the changes that you see in your children's behavior are the result of your intervention with the modules or if they may be caused by other random factors. If behavior problems that you have not intervened with become much better, some other factor, such as the child maturing, may be at work. A continued record can show you when it is not necessary to use the modules for behavior that had been a problem at the beginning of the charting.

∞∞∞

1. What is the reason for keeping a chart during baseline?
2. Who will be responsible for keeping the chart?
3. When will you begin charting and when will you end?
4. What will you do if something unusual happens during the baseline?
5. Will you remind anyone in your family about the chart during baseline?

∞∞∞

2. Getting a Baseline Record for Module 2

Pick a time each day when all clothes and toys should be put away without reminder. Let's say you have picked 5:00 p.m. Now, in the first box in Column 2 above the word *YES* write 5:00 p.m. Beginning tomorrow, walk around the house at 5:00 p.m. and without saying anything to anyone see if your children's clothes, toys, and other belongings have been put away without reminders or scolding. If they have been, put a check in Column 2 in the row for the day's date. If anything is lying around, say nothing and do not put a check in Column 2. Keep this record for all of your children from age 3 through age 17.

∞∞∞

1. At what time each day will you find out if your children's belongings are where they should be?
2. What will you do if nothing is lying around?
3. What will you do if things are not where they belong?
4. Will you remind or scold any child who has left things lying around the house?

∞∞∞

3. Getting a Baseline Record for Module 3

Column 3 is labelled "Bedtime problems." Tomorrow night and every night after that put a check in Column 3 in the small box labelled *NO* if none of your children from age 3 through age 13 had to be reminded to get ready for bed or to go to bed; none went to bed at what you believe to be an inappropriate time; none did not stay quietly in the bedroom until morning, making only brief, quiet trips to the bathroom; and none expressed problems with bad dreams or fear of monsters.

∞∞∞

1. To which children in your family does Column 3 apply?
2. What do you believe to be appropriate times for each child to be in bed? Why?
3. When will you put a check in Column 3?

∞∞∞

4. Getting a Baseline Record for Module 4

Column 4 is labelled "Toileting problems." If any of your children from age 3 through age 13 has trouble with wetting or soiling, keep track of his accidents. Each time the child has an accident put the child's initial followed by W for wetting or S for soiling and the approximate time of day in Column 4 in the box labelled *Accidents, good behavior, rewards given.* Put a check in the box labelled *NO* only if no child age 3 to 13 had problems with soiling or wetting that day.

∞∞∞

Figure 1. One Family's Home-Problem Assessment Chart

1. DATE	2. Clothes, toys away (5:00pm YES)	NO	3. Bedtime problems (Earned, owed bedtime for all modules)	NO	4. Toileting problems (Accidents, good behavior, rewards given)	NO	5. Temper tantrums (Timeouts called, completed)	NO	6. Fights (Timeouts called, completed)	YES	7. Instructions followed (Timeouts, called, completed)
1/20/85	✓	✓			M-W 7pm	X		X		X	
1/21/85	✓	✓		✓		X		X		✓	
1/22/85		✓			M-W 8pm	✓		X		✓	
1/23/85	✓	✓			M-W 7pm	X		✓		✓	
1/24/85	✓	✓		✓		✓		✓		X	
1/25/85	✓	✓			M-W 7pm	✓		✓		✓	
1/26/85	✓	✓			M-W 7pm	X		✓		✓	

8. Good behavior away from home		9. On time to school		10. Chores done		11. Homework done		12. Loneliness, unhappiness, fearfulness, self-injury		13. Swearing, lying, cheating, stealing, fire setting, violence	
YES	Timeouts called, completed	YES	Good behavior, rewards given	YES	Good behavior, rewards given	YES	Good behavior, rewards given	NO	Problems, good behavior, rewards given	NO	Timeouts called, completed. Problems, good behavior, rewards given
✓			—	✓			—	✓			D-LY
✓		✓		✓		✓		✓			C-C
✓		✓		✓				✓			D-LY C-C
	✓								c-u	✓	
✓						✓		✓			D-LY
✓		✓		✓		✓		✓		✓	
✓			—	✓			—	✓			C-C

1. To which children in your family does Column 4 apply?
2. How will you record problems with wetting and soiling?
3. When will you put a check in Column 4?

∞∞∞

5. Getting a Baseline Record for Module 5

Column 5 is labelled "Temper tantrums." You know that a temper tantrum is taking place when a child, who has not been mistreated, is out-of-control for at least 1 minute, screaming, crying, throwing things, or hitting. Tomorrow night and every night after that put a check in Column 5 in the box labelled *NO* if no child from age 3 through age 13 had a temper tantrum that day.

If you like, mark an *X* in the box when you see a temper tantrum. The *Xs* will remind you not to put a check in the box that evening.

∞∞∞

1. When will you put a check in Column 5?
2. Will you put a check in Column 5 if one child has a temper tantrum and the other does not?
3. What can you do to remind yourself that you saw a temper tantrum during the day?

∞∞∞

6. Getting a Baseline Record for Module 6

Column 6 is labelled "Fights." You know that a fight is taking place when you think children are fighting and you can hear their voices from the room next to where they are, when one child complains to you that another is picking on or hitting him, and when you see one child hitting another. Tomorrow night and every night after that put a check in Column 6 in the box labelled *NO* if there were no fights between children from age 3 through age 13 that day.

If you like, mark an *X* in the box when you see a fight. The *Xs* will remind you not to put a check in the box that evening.

∞∞∞

1. When will you put a check in Column 6?
2. What will you do if only one fight occurs even though there are usually many more fights in your house?
3. What can you do to remind yourself that you saw a fight during the day?

∞∞∞

7. Getting a Baseline Record for Module 7

Column 7 is labelled "Instructions followed." Tomorrow night and every night after that put a check in Column 7 in the box labelled *YES* if all the instructions you gave that day to children from age 3 through age 13 were followed.

If you like, mark an *X* in the box when a child doesn't follow your instructions. The *X*s will remind you not to put a check in the box that evening.

∞∞∞

1. When will you put a check in Column 7?
2. What can you do to remind yourself that a child didn't follow instructions during the day?

∞∞∞

8. Getting a Baseline Record for Module 8

Column 8 is labelled "Good behavior away from home." Tomorrow night and every night after that put a check in Column 8 in the box labelled *YES* if all the behavior away from home of children from age 3 through age 13 was good.

If you like, mark an *X* in the box when a child acts inappropriately in public. The *X*s will remind you not to put a check in the box that evening. Draw a line through boxes for the days children were not in public with you to show that you did not keep track on those days.

∞∞∞

1. When will you put a check in Column 8?
2. What can you do to remind yourself that a child behaved poorly in public during the day?
3. How will you mark days when children were not in public with you?

∞∞∞

9. Getting a Baseline Record for Module 9

Column 9 is labelled "On time to school." Tomorrow night and every night after that (Monday through Friday) put a check in Column 9 in the box labelled *YES* if all children who attend school from age 4 through age 17 got to school on time that day and stayed at school without any reminders or special help from you. If you prefer, you can enter the check right after the morning is over. Draw a line through the boxes for Saturday and Sunday to show that you did not keep track on those days.

∞∞∞

1. When will you put a check in Column 9?
2. How will you show that you did not keep track of school attendance on Saturday and Sunday?

coococo

10. Getting a Baseline Record for Module 10

Column 10 is labelled "Chores done." Tomorrow night and every night after that put a check in Column 10 in the box labelled *YES* if all children from age 4 through age 17 did their assigned chores on time, up to your standards, and with no reminders.

coococo

1. When will you put a check in Column 10?
2. Will you remind children to do their chores?

coococo

11. Getting a Baseline Record for Module 11

Column 11 is labelled "Homework done." Tomorrow night and every night after that (Monday through Friday) put a check in Column 11 in the box labelled *YES* if all children from age 6 through age 17 quietly did their homework or read a library book for at least 1 hour with no television on and no reminder. Draw a line through the boxes for Saturday and Sunday to show that you did not keep track on those days.

coococo

1. When will you put a check in Column 11?
2. How will you show you did not keep track of homework on Saturday and Sunday?

coococo

12. Getting a Baseline Record for Module 12

Column 12 is labelled "Loneliness, unhappiness, fearfulness, self-injury." Tomorrow night and every night after that put a check in Column 12 in the box labelled *NO* if no child from age 3 through age 17 complained about loneliness, unhappiness, or fearfulness and if no child injured himself needlessly on that day. On days when a problem occurred, put the child's initial in the box labelled *Problems, good behavior, rewards given* followed by a letter to indicate the problem (L = loneliness, U = unhappiness, F = fearfulness, I = self-injury).

coococo

1. When will you put a check in Column 12?
2. How will you indicate that a child had a problem with loneliness, unhappiness, fearfulness, or self-injury?

∽∽∽

13. Getting a Baseline Record for Module 13

Column 13 is labelled "Swearing, lying, cheating, stealing, fire setting, violence." Tomorrow night and every night after that put a check in Column 13 in the box labelled *NO* if no child from age 3 through age 17 was involved in swearing, lying, cheating, stealing, fire setting, or violence on that day. On days when a problem occurred, put the child's initial in the box labelled *Timeouts called, completed. Problems, good behavior, rewards given* followed by a letter or letters to indicate the problem (SW = swearing, LY = lying, C = cheating, S = stealing, FI = fire setting, V = violence).

∽∽∽

1. When will you put a check in Column 13?
2. How will you indicate that a child had a problem with swearing, lying, cheating, stealing, fire setting, or violence?

∽∽∽

14. Moving On to Module 2

Once you have a baseline record lasting between 7 and 14 days, check over the record and decide if it represents the way things usually go in your house. If it does, begin working on Module 2. If the baseline record does not seem to give an accurate picture, continue until you have 7 reasonably accurate days charted. Then begin working on Module 2.

∽∽∽

1. Is your baseline record reasonably accurate? If yes, what will you do next? If no, what will you do next?
2. If your baseline record is not accurate, why do you think it is not?
3. What could you do to ensure that the rest of the baseline record will provide a more accurate picture?

∽∽∽

Module 2: Putting Clothes and Toys Away

Almost all parents have some complaints about their children's messiness and disorganization. Telling children to put their things away repeatedly doesn't seem to teach them to care for their belongings without reminders but can cause arguments and resentment between parents and children. When children take responsibility for their own belongings, they contribute to family harmony because no one else has to find their lost possessions. They also prepare for school, where organization and planning are important skills.

This module explains how you can encourage your children to put their belongings away without nagging or threatening them. The behavior-change procedures in this module are modeled after the Sunday Box described by Ogden Lindsley in a 1966 article in the *Johnstone Bulletin*. Children's belongings that are not put away every day are put in a box and not returned until Sunday. This module is appropriate for children from age 3 through age 17.

Putting clothes and toys away as a problem in a competent family. Family members include two parents in their early 40s, a 7-year-old son, and a 5-year-old daughter. Father is a member of a symphony orchestra and Mother, a high school teacher. Both are active in community life; they are patrons of the arts and highly regarded for their involvement in local and state politics. The family travels together to foreign countries to attend Father's performances whenever schedules permit. When both parents are working or traveling, a live-in housekeeper cares for the children. Mother and Father are worried about their children's messiness; the children rely on the housekeeper to pick up after them. The housekeeper, who sees organizing the children's rooms as part of her job, discourages the children from putting their things away despite requests from the parents to leave this responsibility for the children.

Putting clothes and toys away as a problem in a less competent family. This family includes two parents, both in their late 40s, 16- and 14-year-old daughters, and a 12-year-old son. Mother, who taught school before she married, is now a homemaker. Father owns a chain of drugstores. The whole family spends almost all of their free time together in religious activities and at their lakeside vacation home. The parents rarely spend time alone with each other or socialize with other couples. The three children dress and act as if they were several years younger than they are. Both girls seem much less mature than other girls their ages. They cling to their mother and demand that she do things for them that most teenaged girls want to do for themselves, such as fixing their hair and choosing their clothes. The son has no friends, is very fearful, and engages in many rituals, such as closing doors in a certain way. All three children leave their things around the house and wait for Mother to put them away. She usually does this quietly but angrily. She eventually complains to Father, who orders one of the children to clean up and uses physical punishment if the child doesn't obey.

1. Deciding if You Need to Work Through This Module

Look at your baseline record in Column 2. You need not work through Module 2 if: (*a*) you are sure your baseline record was fairly typical for your family, (*b*) there was a check in Column 2 for 6 out of 7 baseline days, (*c*) children were not nagged or threatened to put things away, (*d*) children put their things away by themselves, and (*e*) no family member is unhappy about the way children care for their belongings.

If you decide to work through Module 2, draw a horizontal line across Column 2 underneath your last baseline day. The line will separate your baseline record from the record of your progress during Module 2. If you decide not to work through Module 2, continue filling in all columns of your chart, and move on to Module 3. If at any time fewer than 6 out of 7 days in Column 2 have checks, complete Module 2.

∞∞∞

1. Do you need to work through Module 2? If not, why not?

∞∞∞

2. Preparing to Use a Sunday Box

Pick a time by which children's belongings should be put away every day. Many parents choose 5:00 p.m., right before dinner. You could use the same time that you chose while getting the baseline measure. Write this time on your assessment chart in Column 2 above the label *YES*.

Get a box large enough to hold many items, but small enough to be locked in a closet, cupboard, or car trunk. Decide where you will lock the Sunday Box so that your children will not be able to get into it.

∞∞∞

1. At what time have you decided that children's belongings should be put away?
2. What container will you use for the Sunday Box? Where will you lock it away?
3. Why is it a good idea to lock up the Sunday Box?

∞∞∞

3. Using the Sunday Box

The first time you use the Sunday Box, for example at 5:00 p.m. on Monday, quietly walk around and put any of your children's possessions that are not where they should be in the box. Then, lock the Sunday Box away. Take the box around at 5:00 p.m. every day after that, putting in the box anything that is not where it belongs and then locking the box away. If you are one of two parents, share the responsibility for daily collection with your partner.

Once an item is in the Sunday Box, it stays there until Sunday. Do not return items to children before Sunday even if they whine or complain. On Sunday morning, empty the box in a room used by the whole family. Always use the same room. When you bring the Sunday Box around that evening, put any unclaimed items back in the box.

Donate any items that stay in the Sunday Box for two Sundays in a row to your favorite charity. If you cannot afford to give up these items, store them and return them as birthday gifts.

Once you've started using the Sunday Box and see good results, don't stop. If you do, the good results will vanish. When you are travelling, bring the Sunday Box along with you, or create one at your destination. Keep using the Sunday Box until your children are grown up and living away from home.

∞∞∞

 1. Will you warn children before you bring the Sunday Box around?
 2. Will you talk about putting things in the Sunday Box as you are doing it?
 3. What will you put in the Sunday Box?
 4. Will you return things to children if they whine or complain?
 5. What will you do with the Sunday Box when you are finished collecting for the day?
 6. How long do things stay in the Sunday Box?
 7. Where will you return the contents of the Sunday Box and when?
 8. What will you do with items that you returned Sunday morning but are still not put away that night?
 9. When will you donate items from the Sunday Box to a charity? To what charity will you donate these things? If you decide not to donate these items to charity, what will you do with them?
10. When should you stop using the Sunday Box?
11. What will happen if you stop using the Sunday Box before your children are grown up and living away from home?

At 4:30 p.m. every day, one mother begins reminding her two boys that the Sunday Box will soon come around. By 5:00 when she brings the Sunday Box around, they have generally put most of their things away. One day she came home late from work and didn't remind the boys about the Sunday Box. By 5:15, the box was full of the boys' favorite toys. Why? Is Mother really being kind to her boys by reminding them to put their things away? Why not?

∞∞∞

4. Explaining the Sunday Box to Your Children

Before you begin using the Sunday Box, explain it once to your children. You might say something like this:

"Jenny and Sue, I've decided to use something new to help you learn to put your things away. It's called the Sunday Box. Every day at 5:00 I will walk through the house and put anything that is not put away into this box. I'll keep things in the box until Sunday morning at 9:00 when I'll put whatever is in the box on the table in the family room. You can have your things back then. If something is still on the family room table by 5:00 on Sunday, though, it goes back into the box. Whatever is in the box for two Sundays in a row will be given away to the Salvation Army. Now, let's go in your room and decide where all of your things should be put away."

Make sure that you include in your explanation:

1. Why you will use the Sunday Box.
2. What will go into the Sunday Box.
3. When the box will be used.
4. When and where the contents of the box will be returned.
5. What will happen to anything that is in the box twice in a row.

Also explain to your children where their belongings should be put. What you expect of your children will depend on each child's age, strength, and motor skills. Help your children succeed by providing easily reached hooks, closet rods, and book and toy shelves. Have your children repeat your explanation of the Sunday Box and where their belongings should be put away to make sure they understand what you've told them. Even if they don't seem to understand, follow through with your plan. They will understand once they're experienced the Sunday Box procedure a few times.

∞∞∞

1. How many times will you explain the Sunday Box to your children?
2. What five things will you tell your children about the Sunday Box?
3. How will you make sure they understand what you have told them? What if they don't seem to understand?

∞∞∞

5. Helping Children Get Used to the Sunday Box

Children are responsible for the consequences of losing items to the Sunday Box. Your children may complain that teachers will punish them for appearing at school without their homework or gym equipment. If you merely listen sympathetically, but give no advice, your children will figure out how to deal with teachers and will put their homework and gym equipment away before the Sunday Box comes around again. If children lose items such as winter coats to the Sunday Box, provide warm, but not equally attractive, substitutes.

∞∞∞

1. What will you do if homework or gym equipment lands in the Sunday Box?
2. What will you do if a winter coat lands in the Sunday Box?

∞∞∞

6. What to Do About Parents' Belongings

Children often ask whether their parents' things go in the Sunday Box. If your children ask this question, explain once that because you have more responsibilities than they have, you also have more power. For this reason you will not put parents' things in the Sunday Box. Tell them that when they have children, they can put their children's things in the Sunday Box.

You can also explain once that you will not abuse your power. Make sure that you do put all of your belongings away each day to provide a good example for your children.

∞∞∞

1. If your children ask whether parents' things go in the Sunday Box, what will you say?
2. How will you provide a good example to your children?

When Jeff and Debbie come home from work, they each change into comfortable clothes, spend a few minutes relaxing and then make sure that their own belongings are put away. Then one of them takes the Sunday Box around, while the other starts dinner. Matthew and Elizabeth, their children, rarely lose anything to the Sunday Box, although neither child is compulsively neat. Why?

∽∽∽

7. Moving On to Module 3

After you have used the Sunday Box every day for 1 week, continue using the Sunday Box and move on to Module 3. Make sure to continue using these procedures and charting for this module when you move on. Note that success with this module occurs when you regularly use the Sunday Box every day as directed, not when children put their things away every day (or even most days). Perfect tidiness on children's part should never be expected, since it is not particularly healthy. It is very likely that regular, appropriate use of the Sunday Box will encourage much more tidiness and organization by children. The speed with which this change occurs will vary depending upon children's ages, past experience, and with the manner in which you use the Sunday Box. To avoid putting undue pressure on children and to contribute to your family's progress through training, you can move on to the next module after you have consistently used the Sunday Box for a week. When children's messiness is a very troubling problem, delay moving on to the next module until there are at least twice as many checks in Column 2 after implementing Module 2 as there were during baseline.

If you start using the Sunday Box and then stop, if you think you aren't using the Sunday Box correctly, or if you aren't consistently using the Sunday Box every day, return to the beginning of this module.

∽∽∽

1. How will you know when you are ready to move on to Module 3?
2. When is it a good idea to begin Module 2 again?

∽∽∽

Module 3: Bedtime

Although most parents would like children to go to bed in a peaceful manner, a surprising amount of arguing takes place in many households as children get ready for and into bed. For these children, arguing about sleeping may produce restlessness and nighttime fears. Other children, who have no set bedtimes, watch television until they fall asleep and are irritable in the morning.

When children get ready for bed on their own and amuse themselves until they fall asleep, they learn habits that will be useful when they are older. Children who can amuse themselves until they fall asleep are prepared for the delays and boredom that are a part of many school days.

This module explains how you can teach children to get ready for and into bed on their own at a reasonable hour every night and to amuse themselves until they fall asleep. It also includes sections that explain what to do about bad dreams and fear of monsters. This module is appropriate for children from age 3 through age 13.

Bedtime as a problem in a competent family. Members of this family include Father, a 45-year-old policeman, Mother, a 40-year-old homemaker, a 10-year-old son, and an 8-year-old daughter. Mother's parents live upstairs from the family, and Father's parents live down the street. Father is going to night school to prepare for promotion. Mother is very active in her church and in the school's parent-teacher organization. Sundays and holidays are spent with grandparents, aunts, and cousins. For several years, both children have refused to sleep in their own beds; they sleep on couches in the living room and, every once in a while, in their parents' bed. The parents' repeated efforts to get the children to sleep in their bedrooms end with one or both children crying and shaking with fear.

Bedtime as a problem in a less competent family. Members of this family include Father, a 46-year-old plumber, Mother, a 37-year-old homemaker, and an 8-year-old son. Father spends his free time at the racetrack. Mother, who has been depressed since her son was born, spends as much time as she can with her son, who in her opinion is a disturbed child. This is Father's second marriage. Over the last 9 years, several of Father's teenaged sons from his first marriage have lived with the family. In each case, the boys left home after a violent argument. The 8-year-old son has a television in his bedroom and watches it whenever he can. He rarely falls asleep before midnight and often appears sleepy and distracted at school. When Father is late coming home, Mother often lets her son sleep in her bed. Neither parent is worried about their son's bedtime routine.

1. Work Through This Module Even if Bedtime Is Not a Problem

Later modules in this chapter concerned with temper tantrums and fights build on this module. For this reason, you should read through each step in this module and answer each question even if bedtime is not a problem in your family. If your child's baseline record has checks for fewer than 6 out of 7 days, you need to use this module to establish bedtime routines. In that case, work through the module and apply its procedures. Draw a horizontal line across Column 3 underneath your last baseline day. The line will separate your baseline record from the record of your progress during Module 3.

∞∞∞∞

1. Does your baseline record indicate bedtime problems?
2. Why is it important to work through this module even if your children don't have bedtime problems?

∞∞∞∞

2. Establishing a Bedtime for Each Child

Decide on a bedtime for each child through age 13. Use the same bedtime for weekdays and weekends. As often as possible, make travel plans that respect regular bedtimes.

Set a bedtime consistent with each child's age. For example, ages 3 through 4—7:00 p.m., ages 5 through 7—7:30 p.m., ages 8 through 10—8:00 p.m., ages 11 through 12—8:30 p.m., and age 13—9:00 p.m.

Once children are in bed, keep the area near their rooms quiet. Lower your voices and the television volume. This is an opportunity to respect your children as you would like them to respect you.

Never set bedtime later because children whine or complain. Listen, but say nothing, when children whine or complain. If you extend bedtime after a child whines or complains, you will have more bedtime problems and more whining and complaining in the future. Always discuss a reasonable request the first time it is made. Once you've told the child your decision, do not discuss that same request again. Save later bedtimes for a treat that is either earned by the child or comes at a special time of year (for example, during a holiday or a visit by a special relative). Do not set bedtime later because of a special television program. Any television program shown after your child's bedtime is meant for older children.

Establishing bedtimes for children also involves providing a good example of nighttime behavior. Parents who fall asleep on the living room couch night after night tend to have children with poor bedtime routines. Decide how many hours of sleep you need each night and work on establishing a routine for getting ready for bed and into your bedroom at approximately the same time each night.

∞∞∞∞

1. What bedtimes have you chosen for each of your children?
2. What can you do to help your children fall asleep once they have gone to their rooms?
3. Why is it not a good idea to change children's bedtimes after they whine and complain?
4. When is it a good idea to give children later bedtimes?
5. What can you tell children when they want to stay up late to watch special television programs?
6. What kind of an example do your bedtime habits provide to your children? What could you do if you need to improve your example?

   Jack works the night shift at a newspaper plant. Ruth watched television, nibbled on snacks, and fell asleep on the living room couch every night waiting for Jack to get home. When she noticed that their children, Ellen and Susan, had trouble getting to bed on time, she started going to bed shortly after them and setting an alarm clock to wake her up just before Jack was due home. How do you think the children were affected by Ruth's solution? What do you feel were the effects on Ruth's health and her relationship with Jack?

∞∞∞∞

3. How to Help Children Who Don't Tell Time Get Ready for Bed on Their Own

Show young children who cannot tell time what the clock looks like at bedtime and at the time when they should be preparing for bed. Draw pictures with them of the clock at both times and hang the pictures near a clock. When it is time to give a young child a gift, give an inexpensive digital watch or clock.

Together with young children, figure out what happens just before they should get ready for bed. For example, a favorite television program may end at the time children should start washing and putting on pajamas. Read a special bedtime story to young children who get ready for bed independently.

∞∞∞∞

1. Can all of your children tell time?
2. How will you prepare children who can't tell time to get ready for bed on their own?
3. How can you reward young children for getting ready for bed independently?

∞∞∞

4. What to Do When Children Go to Bed On Time

When children get ready for bed on their own, tell them before they go to bed what they are doing that you like. You might say, "I see that you've washed and dressed for bed without reminder and come to say 'Goodnight.' I'm very pleased with what you've done."

When children go to bed on time and amuse themselves quietly until they fall asleep, tell them the next morning that you liked what they did the night before. You might say, "Last night you went to bed on time and stayed in your bedroom the rest of the night. I like that. Do you feel proud of yourself?"

∞∞∞

1. What will you say when your children get ready for bed on their own, and when will you say it?
2. What will you say when they go to bed on time, and when will you say it?

Four-year-old Adina loves to have her back rubbed. Every once in a while when Adina has gone to bed on time with no reminder, Mom comes in to her bedroom and gives Adina a back rub. Adina never has any trouble falling asleep, even at the end of a hard day at nursery school. Why not?

∞∞∞

5. What to Do When Children Don't Go to Bed On Time

Talk to children as little as possible if they are not in bed on time. Never answer children who call to you from their rooms unless they are very sick. Do not point out that they are late for bed or, if they are in their bedrooms, that they are noisy. Do not remind children of the consequences for going to bed late. When toddlers wander out of their rooms, put them back in their bedrooms without a word until they stay there for the rest of the night.

Make a note of how long it takes children beyond their bedtimes to go to their bedrooms and stay there without reminder. Bedtime owed is the difference between a child's regular bedtime and the time the child finally went into the bedroom and stayed there for the rest of the night.

When a child owes bedtime, wait until the child asks to be taken somewhere special or to be given a special privilege before discussing it. Gently remind the child once that the child owes you some bedtime. As soon as the child pays back the bedtime by going to bed earlier on 1 or several nights, comply with the child's special (and reasonable) requests. Let children initiate paying back bedtime. Let them decide on what nights to go to bed early and how early to go to bed. A conversation about bedtime might sound like this.

> **Lee:** Dad, all the kids are going to the skating rink tonight. Can I have a ride over there?

> **Dad:** Lee, the chart says you owe 1 hour of bedtime, so I won't take you to the rink tonight. As soon as you've paid back the bedtime you owe, I'll be happy to take you to the rink.

∞∞∞

1. Should you talk to children after their bedtimes?
2. What will you say to children who call out to you from their bedrooms?
3. Will you remind children about the consequences of going to bed late?
4. How can you help toddlers learn to stay in their bedrooms at night?
5. When will you consider children late for bed?
6. Will you remind children that they owe bedtime?
7. If children owe bedtime, will you do special things for them?
8. What will you say to a child who asks for a special privilege and owes bedtime? How often will you say this?
9. Who will decide when bedtime will be paid back?

∞∞∞

6. Explaining Bedtime to Your Children

Before you begin keeping track of bedtime owed, explain bedtime once to your children. You might say something like this:

> "I think it would be a good idea if each of you had a regular bedtime and got used to going to bed without reminder. That way you won't be as tired in school and I won't have to nag you to go to bed. Chris, I'd like you to be in bed by 8:00 p.m., John, by 9:00 p.m. Being on time for bed means being washed, dressed for bed,

and in your bedrooms with the doors closed at your bedtimes. Lights may be on, and you may read or play quietly until you decide to go to sleep. You may listen to your radios as long as the radios can't be heard outside your rooms. Trips to the bathroom must be made so quietly that I can't hear you. So long as you do all the things I've just described, I'll consider you on time for bed. If you forget one thing (for example, you make a few noisy trips to the bathroom), I'll consider you late for bed. The bedtime you owe will be the amount of time after your bedtime that it takes you to get into your bedrooms and stay there for the rest of the night (except for very quiet bathroom trips). You will have to make up the time you are late to bed by going to bed early on another day."

Make sure that you include in your explanation:

1. Why you will use bedtime procedures,
2. What your children's bedtimes are,
3. What being in bed on time means,
4. What they may do in their rooms until they fall asleep,
5. What they will have to do if they are late in going to bed,
6. How bedtime owed is calculated.

Have your children repeat your explanation of bedtime to make sure they understand what you've told them. Even if they don't seem to understand, follow through with your plan. They will understand once they've experienced the bedtime procedure a few times.

∞∞∞

1. How many times will you explain bedtime to your children?
2. What six things will you tell your children about bedtime?
3. How will you make sure they understand what you have told them? What if they don't seem to understand?

∞∞∞

7. Dealing with Bad Dreams and Monsters

Once you have successfully established bedtime routines for your children, you may need to take some steps to help children who wake up frightened in the middle of the night or who are afraid to go to sleep because of bad dreams and monsters.

Make sure to provide softly glowing night lights for all children's bedrooms and never lock your children in their rooms. When children wake up and come to your room, gently guide them back to their own rooms if they are toddlers or tell them to go back to their rooms if they are older. Young children may have to be repeatedly guided back to their own rooms. Children who come to your bedroom in the middle of the night for any reason except for a real emergency or illness owe you bedtime (the difference between their bedtime and the time they finally went back to their rooms and stayed there for the rest of the night).

It is not a good idea to sleep with frightened children because this gives children no opportunity to learn to cope with their fears themselves. From this experience, children often come to believe that they are incapable of dealing with fears without parents' physical presence. Sometimes, lonely or fearful parents get satisfaction from sleeping with their children when the children have minor fears. This practice doesn't help the parents and strengthens children's fears. Remember that growing up involves learning how to make it through the night without help from parents.

The day after a child's first nightmare, talk to the child about dreams. Explain that we often dream about our day's activities, especially about problems we haven't solved. Then help the child decide what to do on awakening from a bad dream. The child could turn the light on, go to the bathroom, get a glass of milk or water, and read or play quietly until ready for sleep. Put a drawing pad and crayons beside the bed so that the child can draw a picture of the bad dream. Some children like to show the picture to parents in the morning, others like to tear it up at night to show themselves that they are in control. In the morning, when the child tells you about coping with a bad dream without coming to your bedroom, praise the child and talk at length about the child's clever solution to the problem.

The first time a child mentions a fear of monsters, explain that there are no monsters but that many children imagine monsters. Then, help the child look for monsters under the bed and in the closet to show that there are no monsters. Do not repeat the monster search again, but encourage children to search for monsters on their own whenever they are afraid. Provide bedside lamps and flashlights to aid in this search.

Parents' arguments and sexual activities often wake children up and frighten them. To avoid this problem, close bedroom doors and play soft music to muffle noises.

∽∽∽

1. What will you do if your child wakes up frightened in the middle of the night and comes to your room?
2. Why is it not a good idea to sleep with a frightened child? What does this practice tell children about their ability to deal with fears on their own?
3. How can you prepare a child to deal with bad dreams?
4. How can you prepare a child to deal with monsters?

5. How will you muffle noise that might wake up children and frighten them?

Julia, a divorced mother, has noticed that her 9-year-old son, Raoul, often has nightmares on nights when she has invited a date over for dinner. Julia decided to explain to Raoul about nightmares and talk to him about how he feels when she has a date. She also has started preparing Raoul's favorite breakfast on mornings following an evening on which she had a dinner guest and Raoul got to bed and stayed there without any problems. What do you think Raoul will gain from this experience other than learning to get to bed on time?

∞∞∞

8. Keeping a Record for This Module

While working through this module, continue as you did during baseline to put a check in the small box in Column 3 labelled *NO* when none of your children (from age 3 to 13) were late going to bed or had bedtime problems that night. You will also want to keep track of bedtime owed in the box in Column 3 labelled *Earned, owed bedtime for all modules.* For example, if a child's bedtime is 8:00 and he finally went into his bedroom and stayed there at 10:00, he owes 2 hours of bedtime. If a child went to bed on time at 7:00 but got up at 8:30 and didn't go back in his bedroom until 9:00, he owes 2 hours of bedtime. Mark bedtime owed with the child's initial, a minus sign, and the number of minutes or hours owed. When a child makes up the bedtime, cross out the notation.

The example on the following page shows how Column 3 might look on a family's assessment chart after they have begun using Module 3. In this family there are two children, Andy and Bridget. On the first day of charting, Andy did not go to bed until 1 hour after his bedtime. This is marked in the first box by his initial, a minus sign, and the time (*A-1hr*). Andy made up the bedtime owed the next day, so the notation was crossed out. On the second day, Andy and Bridget both went to bed on time and had no bedtime problems. The check in the small box for this day records this behavior. On the third day, Andy went to bed 1 hour late and did not yet make up the extra time. Bridget went to bed ½ hour late but did make up the time the next day.

∞∞∞

1. Where will you record bedtime owed?
2. How will you record bedtime owed?
3. How will you keep a record of bedtime that your children make up?

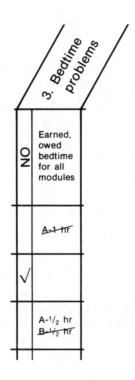

9. Moving On to Module 4

You can move on to Module 4 after you have consistently put bedtime routines into effect every night for at least 1 week. This may only take one family meeting and 1 week of homework for many families. If bad dreams and monsters are problems for your children, it may take more family meetings and homework to consistently put these procedures into effect. Make sure to continue using these procedures and charting for this module when you move on. If bedtime routines are very problematic, don't move on until the checks in Column 3 are twice as many as during baseline.

If you start to establish bedtime routines and then stop, if you think you aren't implementing bedtime procedures correctly, or if you aren't consistently implementing bedtime procedures, return to the beginning of this module.

∽∽∽

1. When can you begin to work on Module 4?
2. If you don't need to work on Module 4, when will you move on to Module 5?
3. When is it a good idea to begin Module 3 again?

∽∞∽∞∽∞

Module 4: Toileting

Children who soil often soil because they are constipated and unskilled in using the sphincter muscle to expel feces. When they are playing or are distracted, they relax and release some feces. Some children who soil never achieved bowel control as toddlers, while others did.

A number of circumstances promote poor bladder control. In some children, the problem is a result of insufficient toilet training. Other children are such deep sleepers that they are not awakened by the sensation of a full bladder. A few children report that they lose bladder control when they are frightened or anxious.

Children need to experience the natural consequences of poor toileting habits, and parents need to interfere less in what should be a self-managed bodily function. Most children learn toileting without any intervention, or with minimal intervention, by their parents. This module is aimed at children who fail to learn toileting in the normal way. It explains how you can promote good toileting habits by making children responsible for cleaning up after accidents and by using a reward system. It is appropriate for children age 3 through age 13.

Toileting as a problem in a competent family. This family consists of a mother and father both in their late 30s, who are high school teachers, and a 5-year-old girl. The girl is bright and outgoing. With her parents' help, she writes stories, illustrates them, and sometimes composes piano music to go along with the stories. Her parents find it hard to resist her requests because she is such a charmer. Toilet training is the only developmental task that she hasn't mastered. The girl soils her pants about once a day and wets her bed most nights. She is upset about both kinds of accidents and has asked her parents to find a doctor who can help her with this problem.

Toileting as a problem in a less competent family. This family consists of 40-year-old parents, a 10-year-old son, and a 7-year-old daughter. The boy, like his younger sister, has been wetting his pants at school and his bed at night since kindergarten. Mother is a homemaker, and she finds the responsibilities of caring for her home, two children, and husband—a busy, successful executive—overwhelming. She maintains that her son will outgrow his problem with wetting but panics when he comes home from school crying because he's been teased about his bad smell. Father is generally not worried about his son's problem, but he becomes irate when his wife calls him at the office or on a business trip to complain that the son's problem is the result of Father's frequent absence from home.

1. Deciding if You Need to Work Through This Module

Look at your baseline record in Column 4. You need not work through Module 4 if: (*a*) you are sure your baseline was fairly typical for your family, (*b*) you are satisfied with the progress of the normal toilet-training process with your children from 3 to 5 years old, (*c*) daytime soiling or wetting occurred less than once a week in a child 5 years old or older, (*d*) nighttime wetting occurred no more than once a week for children between the ages of 5 to 8 and less than once a week for children over age 8, (*e*) your pediatrician recommends letting the child outgrow wetting, and (*f*) your child expresses no concern about the problem of wetting.

Before beginning this module, have your child examined by a pediatrician. If the pediatrician tells you that the child needs to learn better bowel or bladder habits or to be more aware of a full bowel or bladder, use this module. If your pediatrician recommends that your child be allowed to grow out of the problem, agree with your pediatrician on an amount of time during which you will not pay any attention to the problem. Together with your pediatrician, institute the procedures described here if the problem has not resolved itself during the agreed upon waiting period. If the child has a physical problem that cannot be completely corrected with surgery or if drug therapy has been tried and has been unsuccessful or has had poor side effects, you can also use this module. Under these conditions, make sure that you are very consistent in instituting recommended changes and very patient with your child. Consider consulting a psychologist skilled in behavioral pediatrics. With poor feedback from sphincter muscles or bladder, learning of self-control may be very difficult and slow using these procedures alone.

If you decide to work through Module 4, draw a horizontal line across Column 4 underneath your last baseline day. The line will separate your baseline record from the record of your progress during Module 4. If you decide not to work through Module 4, continue filling in all columns of your chart and move on to Module 5. If at any time soiling or wetting occurs more frequently than stated in the previous guidelines, complete Module 4.

∞∞∞

1. Do you need to work through Module 4? If not, why not?

∞∞∞

2. Making Your Children Responsible for Cleaning Up After an Accident

After nighttime soiling or wetting, have children wash themselves, put on clean clothes, change the sheets on their beds, and go to sleep without waking you. In the morning, children should wash the sheets and night clothes as you would ordinarily do. After daytime soiling or wetting, have children wash themselves, put on clean clothes, and wash the dirty clothes as you would ordinarily do.

Explain to all of your children (not just to the child with toileting problems) that from now on they are responsible for cleaning up when they get dirty. Lead each of them through the steps required for bathing, stripping and making beds, and soaking and washing laundry. Make washcloths, soap, and other supplies readily available. Give ample praise when children clean up on their own. Only when their efforts are obviously inadequate should you ask them to redo their work (or wash themselves again). You should never do the work for them unless it is physically impossible for them to do it.

∞∞∞

1. What will you have children do after nighttime soiling or wetting?
2. What will you have children do after daytime soiling or wetting?
3. How will you help children learn to clean up after accidents?
4. How will you reward children for cleaning up on their own?
5. What will you do when their efforts to clean up are inadequate?
6. When will you do the cleaning up for your children?

∞∞∞

3. Making Bowel Movements in the Toilet More Likely

There are several things you can do to make bowel movements in the toilet by your children more likely. First, if the pediatrician says that your child is constipated, ask for an enema for the child. Also, ask the pediatrician to prescribe a very mild dose of laxative that your child can take nightly for the next few weeks while getting into the habit of a daily bowel movement in the toilet. Begin serving a high-fiber diet, including whole-grain breads and cereals, to all family members.

Second, make sure that the bathroom your child uses is warm, comfortable, and free from harassment, such as other family members telling the child to hurry up. Make sure that the school bathroom is equally free of harassment and that the teacher excuses the child to use the bathroom on request.

Third, pick out a number of toys and books with your child that are to be used only when the child is seated on the toilet. Place a timer in the bathroom and show the child how to set it for 5 minutes. Ask the child to sit on the toilet for 5 minutes once a day after a meal eaten at home. Choose the meal after which the child is most likely to have a bowel movement. The child need not go to the toilet immediately after leaving the table. Ask the child to set the timer so that the child will know when 5 minutes are up. Remind the child only one time a day, after the meal that usually precedes soiling (most often this is breakfast), to sit on the toilet after meals. Whenever the child sits on the toilet for 5 minutes, praise the child lavishly for working on a new and important habit.

∞∞∞

1. What will you do if your child is constipated?
2. What should you check about your bathroom at home and the child's bathroom at school?
3. How will you encourage your child to have a bowel movement after meals?
4. What will you do when your child sits on the toilet for 5 minutes after meals?

∞∞∞

4. Rewarding Your Child for Bowel Movements in the Toilet

One way to reward a child for bowel movements in the toilet is by using a goodie bag. With your child, buy a number of small toys and treats, wrap each one up, and put them in a paper bag. Let the child choose a goodie each time there is a bowel movement in the toilet. Another way to reward the child is by agreeing with the child on a movie or activity for the weekend and then agreeing upon how many bowel movements will be needed to earn that activity. Your child's age and interests should determine how you reward a bowel movement in the toilet. Explain to the child that these rewards are designed to help build an important, but hard to acquire, habit. Once the habit is very well established, the rewards will no longer be needed.

Do not reward the child for clean pants or for no evidence of soiling. Such a reward system encourages withholding of feces, constipation, and ultimately more soiling.

Getting the cooperation of teachers, babysitters, and anyone the child spends a lot of time with will help the child improve more quickly. Be patient. You are likely to see gradual improvement over a period of 2 months or more. Any changes in routine, including illness and vacations away from home, are likely to slow improvement or cause a setback.

As soon as you have had 2 months during which no soiling occurred along with daily bowel movements in the toilet, begin to gradually phase out the rewards you are providing for bowel movements in the toilet. The same reward that was once earned by a bowel movement in the toilet on 1 day will now require a bowel movement in the toilet on 2 days. After another month of continued success, introduce some more inflation so that the reward requires 3 days of bowel movements in the toilet. Discontinue all material rewards and switch to praise alone after 6 months of uninterrupted success. Continue to praise daily visits to the toilet after a meal and bowel movements in the toilet for another few months and then gradually notice these habits less and less often. At the same time, encourage your child to praise himself (aloud at first, silently later) for demonstrating grown-up, healthy habits.

∞∞∞∞

1. How will you reward your child for bowel movements in the toilet?
2. Why is it not a good idea to reward a child for clean pants?
3. How quickly should you expect your child to improve in bowel movements in the toilet?
4. When will you begin to phase out rewards for bowel movements?
5. How will you phase them out?

> Sandy, age 3, insists on having bowel movements in a diaper. She has her mother change her from underpants to a diaper whenever she is ready for a bowel movement. Sandy refuses to sit on the toilet at these times. Sandy's mother and father talked the problem over and decided to stop changing Sandy after a bowel movement and to require her to clean up after herself when she soils her pants. What do you think of this approach? What good results do you expect? What else could Sandy's parents do to help with toilet training?

∞∞∞∞

5. Explaining Rewards for Bowel Movements in the Toilet to Your Child

Before you begin rewarding your child for bowel movements in the toilet, explain once what you will be doing. You might say something like this:

"Tim, you and I are going to start working on something important for you to learn. That is to make bowel movements in the toilet instead of in your pants. Using the toilet is a very grown-up thing to do, but it's not always easy to learn. To help you learn, I would like you to sit on the toilet for 5 minutes after lunch. Here is a timer that I will teach you to set for 5 minutes. When you do make a bowel movement in the toilet, you will get a treat. This afternoon we will go buy some treats, wrap them up, and put them in a goodie bag."

Make sure that you include in your explanation:

1. Why you will reward the child for bowel movements in the toilet,
2. When you want the child to use the toilet for 5 minutes,
3. How the child will be rewarded for bowel movements in the toilet.

Have your child repeat your explanation to make sure he understands you. Even if your child doesn't seem to understand, follow through with your plan. He will understand after he has experienced the procedures a few times.

∞∞∞

1. How many times will you explain bowel movements in the toilet to your child?
2. What three things will you tell your child about bowel movements in the toilet?
3. How will you make sure your child understands what you have said? What if your child doesn't seem to understand?

∞∞∞

6. Making Dry Days and Nights More Likely

If your pediatrician assures you that your child will outgrow the problem of wetting, continue to make the child responsible for cleaning up after accidents and stop worrying about the problem. Continue with the steps in this module only if your child expresses discomfort with wetting because of embarrassment at school or at friends' houses.

To make dry days and nights more likely, first make sure that the bathroom at home is warm and comfortable, and that the child is not harassed by other family members while using the bathroom. Make sure the bathroom at school is equally free from harassment and that the teacher excuses the child to use the bathroom upon request.

Second, make sure that you are following earlier procedures in Module 3 regarding bedtime. When children go to bed at the same time each night and are allowed to fall asleep at their own pace, they are less likely to wet the bed. Children who can fall asleep when they are ready tend to be more aware of a full bladder.

Third, if your child is a very deep sleeper and nighttime wetness is the problem, purchase a conditioning device available through the Sears catalog (Sears Wee Alarm or Sears Lite Alarm). These products use a buzzer or bell attached to a pad placed beneath the child's sheet. When the pad is wet, the circuit is closed and the alarm goes off, awakening the child. After several nights, the child begins to anticipate the alarm by waking up before wetting and going to the toilet. Teach the child how to turn off the alarm and replace the wet pad with a dry one. Do not turn the alarm off even if it wakes you up. Wait for the child to turn it off. Use of one of these devices can easily be combined with the reward system described in the next section.

∞∞∞

1. What will you do if your pediatrician tells you not to worry about your child's wetting, and your child isn't upset about wetting?
2. How do conditioning devices work? How do they train children to empty their bladders in the toilet? Why is it unwise for you to turn off the alarm if your child does not?

∞∞∞

7. Rewarding Your Child for Dry Days and Nights

Together with your child, decide on a "reward menu" for a dry day or dry night. A reward menu is a list of rewards that a child can choose from and that you and the child decide upon. Choose rewards that you will be able to give repeatedly, that are age appropriate, that the child values, and that you feel comfortable giving only when earned and withholding when not earned. If you like, include one or more choices on the reward menu that require 7 dry days or nights. Give these as bonuses beyond the daily rewards.

Include some items that the child will be able to share with siblings so that they will benefit when the child has a dry day or night. Siblings have enormous influence, for better or for worse, over one another's behavior. When siblings can benefit from one child's success, they work hard to contribute to that success. For example, if the child puts pancakes for breakfast on the menu, keep supplies for pancakes on hand, only provide pancakes for breakfast when they are earned, and provide pancakes for breakfast to other family members also when the child earns and selects this reward.

Decide how many choices from the menu the child will be able to make when the child has a dry day or night. Develop a lengthy written reward menu, so that the child will not tire of available rewards over the next few months. Post this reward menu where the child can see it. Physical affection and praise need not be listed on the menu, since you should praise your child after dry days or nights whether the child asks or not. Figure 2 shows a sample reward menu for dry days.

Watch for gradual improvement over the first month of your behavior-change program. After each week, fine-tune the program as needed and make necessary changes in the reward menu.

Figure 2. Sample Reward Menu for Dry Days

Jane Ann's Reward Menu
(Choose any two of the following after a dry day.)

Ice cream sundaes for dessert after dinner for the whole family

One hour of play with Dad when he comes home from work

One hour of bike riding with Mom

25¢ toward a toy

Two scratch-and-sniff stickers

One 3-minute phone call to Grandma

One friend can sleep over

Mom's special spaghetti with meat sauce for the whole family

Baking chocolate chip cookies with the rest of the family

After a month of continuous dryness, provide the same rewards after 2, rather than 1, dry days or nights. If nighttime and daytime wetting are both problems, after a month of continuous dry days provide the same rewards for a dry night and day, rather than just after a dry day. After an additional month of success, introduce more inflation. Make the same rewards available after three dry intervals, rather than two. Continue increasing the dry intervals needed to earn a reward each month until 6 successful months have passed. Then, stop the material rewards and provide lots of praise for dry intervals until several more successful months have passed. Also, encourage your child to praise himself (aloud at first, silently later). At that point, praise dryness only when the child calls attention to it.

∞∞∞

1. What type of rewards should you include on the reward menu?
2. Why don't you need to include physical affection and praise on the reward menu?
3. When should you give your child rewards?
4. What will you do after a month of continuous dry days or nights?
5. What will you do after 2 months of continuous dry days or nights?
6. When will you discontinue material rewards for dry days or nights?

Karen was very successful at setting up a program to increase Tim's dry nights. After the 1st month of complete dryness, she was so pleased that she stopped all material rewards. By the middle of the 2nd month, Tim started wetting his bed again. What went wrong? What should Karen have done at the end of the 1st month? What should she do now?

∞∞∞

8. Explaining Rewards for Dry Days and Nights to Your Child

Before you begin rewarding your child for dry days or nights, explain once what you will do. You might say something like this:

"Bob, you've told me how you wish you didn't wet the bed at night, so that you could sleep over at your friends' houses without embarrassment. Let's work together to teach you to wake up when your bladder is full and use the toilet. I've bought a sheet with an alarm attached that will wake you up when you wet the bed. After a few nights of being woken up after you wet the bed, you'll start waking up before you wet, when your bladder is full. Now I'm going to show you how the sheet works, how to change your bed when you do wet, and then we'll agree on a whole list of rewards that you can choose from when you wake up dry."

Make sure that you include in your explanation:

1. Why you will reward the child for dry days or nights,
2. How the nighttime conditioning device works (if you are using one) and what the child should do when the alarm goes off,
3. How the child will be rewarded for dry days and nights.

Have your child repeat your explanation to make sure he understands what you've told him. Even if your child doesn't seem to understand, follow through with your plan. He will understand after he has experienced the procedures a few times.

∞∞∞

1. How many times will you explain dry days and nights to your child?
2. What three things will you tell your child about dry days and nights?
3. How will you make sure your child understands what you have said? What if your child doesn't seem to understand?

∞∞∞

9. Keeping a Record for This Module

While working through this module, continue as you did during baseline to put a check in the small box in Column 4 labelled *NO* when none of your children (age 3 through age 13) had problems with soiling or wetting that day. You will also want to chart accidents as you did during baseline by writing down the child's initial, a W or S for wetting or soiling, and the time of the accident. In addition, you will want to keep track of bowel movements in the toilet and dry days or nights for your children who are being rewarded for these behaviors, and you will want to note when they are rewarded. On days when your child makes a bowel movement in the toilet or has a dry day or night, write the child's initial in the box labelled *Accidents, good behavior, rewards given* and put a star by the initial. This will remind you to reward your child for the behavior. When you reward your child, lightly cross out the initial and the star.

The example on the following page shows how Column 4 might look on a family's assessment chart after they have begun using Module 4. In this family there are two children, Andy and Bridget. On the first

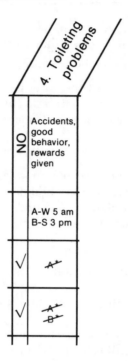

day of charting, Andy wet at 5:00 a.m. (*A–W 5am*) and Bridget soiled at 3:00 p.m. (*B–S 3pm*). On the second day there were no accidents by Andy or Bridget. This was indicated by the check in the small box in Column 4. In addition, Andy had a dry night and his initial and a star were marked down to show this (*A**). The initial and star were crossed out lightly when he was rewarded. On the third day, there were no accidents, Andy had a dry night and was rewarded, and Bridget made a bowel movement in the toilet and was rewarded.

∞∞∞

1. Where will you record your children's accidents?
2. How will you record your children's accidents?
3. How will you record your children's bowel movements in the toilet and dry days or nights?
4. How will you keep a record of the times that you reward your children?

∞∞∞

10. Moving On to Module 5

The establishment of long-term success with soiling and wetting requires a few months. You can move on to Module 5 when you have consistently used the procedures described in this module for at least 1 week. If toileting problems are extremely troublesome, don't move on until there are twice as many checks in Column 4 as there were during baseline. Putting these procedures into effect may be difficult. It may take a family two or three family meetings and 3 to 4 weeks of work before they are consistently putting these procedures into effect and are ready to move on to Module 5. Make sure to continue following the procedures in this module and to keep charting for this module when you move on to Module 5.

If you start to establish toileting routines and then stop, if you think you aren't implementing toileting procedures correctly, or if you aren't consistently implementing toileting procedures, return to the beginning of the module.

∽∽∽

1. How will you know when you are ready to move on to Module 5?
2. When is it a good idea to begin Module 4 again?

∽∽∽

Module 5: Temper Tantrums

A child's temper tantrums can make life miserable for family members. Tantrums indicate that a child lacks important skills—the ability to cope with anxiety, boredom, and frustration and the ability to solve problems with people and with objects. As a result, children who often resort to temper tantrums are at risk for problems at home, with peers, and at school.

This module explains what you can do when children have temper tantrums in order to reduce the number of temper tantrums and teach your children self-control and problem-solving skills. It explains the "timeout" procedure. In timeout, children who misbehave go to a "timeout room" for a fixed amount of time. Timeout can be used to remedy temper tantrums and many other problems. This module is appropriate for children from age 3 through age 13.

Temper tantrums as a problem in a competent family. A 35-year-old widowed commercial airlines pilot and her 5-year-old daughter make up this small family. Until her father's death in a car accident 2 years before, the daughter was a happy, well-adjusted little girl. Soon after her father's death, the daughter began having violent, prolonged temper tantrums. Her tantrums have always occurred when she is alone with her mother. At school or with babysitters and playmates, she never has temper tantrums. Mother has worked hard to adjust to her husband's death. She is terribly frustrated by her daughter's outbursts and ashamed that she sometimes avoids being alone with her daughter.

Temper tantrums as a problem in a less competent family. This family includes a 23-year-old pregnant mother on public assistance and her 3-year-old daughter. Mother, who was raised by an aunt, left home to live with her boyfriend when she was 17. Her boyfriend drinks heavily and often beats her and their daughter. Two times in the last few years, Mother has left her boyfriend's apartment and moved in with another man. According to Mother, her daughter is a wild animal, not a little girl. Mother claims that her daughter's temper tantrums are so violent that friends have advised her to put the child in a cage. The child, who is dirty, poorly dressed, and speaks very little, is quite docile with strangers.

1. Work Through This Module Even if Temper Tantrums Are Not a Problem

This module teaches timeout, a procedure which is necessary for dealing with temper tantrums and with problems presented in later modules in this chapter. Even if your child does not have temper tantrums, you will need to learn how to use timeout to deal with other problems, such as fighting between siblings. For this reason, you should read through each step in this module and answer each question even if your child has never had a temper tantrum. If your child's baseline record has checks for fewer than 6 out of 7 days, you need to use this module to reduce temper tantrums. In that case, work through the module and apply its procedures.

Draw a horizontal line beneath the last day in Column 5 on your assessment chart. The line will separate your baseline record from the record of your progress during Module 5.

∞∞∞

1. Does your baseline record show that temper tantrums are a problem in your family?
2. If temper tantrums are not a problem, why is it still important to work through this module?

∞∞∞

2. Recognizing a Temper Tantrum

A temper tantrum takes place when a child, who has not been mistreated, is out-of-control for at least 1 minute, screaming, crying, throwing things, or hitting. Most parents recognize when a temper tantrum is taking place. Usually tantrums occur when a child has been told no or when a child is very tired.

Only rarely is a temper tantrum the result of illness or serious injury. Whenever you believe that a child having a tantrum is ill or hurt, quickly and quietly get the information you need to make a decision and provide whatever care is needed. If the tantrum is not a one-time event but is a repeating problem, provide whatever care the child needs and follow the next steps in this module, even if the child having the tantrum is ill or hurt.

Temper tantrums can occur with or without self-destructive behavior that causes physical injury, such as head banging or hair pulling. Most temper tantrums do not involve self-injury, although parents often deal poorly with temper tantrums because they fear children will hurt themselves. Parents of otherwise well-adjusted children can learn to respond successfully to temper tantrums without professional help if no self-destructive behavior is involved. However, a self-destructive tantrum signals problems best handled with the help of a mental-health professional. For more information on the topic, consult Module 12 in this chapter.

∞∞∞

1. What do your children's temper tantrums look like? Are there differences among your children in the way they have temper tantrums?
2. What usually happens right before your children have temper tantrums? What usually happens right after?
3. What is the thing to do if a child having a temper tantrum seems ill or hurt?
4. Do your children ever have self-destructive temper tantrums? If so, how do they injure themselves?
5. Why should self-destructive tantrums be approached differently than tantrums that are not self-destructive?

∞∞∞

3. Preparing Timeout Rooms

Pick a timeout room for each child in your family. The rooms should have doors that close but do not lock. The best timeout room is the child's own bedroom. If your children have televisions in their rooms, remove them along with anything that might harm an out-of-control child.

If children do not have their own bedrooms, assign a timeout room to each child, making sure that the room has no television or dangerous items in it, such as sharp objects, poisons, or small objects that can be swallowed, but does have interesting toys and books. Do not use the bathroom for timeout. In a small apartment, assign a timeout spot to each child.

Leave children's toys and books in the timeout room, since you want children to calm down and distract themselves in timeout. It is not unusual for a tired child to fall asleep during timeout and wake up refreshed. Many children who become accustomed to timeout as described in this module gradually start going to their rooms when they feel angry or upset as a way of avoiding a timeout.

∞∞∞

1. Describe the timeout room you've chosen for each child in the family.
2. Why is it a good idea for the child's room to be the timeout spot?

Rosa, a single mother, lives with her two sons in a one-bedroom apartment. The television is usually on in the living room, and it can be heard and seen from the small kitchen. Suggest what Rosa must do to send one or both boys to timeout in her apartment. What problems will she probably encounter? How can she solve them?

∞∞∞∞

4. Calling Timeout for Temper Tantrums

Call timeout as soon as a temper tantrum begins. Do this by saying "timeout" and waiting silently for the child to go to the timeout room. Do not warn or threaten the child that timeout will be called soon. Just call timeout as soon as the temper tantrum begins. It is unwise to warn a child about a possible timeout, because such warnings prevent children from learning to think before they act and from warning themselves: "If I do this, then I'll get a timeout."

Do not tell children to think over the reasons for their misbehavior while they are in timeout. Children who are mature enough to think before they act will rarely need timeout. When they do experience timeout, they will think over what led up to the timeout without being told. Timeout is not designed to instill guilt, since guilty children are not necessarily well-behaved children.

Children under the age of 5 can be picked up and put in their rooms for timeout after you have said "timeout." If toddlers wander out of their rooms, pick them up quietly and put them back in their rooms.

If you are away from home and no timeout room is available, you can hold children under the age of 4 who are out-of-control until they are quiet for at least 1 minute. During this time do not talk to the child. You may position the squirming child face down over your lap with one hand on the child's back and one hand grasping the child's two hands. Or, you may stand or sit and hold the child facing away from you, with your hands holding the child's hands.

If there is no time to call timeout and to wait for the child to complete the timeout, call a delayed timeout by simply saying "Time-out at bedtime" and subtracting ½ hour from the child's bedtime that night. For example, when you are rushing to get off to work, call a delayed timeout. When you are in a place where there is no timeout room, call a delayed timeout. Module 8 explains more about how to call timeout away from home.

Remember to call timeout every time you see a temper tantrum begin, even if the child has just completed a timeout. You may have to call timeout six or seven times a day for a few weeks if your children often have temper tantrums.

When your children have friends come over, apply timeout for temper tantrums and other behaviors to guests as well. Explain house rules one time to the guests when they first arrive. Do this in a friendly, humorous way. Apply timeout with guests as you do with your children.

∞∞∞

1. How far along should the temper tantrum be before you call timeout?
2. How do you call timeout?
3. What is the first thing to do after calling timeout?
4. Why is it unwise to warn a child before calling timeout?
5. Why is it a bad idea to tell children to think over what they've done wrong while they are in timeout?
6. What should you do when there is no time for a timeout?
7. What should you do when there is no place for a timeout?
8 How soon after a child comes out of timeout will you call timeout again?
9. What should you do when your children have guests?

∞∞∞

5. What to Do When a Child Goes to Timeout as Requested

When you call timeout, expect children to go to timeout within 1 minute after you call timeout and stay there quietly until a buzzer goes off or an adult says that timeout is over. As soon as a child has gone to timeout and is quiet, set a timer for 5 minutes if the child is 5 years old or under, for 10 minutes if the child is from 6 through 10 years old, or for 15 minutes if the child is from 11 through 13 years old. The timeout procedure described in this module is appropriate for children through age 13. After that age, the amount of external control involved in timeout is bad for the child and often unworkable. Management of older children who have temper tantrums is too complex for discussion here. If you have such a problem consult a mental-health professional.

Reset the timer whenever you hear noise from the child's timeout room. If the buzzer cannot be heard from the child's room, announce the end of timeout by saying "Timeout is over."

When a child older than 5 leaves the room before timeout is over, say "Timeout at bedtime" and subtract ½ hour from bedtime. When a child younger than 5 wanders out of the room before the buzzer goes off, pick the child up quietly, put the child back in the timeout room, and reset the timer.

When timeout is over, the child may come out of the timeout room and resume regular activities. Allow children to stay in their rooms after timeout is over if they wish.

Do not talk to the child about what the child did before timeout or why you decided to call timeout. This would punish the child for going to timeout as you've asked. Later in the day, if the child asks, explain why you called timeout. Explain this only once.

When a child goes into timeout as soon as you have said "timeout" and remains there until the buzzer goes off, tell the child when timeout is over "You did a good job. You went into timeout on time and you were quiet."

∞∞∞∞

1. How long will timeout be for each of your children?
2. After you have called timeout, when will you set the timer?
3. What's wrong with using timeout with a child older than 13?
4. What will you do if your child goes quietly to timeout but starts yelling after a minute in timeout?
5. How will you let your child know that timeout is over?
6. What if a child does not come out of the timeout room even though timeout is over?
7. Is it a good idea to discuss the cause of timeout right after timeout is over? Why not?
8. What will you say when a child has gone to timeout quickly and quietly and comes out when you've announced that timeout is over?

∞∞∞∞

6. What to Do When a Child Doesn't Go to Timeout

When a child does not go to timeout within 1 minute of when you call timeout, ignore the temper tantrum and make the child's bedtime ½ hour earlier that night. Do not force the child to go into timeout, nor discuss the timeout with the child until it is time to remind the child about the earlier bedtime. When children are physically forced to go to timeout, they don't learn to go to timeout on their own. Even if the use of physical force was a good idea, some children are too big to be forced into timeout, especially by their mothers. For each timeout you call during the day that a child ignores, subtract ½ hour from that night's bedtime.

Bob, a 7-year-old, had a temper tantrum. When the tantrum began, Dad said "timeout." Bob did not go to his timeout room. During the remainder of the tantrum, Dad and everyone else in the house ignored Bob completely, neither looking at him nor talking to him. They paid attention to him again as soon as the tantrum was over and his behavior was appropriate. At 6:00 p.m., Dad said, "Time to get ready for bed. Bedtime tonight is at 7:00." Bob's regular bedtime is 7:30. Bob did not go to bed until 8:00, and so Dad noted on the assessment chart that Bob owes 1 hour of bedtime. Next time Bob asks for a special favor, Dad will remind Bob that he must first pay back the extra bedtime.

∞∞∞

1. What will you do if a child does not go to timeout on time?
2. What will you say to a child after you've called timeout, and the child does not go to timeout?
3. Why is it a bad idea to use physical force to put an older child in timeout?
4. What will you do if you call timeout three times during the day, and the child ignores each request?
5. What will you do if the child does not go to bed at the earlier bedtime?

∞∞∞

7. Rewarding for No Timeouts

On a day when a child was never asked to go to timeout, set the child's bedtime 1 hour later. A later bedtime is a particularly good reward for no timeouts because it is always available and is something most children will work for. Allow children to save up bedtime they earn.

∞∞∞

1. How will you reward a child who has had no timeouts?

∞∞∞

8. Dealing with Property Damage

Most children go to timeout quickly and without causing any harm to themselves or their surroundings. A few children destroy things on the way to timeout or in timeout. Children are particularly likely to be destructive before or during timeout if their parents are very worried about property damage. Under these circumstances children may threaten their parents by saying something such as, "If you make me go to timeout, I'll break this vase." It is a good idea for these children to learn through their parents' use of timeout that their parents love them more than they love their possessions.

Property damage will stop as children learn self-control through exposure to timeout, but there is no way to prevent all property damage and to still use timeout successfully. It is best to put precious items in a safe place until your children gain self-control. Your children, not your property, should be your first priority.

When children destroy your property, you can deduct the cost of repairs or replacement from their allowances. If you anticipate a certain kind of damage because it has happened several times before, find out what the repairs will cost and tell the child when you explain timeout. You will learn about ways that children can earn money from Module 10. Do not replace children's belongings that they destroy on the way to or in timeout. It is their choice to destroy their belongings.

∞∞∞

1. Do you expect your child to be destructive when you call timeout? If so, why?
2. If you have to choose between teaching your child self-control and safeguarding your property, what will you do?
3. How can you minimize property damage while your child is getting used to timeout?
4. What will happen if your children learn that they can intimidate you with threats of property damage?

Bill's mother and father have had a lot of fights recently. During these fights, Bill's father often breaks dishes or furniture. Bill's mother is learning to use timeout to control Bill's temper tantrums, during which Bill frequently threatens to (but never actually does) break household objects. What should Bill's mother do about property damage during timeout?

∞∞∞

9. Explaining Timeout for Temper Tantrums to Your Children

Before you begin using timeout for temper tantrums, explain it once to your children. You might say something like this:

"Willie, sometimes you have temper tantrums, screaming a lot and throwing your things around. I think that your temper tantrums cause a lot of tension between you and me and you and your sister, Betty. From now on, as soon as I see you starting a temper tantrum, I'll say 'Willie, timeout.' When you hear me say that, go right away to your room and rest or play quietly so I can't hear you. I'll tell you that you can come out after you've been quiet in your room for 10 minutes. When you come out after 10 quiet minutes, I'll tell you how pleased I am that you went to timeout quickly and stayed there quietly. If you don't go to timeout when I call it, or if you come out before 10 quiet minutes are over, you will have to go to bed a half-hour early. If you have a temper tantrum at a time when or in a place where I can't call timeout, I'll say 'Timeout at bedtime' and you will have to go to bed a half-hour early that night. On a day when you do not have to go to timeout, I'll add an hour to your bedtime. If you break anything of yours during timeout, that's your business. If you break anything of mine, I'll deduct the cost from your allowance until you've paid for the breakage."

Make sure that you include in your explanation:

1. What your definition of a temper tantrum is,
2. Why you will call timeout for temper tantrums,
3. When you will call timeout for temper tantrums,
4. What going to timeout means,
5. What children can do during timeout,
6. What will happen if they go to timeout on time,
7. What will happen if they don't go to timeout or leave timeout early,
8. What you will do if you can't send them to timeout right away,
9. What you will do if children destroy property during timeout,
10. What will happen on a day when a child is not sent to timeout.

Have your children repeat your explanation of timeout for temper tantrums to make sure they understand it. Even if they don't seem to understand, follow through with your plan. They will understand timeout for temper tantrums after they've experienced it a few times.

∞∞∞

1. How many times will you explain timeout for temper tantrums to your children?
2. What 10 things will you tell your children about timeout?
3. How will you make sure they understand what you have told them? What if they don't seem to understand?

∞∞∞

10. Keeping a Record for This Module

While working through this module, continue as you did during baseline to put a check in the small box labelled *NO* in Column 5 when none of your children (age 3 to 13) had a temper tantrum that day. You will also want to keep track of timeouts and bedtime owed. For this system to work, you must keep a careful record on paper. No parent can possibly remember all of the information necessary to administer time-out fairly and to decide about the effects of timeout.

Each time you call a timeout for a temper tantrum, write down the child's initial in Column 5 of your assessment chart in the box labelled *Timeouts called, completed.* When the child does not go to timeout, leaves timeout early, or when you cannot call an immediate timeout, write the child's initial and *-½ hr.* in Column 3, "Bedtime problems," under the box marked *Earned, owed bedtime for all modules.* When no timeouts are called for any child for any reason during the day, mark down each child's initial and *+1hr.* in Column 3.

Many children like to save up later bedtime hours for a special occasion. This is a very good idea. Keep track of later bedtime hours that children have used up by drawing a line through the extra time you've entered in Column 3.

The example on the following page shows how Columns 3 and 5 might look on a family's assessment chart after they have begun using Module 5. In this family there are two children, Andy and Bridget. On the first day of charting temper tantrums, neither Andy nor Bridget had a tantrum. This was indicated by a check in the small box in Column 5. Since no timeouts were called during the day for temper tantrums or other problems, each child earned a 1 hour later bedtime. This was marked in Column 3 with the child's initial and *+1hr. (A+1hr. B+1hr.).* Each child used the hour of later bedtime that night, so a line was drawn through the notations to show that the bedtime had been used.

On the second day, Andy was sent to timeout and he went. His initial was written in the second box in Column 5 to show that a timeout was called for him, and his initial was crossed out to indicate that he went to timeout.

On the third day, another timeout was called for Andy. This time, he did not go to timeout. His initial was entered in Column 5 when the timeout was called, and *-½ hr.* was entered for him in the bedtime column when he did not go to timeout. Andy did not go to bed ½ hour early that night so the notation was not crossed out and he will have to make up the bedtime that he owes some other time. Note that a child may owe more than ½ hour of bedtime for a particular day. Each time

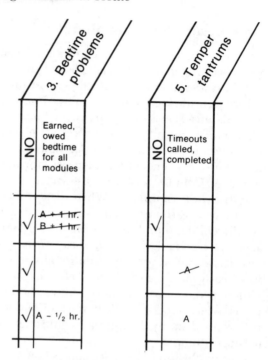

that a timeout is called and ignored or a delayed timeout is called, another ½ hour of bedtime is owed. On the other hand, only 1 hour of later bedtime can be earned by each child per day, as this is given to each child only when no timeouts have been called for any children for any reason during the day.

∞∞∞

1. Why is it important to keep track of timeouts on paper?
2. Where will you keep track of timeouts for temper tantrums you've called?
3. How will you indicate that a child went to timeout?
4. How will you keep track of timeouts you've called that children have ignored or delayed timeouts?
5. How will you keep track of earned extra bedtime? How will you keep track of used extra bedtime?

∞∞∞

11. Moving On to Module 6

You can move on to Module 6 when you have consistently used timeout as described here for at least 1 week and the number of days without temper tantrums is at least 6 per week. While some families quickly get used to timeout procedures, it takes other families as much as 6 weeks to consistently use timeout procedures. If temper tantrums are not a problem in your family, you can move on to Module 6 after you have read this module and answered all the questions in it correctly. Review this module when you are ready to use timeout. Remember to continue using these procedures and charting for this module when you move on.

If you start using timeout and then stop, if you think you aren't using timeout correctly, or if you aren't consistently using timeout, return to the beginning of this module.

∞∞∞

1. How will you know when you are ready to move on to Module 6?
2. When is it a good idea to begin Module 5 again?

∞∞∞

Module 6: Fights Between Children

Disagreements between sisters and brothers that children learn to re-solve themselves are a normal part of growing up in a family. Younger and older, weaker and stronger siblings cannot learn conflict-resolution skills when parents interfere to protect one child or to determine who started the fight. Parents who mediate children's dis-putes or always make one particular child give in and walk away take the chance of encouraging lifelong emnity between siblings.

This module explains how you can reduce the frequency of violent and loud fights between your children and encourage them to resolve their disagreements without involving adults. It uses timeout and earlier bedtime and is appropriate for children from age 3 through age 13.

Fights between children as a problem in a competent family. This family is headed by two parents. Mother, a 35-year-old homemaker, takes courses at night school toward a college degree. Father is a 39-year-old midlevel executive in a large manufacturing company. They have two daughters, one age 6 and one age 13, who fight constantly. Attempts by Mother to discourage her older daughter from getting upset with the younger daughter often lead to bitter arguments be-tween Mother and the older daughter. Both parents are aware that the arguments between the two girls divert their attention away from more serious problems: Mother's fears that she will be too old to use her education when she finishes school, Father's concerns that he is not moving up as quickly in his company as he should, and arguments between them about the time Father spends away from the family and about Mother's disinterest in sex.

Fights between children as a problem in a less competent family. A 32-year-old homemaker mother and a 40-year-old father, who is an executive in an advertising agency, a boy of 12, and girls of 8 and 5 make up this family. Fights between the children are frequent and often end with an injury to one of the girls. The girls often ask Mother to intercede. Lately, when Mother does get involved, her son threatens her and sometimes hits her. From time to time, Mother calls Father at work to complain about the fighting. Father accuses Mother of not knowing how to control the children. Mother accuses Father of not teaching their son to be respectful of adults. The couple seem unaware that their disagreement about the children's fighting exemplifies how they feel about themselves and each other; Mother feels Father sees her as inadequate no matter what she does, and Father is frustrated by what he sees as Mother's passivity and dependence upon him.

1. Deciding if You Need to Work Through This Module

Look at your baseline record in Column 6. You need not work through Module 6 if: *(a)* you are sure your baseline was fairly typical for your family, *(b)* there was a check in Column 6 for 6 out of 7 baseline days, *(c)* children were not punished for having fights or threatened about the consequences of fights, *(d)* no child was injured in a fight during baseline, *(e)* no disputes between children were settled by adults during baseline, and *(f)* no family member is unhappy about the way the children get along together.

If you decide to work through Module 6, draw a horizontal line across Column 6 underneath your last baseline day. The line will separate your baseline record from the record of your progress during Module 6. If you decide not to work through Module 6, continue filling in all columns of your chart and move on to Module 7. If at any time fewer than 6 of 7 days in Column 6 have checks, complete Module 6.

ωοωοωο

1. Do you need to work through Module 6? If not, why not?

ωοωοωο

2. Recognizing a Fight Between Children

There are three ways to recognize a fight between children (your children and your children and their guests). If you hear children's voices from another room when you are inside the house and think a fight is beginning, walk into the room next to where the children are. If you can hear the children's voices or, in a small apartment, if you are bothered by the noise, a fight is taking place. Involved in the fight are all the children in the other room. This practice teaches children to talk and fight quietly.

A fight is also taking place if a child complains to you that another child in the family is picking on or hitting her or if one child tattles to you about any aspect of another child's behavior. Involved in the fight are the complainer and the other child. Ignore fights that take place outside of the house unless a child comes in and complains about another child. If that happens, a fight is taking place outside. Involved in the fight are the complainer and the children complained about. A fight is also taking place if you see children hit each other. Involved in the fight are the aggressor and the victim.

ωοωοωο

1. What three things tell you that a fight is taking place?
2. If children are saying nasty things to each other indoors but you can't hear their voices from the next room, are they fighting?
3. If children are yelling at each other and you can hear their voices from two rooms away, are they fighting? Who is involved in the fight?
4. If children are talking quietly to each other and one child complains to you that the other child is picking on her, are they fighting? Who is involved in the fight?
5. If children are yelling at each other outside but nobody complains to you, are they fighting?

Kevin and Judy live with their mother and father in a small two-bedroom apartment. When Kevin has friends over, his mother, who is recovering from surgery, can hear the boys' voices wherever she goes in the apartment. She has decided to call timeout whenever she can hear the boys' voices from another room. Considering Mother's options, what do you think of her decision? What problems will she encounter? How can she solve these problems?

∞∞∞

3. Calling Timeout for Fights

Once a fight begins, do not talk to the children about the fight, try to find out what happened, or scold or comfort those involved. Call timeout (using the method described in Module 5) for *all* children involved in the fight as soon as the fight begins. Victims need to learn to avoid aggressors as much as aggressors need to learn self-control. The length of timeout depends upon the age of the oldest child in the fight. For example, when a 9-year-old fights with a 4-year-old, timeout for both of them lasts 10 minutes, the normal timeout for a 9-year-old. After timeout is over, call timeout immediately if you spot another fight. Remember to call timeout for fights with your children's guests as well. Calling timeout for fights will not only reduce the number of fights, it will also gradually teach children the skills they need in order to avoid fights, such as negotiation, problem solving, compromise, and self-control.

∞∞∞

1. What is the thing to do when you spot a fight?
2. How soon after you spot a fight will you call timeout?
3. Who will you call timeout for in a fight?
4. What's wrong with calling timeout for the one who started the fight and leaving the victim alone?

5. How long should timeout be?
6. How many times a day can you call timeout for fights?
7. What will you do when a child has a fight with a friend in your house?
8. What new skills do you think your children will learn as they try to avoid timeouts and earn later bedtimes?

> Three-year-old Phillip often provokes his older brothers into hitting him by taking away their toys. If Dad calls timeout for Phillip and his brothers when they hit him, what will Phillip learn? What will he learn if Dad only puts his older brothers in timeout?

∞∞∞

4. Explaining Timeout for Fights to Your Children

Before you begin calling timeout for fights, explain timeout for fights once to your children. You might say something like this:

> "Heath and Ginger, Dad and I would like the two of you to learn to fight without involving us. You need to learn to work things out yourselves, so that when you grow up you'll be happy that you have a sister or a brother. From now on, I'll call timeout as soon as a fight begins. I'll know a fight is beginning when I can hear your voices from another room, when I see you hitting each other, or when one of you tattles about the other. I'll always call timeout for both of you. On a day when I call no timeouts, I'll add 1 hour to your bedtimes."

Make sure that you include in your explanation:

1. Why you will call timeout for fighting,
2. When you will call timeout for fighting,
3. What your definition of a fight is,
4. Who will get timeout for a fight.
5. What will happen on a day when a child is not sent to timeout.

If you have not used timeout with your children before, include in your explanation what timeout means and what happens during timeouts as described in Module 5. Have your children repeat your explanation of timeout for fights to make sure they understand what you've told them. Even if they don't seem to understand, follow through with your plan. They'll understand after they've experienced timeout for fights a few times.

∞∞∞

1. How many times will you explain timeout for fights to your children?
2. What five things will you explain to your children about timeout for fights?
3. How will you make sure they understand what you have told them? What if they don't seem to understand?

∞∞∞

5. Keeping a Record for This Module

While working through this module, continue as you did during baseline to put a check in the small box labelled *NO* in Column 6 when none of your children (age 3 to 13) was involved in a fight that day. You will also want to keep track of timeouts and bedtime owed. Each time you call a timeout for a fight, write down the children's initials in Column 6 of your assessment chart in the box labelled *Timeouts called, completed.* When a child does not go to timeout, leaves timeout early, or when you cannot call an immediate timeout, write the child's initial and *-½ hr.* in Column 3, "Bedtime problems," under the box labelled *Earned, owed bedtime for all modules.* When no timeouts are called for any child for any reason during the day, mark down each child's initial and *+1 hr.* in Column 3.

Many children like to save up later bedtime hours for a special occasion. This is a very good idea. Keep track of later bedtime hours that children have used up by drawing a line through the extra time you've entered in Column 3.

The following example shows how Columns 3 and 6 might look on a family's assessment chart after they have begun using Module 6. In this family there are two children, Andy and Bridget. On the first day of charting fights, neither Andy nor Bridget was involved in a fight. This was indicated by a check in the small box in Column 6. Since no timeouts were called during the day for fights or other problems, each child earned a 1 hour later bedtime. This was marked in Column 3 with the child's initial and *+1 hr. (A+1 hr., B+1 hr.).* Each child used the hour of later bedtime that night, so a line was drawn through the notations to show that the bedtime had been used.

On the second day, Andy and Bridget were sent to timeout for fighting and they went. Their initials were written in the second box in Column 6 to show that a timeout was called for them, and their initials were crossed out to indicate that they went to timeout.

On the third day, another timeout for fighting was called for both children. This time, they did not go to timeout. Their initials were

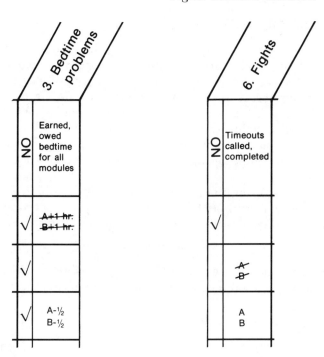

entered in Column 6 when the timeout was called, and -½ *hr.* was entered for them in the bedtime column when they did not go to timeout. Andy and Bridget did not go to bed ½ hour early that night so the notation was not crossed out and they will have to make up the bedtime that they owe some other time. Note that a child may owe more than ½ hour of bedtime for a particular day. Each time a timeout is called and ignored or a delayed timeout is called, another ½ hour of bedtime is owed. On the other hand, only 1 hour of later bedtime can be earned by each child per day, as this is given to each child only when no timeouts have been called for any children for any reason during the day.

∽∽∽

1. How will you record timeouts for fights?
2. How will you keep track of extra bedtime that children earn?
3. What will you do when children use their extra bedtime to stay up or make up bedtime that they owe?

∽∽∽

6. Moving On to Module 7

You can move on to Module 7 when you have consistently used timeout for fights as described in this module for at least 1 week. If fights are a very disruptive problem, don't move on until there are twice as many checks in Column 6 as there were during baseline. If your children have been fighting for a long time and if you have been involved in their fights for a long time, it may take several weeks for you to use timeout for fights effectively. Make sure to continue using these procedures and charting for this module when you move on to Module 7.

If you start using timeout for fights and then stop, if you think you aren't using these procedures correctly, or if you aren't consistently using these procedures, return to the beginning of this module.

∽∽∽

1. How will you know when you are ready to move on to Module 7?
2. When is it a good idea to begin Module 6 again?

∽∽∽

Module 7: Following Instructions

Many parents complain that their children don't follow instructions. Nagging and threatening children only makes the problem worse. The sight and sound of the nagging parent becomes so unpleasant that children avoid listening to anything the parent says. Children who haven't learned to follow adults' instructions are poorly prepared for school and work and are likely to have serious problems with adult authorities during adolescence.

A child who complies with every request made by an adult, no matter how unreasonable, is likely to have problems with anxiety and depression. A democratic society needs citizens who have learned to think for themselves. Authoritarian childrearing, which emphasizes compliance above all else, is poor preparation for adult independence.

This module explains how you can encourage instruction following in children along with responsibility and self-confidence. The module explains how to give instructions so that children are likely to listen and follow through. It uses timeout and earlier bedtime and is appropriate for children from age 3 through 13.

Following instructions as a problem in a competent family. The parents in this family are a 30-year-old father, who is an insurance salesman, and a 28-year-old mother, who is a high-school physical-education teacher. The oldest of the three children, a 6-year-old boy, was adopted at birth. Mother gave birth to twin girls 2 years later. The parents consider their children, particularly their son, spirited and independent. They admire the children's ability to play alone or together for hours at a time without adult involvement. Although their son reads and does simple math problems as part of his play, his teacher regards him as immature and poorly prepared for first grade, mostly because he tends to ignore direct requests made by adults.

Following instructions as a problem in a less competent family. An 8-year-old boy, a 33-year-old father, who is a truck driver, and a 30-year-old mother, who is a homemaker and is taking a secretarial course, make up this family. According to the parents, their son hasn't minded them "since the day he was born." Mother spends all of her free time with her son. Quite a bit of this time involves trying to get her son to do what she tells him. These efforts almost always end with both of them shouting and crying. When Father is home, he uses physical force and yelling to give instructions to his son, but he is just as unsuccessful as Mother. Arguments between Mother and Father about their son's non-compliance, about Father's drinking and occasional beating of Mother, and about the time Father spends away from home are frequent. At school, teachers consider the boy to be a charming, exceptionally well-behaved underachiever.

1. Deciding if You Need to Work Through this Module

Look at your baseline record in Column 7 of your chart. You need not work through Module 7 if: (a) you are sure your baseline was fairly typical for your family, (b) there was a check in Column 7 for 6 out of 7 baseline days, (c) on days you checked, children followed instructions without being threatened with punishment if they didn't follow through, (d) on days you checked, you made a reasonable number of requests of children, neither directing all of the children's moves, nor allowing children to make decisions best left to older people, and (e) no family member has complained that too many instructions are given or that too few instructions are followed.

If you decide to work through Module 7, draw a horizontal line across Column 7 underneath your last baseline day. The line will separate your baseline record from the record of your progress during Module 7. If you decide not to work through Module 7, continue filling in all columns of your chart and move on to Module 8. If at any time fewer than 6 out of 7 days are checked in Column 7, return to Module 7.

∞∞∞

1. Do you need to work through Module 7? If not, why not?

∞∞∞

2. Giving as Few Instructions as Possible

The fewer instructions you give, the more instructions your children will follow and the more pleasant your relationship with them will be. From now on, do *not* give three kinds of instructions:

1. Instructions about chores. Module 10 explains how to set up a system for household chores without reminding or instructing children to do their chores.

2. Instructions already given once. If you repeat your instructions to children, they will quickly learn that they don't have to listen to you the first time you say something. They'll figure out that you'll eventually repeat yourself if they don't listen the first time.

3. Instructions about behaviors with natural, safe consequences. Many things children do have important natural consequences. As long as these consequences are safe for the child, it is a good idea to let the child learn from experience. For example, if a child wears sloppy clothes to school, other children will make nasty comments, and the child will eventually take responsibility for his appearance. Or, if a child rushes off to school without eating his breakfast, later on he may be hungry. If he is, he'll probably eat his breakfast the next morning.

∞∞∞

1. Why is it a good idea for parents whose children are not following instructions to make fewer requests?
2. What three kinds of instructions do you no longer need to give?
3. Why is it unnecessary to give instructions about daily chores?
4. Why should you not repeat instructions once you give them?
5. When can you let children learn from experience?
6. What requests that you frequently make to your children will you eliminate? How will you and your children feel about this change?

Every night the mother of a 12-year-old boy tells her son to wash with soap when he takes his shower even though she knows that he never uses soap and that he gets reasonably clean even so. What kind of relationship might this mother and son have when the son is 18 years old? What would you tell the mother to do?

∞∞∞∞

3. Giving Instructions That Children Can Follow

Take five steps each time you give an instruction:

1. Give specific, brief instructions one time. Good instructions tell the child exactly what to do and when to do it. Some examples of good instructions are: "Hold your sister's hand while we cross the street," "Meet me at the door in 5 minutes," and "Be home for dinner by 5:00." Give a set of instructions only to children who can recall more than one instruction. If you are sure that a child cannot comply with your request, don't make it.

2. Look at the child, smile, and use a pleasant tone of voice when giving instructions. Try not to give instructions when you are angry, since you may be too upset to follow through. Your anger may frighten or confuse children, making it hard for them to follow your instructions. Also, children rarely comply freely with sarcastic or humiliating instructions, and they tend to avoid listening to adults who issue instructions in these ways.

3. When you give instructions, always ask for positive action ("Meet me in front of Grandma's house by 1:00"). Never request negative or "dead-man's" actions ("Stop running in the house" "Be quiet" "Stop bothering me" "Don't pull the cat's tail"). Instead of telling a child to stop doing something, ask the child to engage in a substitute positive behavior. For example, instead of telling a child "Don't interrupt me to show me your drawings while I'm on the phone," ask the child to "Draw a picture for me and show me when I'm finished talking on the phone."

4. Always set a time limit for instructions ("Now" or "By dinner") and wait until the time limit is up to see if the child has followed

through as requested. While waiting, do not remind the child of your request or use threats or bribes to get the child to follow through. If the instruction is to do something right away, wait silently for 1 minute to see if the child does as you ask. If the instruction is to do something by a specific time, wait until that time to see if the child does as you ask.

5. Give instructions only when you are willing and able to follow up on the child's compliance or noncompliance. If there is no way for you to find out if the child has followed your instructions, don't give them.

∞∞∞

1. What five steps should you take each time you give an instruction to a child?
2. What two bits of information are always included in good instructions?

Father works the night shift. Every morning he screams at his children to leave him alone. Why don't they? What could he do to encourage his children to follow his instructions?

Mother asks her children to meet her at the door in 5 minutes. When she first makes this request, they continue playing with their toys. How many times should she repeat her request in the next 5 minutes?

∞∞∞

4. Giving Instructions in an Emergency

In an emergency with young children or with older children who do not follow instructions well, give brief, clear instructions and then do whatever you can to ensure children's safety without waiting for them to follow instructions. For example, if a 2-year-old wanders out into the street, shout "Come here" and run out to rescue him. Or, if a child is about to touch a hot stove, quickly stop him. Do this even if you've explained several times that the stove is hot and dangerous. The child's physical safety and comfort is far more important than compliance with an instruction to stay away from the stove. Abusive parents who value compliance over their children's safety produce unhappy, confused children who are often totally unprepared to follow any reasonable adult instructions.

∞∞∞

1. How should you give instructions in an emergency situation?
2. Give an example of an emergency situation in which you would

not wait for your child to follow instructions. Instead of waiting, what would you do to make sure the child was safe?

∞∞∞

5. What to Do When Children Do What You've Asked

When children follow your instructions on time, tell them what they did that you liked. For example, you could say, "You came home for dinner at 5:00 sharp. I like that because Dad and I are very hungry." If you say nothing when they follow your instructions, they probably won't follow other instructions in the future.

∞∞∞

1. What will you do when children follow your instructions on time?
2. What will happen if nothing is said to children who follow instructions on time?

On Sunday morning, Father asked his children to play in their rooms with the doors closed until 9:00 a.m. The children did what Father asked. What could Father say to the children?

Mother asked her son Donald to hold his sister's hand while they crossed the street. Her son did as she asked. Mother said, "For once you've done what I've asked. It's about time." How do you think the boy felt?

∞∞∞

6. What to Do When Children Don't Do What You've Asked

Wait 1 full minute after giving an immediate instruction or wait until the specified time after giving a delayed instruction. Then, if children haven't done what you've asked, call timeout. When timeout is impossible, either because you are in a hurry to leave the house or because you are in a place without a timeout spot, subtract ½ hour from the bedtime of the child who has not followed instructions.

∞∞∞

1. What will you do when children don't follow instructions on time?
2. What if a child doesn't follow instructions on time while you are rushing to take the child to the dentist?

Father and 9-year-old Jim were shopping for school supplies. Jim saw a glass fish tank and picked it up to look at it more closely.

Father said, "Jim, put that fish tank back on the shelf right now."
Father looked at his watch and waited for 1 minute. He looked at
Jim again and saw that Jim was still holding the fish tank. What
should Father do to encourage Jim to follow instructions in the
future?

∞∞∞

7. Explaining Timeout for Not Following Instructions to Your Children

Before you begin calling timeout for not following instructions, explain it once to your children. You might say something like this:

> "Marilyn, I want you to learn to follow instructions without me
> nagging you. From now on when I ask you to do something and
> you do what I ask, I'll tell you how happy I am. If you don't do
> what I ask when I tell you to, I'll call timeout. I'll only tell you to
> do things one time, and I'll always tell you when to do things. If I
> say 'Now,' I'll give you 1 minute to get started. If I don't call
> timeout for any reason during the day, I'll add 1 hour to your
> bedtime."

Make sure that you include in your explanation:

1. Why you will use timeout for not following instructions,
2. How many times you will give instructions,
3. How long you will wait for children to follow instructions,
4. What you will do if instructions are followed,
5. What you will do if instructions are not followed,
6. What will happen when a child is not sent to timeout.

If you have not used timeout with your children before, include in your
explanation what timeout means and what happens during timeouts
as described in Module 5. Have your children repeat your explanation
of timeout for not following instructions to make sure they understand
what you've told them. Even if they don't seem to understand, follow
through with your plan. They will understand after they've experienced
timeout for not following instructions a few times.

∞∞∞

1. How many times will you explain timeouts for not following
   instructions to children?
2. What six things will you tell children about following instructions?

3. How will you make sure they understand what you have told them? What if they don't seem to understand?

∞∞∞

8. Keeping a Record for This Module

While working through this module, continue as you did during baseline to put a check in the small box labelled *YES* in Column 7 when all of your instructions to children (age 3 to 13) are followed that day. You will also want to keep track of timeouts and bedtime owed. Each time you call a timeout for not following instructions, write down the child's initial in Column 7 of your assessment chart in the box labelled *Timeouts called, completed.* When the child does not go to timeout, leaves timeout early, or when you cannot call an immediate timeout, write the child's initial and -½ hr. in Column 3, "Bedtime problems," under the box labelled *Earned, owed bedtime for all modules.* When no timeouts are called for any child for any reason during the day, mark down each child's initial and +1hr. in Column 3.

Many children like to save up later bedtime hours for a special occasion. This is a very good idea. Keep track of later bedtime hours that children have used up by drawing a line through the extra time you've entered in Column 3.

The following example shows how Columns 3 and 7 might look on a family's assessment chart after they have begun using Module 7. In this family there are two children, Andy and Bridget. On the first day of charting for following instructions, both Andy and Bridget followed all instructions they were given. This was indicated by a check in the small box in Column 7. Since no timeouts were called during the day for not following instructions or other problems, each child earned a 1 hour later bedtime. This was marked in Column 3 with the children's initials and +1hr. (A+1hr., B+1hr.). Each child used the hour of later bedtime that night, so a line was drawn through the notations to show that the bedtime had been used.

On the second day, Bridget was sent to timeout and she went. Her initial was written in the second box in Column 7 to show that a timeout was called for her, and her initial was crossed out to indicate that she went to timeout.

On the third day, another timeout was called for Bridget. This time, she did not go to timeout. Her initial was entered in Column 7 when the timeout was called, and -½ hr. was entered for her in the bedtime column when she did not go to timeout. Bridget did not go to bed ½ hour early that night so the notation was not crossed out and she

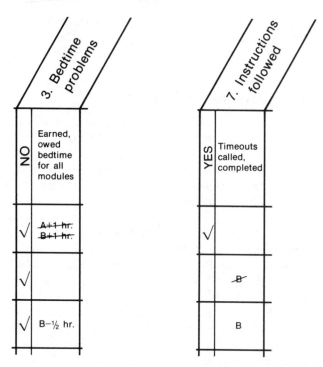

will have to make up the bedtime that she owes some other time. Note that a child may owe more than ½ hour of bedtime for a particular day. Each time that a timeout is called and ignored or a delayed timeout is called, another ½ hour of bedtime is owed. On the other hand, only 1 hour of later bedtime can be earned by each child, as this is given to each child only when no timeouts have been called for any children for any reason during the day.

∽∾∽∾∽∾

1. How will you record timeout for not following instructions?
2. How will you keep track of the extra bedtime that children earn?
3. What will you do when children use their extra bedtime to stay up late or when they make up bedtime that they owe?

∽∾∽∾∽∾

9. Moving On to Module 8

You can move on to Module 8 when you have consistently used timeout for not following instructions as described in this module for at least 1 week. If noncompliance is a very disruptive problem, don't move on until there are twice as many checks in Column 7 as there were during baseline. If you have had longstanding problems with instruction following, it may take several weeks for you and your children to get used to the new procedures described in this module. Make sure to continue using these procedures and charting for this module when you move on to Module 8.

If you start using timeout for not following instructions and then stop, if you think you aren't using the procedures correctly, or if you aren't consistently using these procedures, return to the beginning of this module.

∞∞∞

1. How will you know when you are ready to move on to Module 8?
2. When is it a good idea to begin Module 7 again?

∞∞∞

Module 8: Good Behavior Away from Home

When children are away from home, their behavior tends to be less predictable than it is at home. Sometimes this is because new settings and people are confusing, exciting, or anxiety provoking. Sometimes this is because parents expect too much of their children in public and are embarrassed to do in public what they do at home. Children who are often out of control in the car, in public places, and with unfamiliar people may begin to dread new places and new people. They may have a hard time controlling themselves at school and making new friends.

This module explains how you can encourage children to show as much self-control in public as they do at home. It uses timeout and earlier bedtime and is appropriate for children from age 3 through age 13.

Good behavior away from home as a problem in a competent family. This small family consists of a 28-year-old divorced accountant and her 5-year-old son. Mother is a good problem solver and considers working and raising her happy, bright son to be a worthwhile challenge. The only problem she hasn't solved concerns her son's behavior in public. When she and her son spend the day with a divorced friend and his three boys, her son quickly gets overexcited and does mischievous things he would never do at home. Mother's concern about her son's behavior in public makes her hesitant about the idea of remarriage.

Good behavior away from home as a problem in a less competent family. This family consists of a 39-year-old mother and 43-year-old stepfather who work in the same factory, a 19-year-old son who has just started college, and a mildly retarded 12-year-old daughter. Mother's first marriage ended when she left her alcoholic husband, who repeatedly beat her and her daughter. Mother and Stepfather both drink to excess, and when Mother drinks she becomes agitated and angry. When Mother and her daughter visit Grandma in a nursing home, Mother likes to spend a few hours talking with Grandma, while her daughter is left to amuse herself in the lobby. After a short time, the daughter becomes restless and begins, for no particular reason, to get angry and swear at the nursing-home residents. She acts the same way when the family visits the stepfather's family, who live in a neighboring town.

1. Deciding if You Need to Work Through This Module

Look at your baseline record in Column 8. You need not work through Module 8 if: *(a)* you are sure your baseline was fairly typical for your family, *(b)* there was a check in Column 8 for 6 out of 7 baseline days, *(c)* children were not punished for misbehavior in public or threatened about the consequences of public misbehavior, and *(d)* no family member is unhappy about children's behavior in public.

If you decide to work through Module 8, draw a horizontal line across Column 8 underneath your last baseline day. The line will separate your baseline record from the record of your progress during Module 8. If you decide not to work through Module 8, continue filling in all columns of your chart, and move on to Module 9. If at any time fewer than 6 of 7 days in Column 8 have checks, complete Module 8.

∞∞∞

1. Do you need to work through Module 8? If not, why not?

∞∞∞

2. Making Good Behavior Away from Home More Likely

You can take several steps to avoid behavior problems away from home. First, try to take children to places where their needs for exploration, company, rest, food, and toileting can easily be met. If you must take children with you to a place that is likely to be uncomfortable for them, expect that their behavior will be less controlled than it is at home and be more patient than usual. For example, avoid restaurants where meals are served slowly, where food is unfamiliar to children, and where behavior that is normal for children would make others uncomfortable. Begin taking your children to such restaurants only when they are able to amuse themselves quietly and to enjoy the food and the setting. Also, avoid movies likely to confuse or frighten children, particularly violent movies or movies with explicit sexual scenes, and avoid shopping with children in places where they can easily get lost in a crowd or frightened by the need to rush around.

Second, whenever you travel with children, allow extra time to get to every destination and be prepared to be late. Both you and the children will be less frustrated if you allow extra time.

Third, on every trip away from home, bring a bag of toys and books that can only be used while you travel and at your destination. When you get home, lock up these toys and books until your next trip. Do not bring expensive toys, toys that might hurt people or ruin property (such as BB guns or oil paints), or toys that are hard to pack up quickly.

Fourth, on all trips tell children where you are going, how long you will be gone, and the purpose of the trip. Keep your word about travel plans and give a prompt, reasonable explanation when you must change plans.

Fifth, when you take more than one older child in a car, let children draw straws or roll dice for the privilege of sitting in the front seat or in a rear window seat each time the family gets into the car. While taking turns seems like a good idea, it is easy to forget whose turn it is, and so reliance on taking turns often provokes an argument.

Sixth, when you travel in a car, buckle your seat belt, make sure children buckle their seat belts, and place infants in safe car seats, approved of by pediatricians. Many hospitals will loan you a safe car seat.

Seventh, do not allow other adults that your family visits to ask your children to do things you don't expect of them. Here are two examples of parents preventing other adults from making unreasonable demands. "Uncle Jim, Sue is too young to take part in this conversation: That's why I told her to go outside and play." "Mother, I disagree. I don't believe that children should be seen but not heard. I like Charlie to express his opinion about things that concern him, as long as he talks in a polite, reasonable way."

∞∞∞

1. What seven things can you do to avoid behavior problems away from home?

When Sally visits her aunt, her aunt heaps food on the children's plates and is annoyed if they don't eat everything they are served. At home, Sally gives the children small portions of food and allows them to eat until they are satisfied. Should Sally say something to her aunt? What should she say?

∞∞∞

3. What to Do about Whining and Complaining

Ignore whining, complaining, and demanding behavior. When a child whines or complains, say nothing and do nothing. As soon as the whining or complaining stops, once again show interest in the child. Never change your plans in response to whining or complaining. If another adult pays attention to your child while she is whining or complaining, you might say something like this: "Let's talk to each other but not to Sarah as long as she is complaining. When she stops complaining, we'll talk to her."

∞∞∞

1. What is the right thing to say to a child who has been complaining off and on for several hours?
2. When should you show interest again in a complaining child?

Christine is in a grocery market with her three children. Her youngest daughter is whining and begging for money for an ice cream bar. Christine says nothing to her after she has said no one time. Then her next-door neighbor comes along, hears Christine's daughter complaining, and starts talking with her in order to comfort her. How could Christine ask the neighbor to help her ignore her daughter's complaining?

Mrs. Jones says that ignoring doesn't work for her. Whenever her son starts whining, Mrs. Jones says, "If you don't stop whining this minute, I'm going to ignore you." Why doesn't ignoring work for Mrs. Jones?

∞∞∞

4. Calling Timeout Away from Home

While traveling in the car, call timeout when children fight, make distracting noises, unbuckle seat belts, have temper tantrums, or don't follow instructions. Call timeout for the length of time you usually set for timeout. Do this as soon as children begin to misbehave by pulling over to the side of the road (or off a highway and on to the side of a road), parking the car, and waiting for the length of the timeout for complete quiet from all passengers. Do not warn children that you will call timeout if they don't stop; just call timeout as soon as the problem begins. During timeout in the car, all passengers may read, play silently, or rest. If you have called timeout for 5 minutes, start the car as soon as 5 quiet minutes have passed. Use timeout as often as needed, just as you do at home. If you follow these procedures, your children will at first amuse themselves during timeout. Later, they will learn to amuse themselves as a way of avoiding timeout. Don't talk to your children about the reason for the timeout. If you instruct children to think about how bad they've been during timeout, they'll feel guilty, but won't be better prepared to avoid timeout. Very guilty children often have poor self-control.

In a grocery store or other public place or at your friends' homes, call timeout for the same reasons you would at home (temper tantrum, fight, not following instructions) and for the same length of time. If you have a car and if the weather is moderate enough to allow you and your child to sit in the car with no bad effects, use the parked car for timeout. *Stay in the car with your child.* If you have called a 15-minute timeout, stay in the parked car with the child until 15 quiet minutes have passed. Both adults and children can read, rest, or play quietly until the timeout is over.

When you are away from home and an immediate timeout is impractical, subtract ½ hour off your children's bedtimes for each timeout you call. Call timeout as often as and for the same reasons that you do at home. With children having tantrums who are under the age of 4, you could hold them over your lap until they settle down for at least 1 minute.

∞∞∞

1. What should you do when children misbehave in the car?
2. Must children sit quietly with their hands folded and eyes closed during timeout in the car?
3. Why is it a good idea for children to be able to amuse themselves quietly during timeout in the car?
4. As you and your children are sitting in the car during timeout, what should you say to your children about the reason for the timeout?
5. Should you instruct children to think about how bad they've been as they sit in the car during timeout? Why not?
6. What will you do when children misbehave in a public place?
7. What precautions will you take when you use a parked car for timeout?
8. What can you do if an immediate timeout is impractical?
9. What can you do with younger children who are having tantrums in public?

   Jenny, a 9-year-old, and her father have taken the bus to the zoo. At the zoo, Jenny has a temper tantrum in front of a crowd of people. What would you recommend that Father do? What would you recommend that he say?

∞∞∞

5. Explaining Timeout for Misbehavior Away from Home to Your Children

Before you begin using timeouts for misbehavior away from home, explain once to your children what you are going to do. You might say something like this:

"Tammy, Bea, and Lisa, I want you to learn to be as well behaved away from home as you are at home. When we are in the car and there is a fight or someone makes distracting noises, takes off her seat belt, has a temper tantrum, or doesn't follow instructions, I'll call timeout and pull the car over to the side of the road. We will sit in the car until we've had 5 quiet minutes. When we are away from home but not in the car and I have to call timeout, we'll use the car as a timeout spot if the weather is good. If the weather is bad so that we can't use the car for a timeout spot, I'll say 'Timeout at bedtime' and take half an hour off your bedtimes that night. On a day when I don't have to call timeout for any reason, I'll add 1 hour to your bedtimes that night."

Make sure that you include in your explanation:

1. Why you will call timeout for misbehavior away from home,
2. What behaviors you will call timeout for in the car and public places,
3. What you will use for a timeout room,
4. What will happen if you cannot use the car for a timeout room,
5. What will happen on a day when a child is not sent to timeout.

If you have not used timeout with your children before, include in your explanation what timeout means and what happens during timeouts as described in Module 5. Have your children repeat your explanation of timeout for misbehavior away from home to make sure they understand what you've told them. Even if they don't seem to understand, follow through with your plan. They will understand after they've experienced timeout for misbehavior away from home a few times.

∞∞∞

1. How many times will you explain good behavior away from home to your children?
2. What five things will you tell your children about good behavior away from home?
3. How will you make sure they understand what you have told them? What if they don't seem to understand?

∞∞∞

6. Keeping a Record for This Module

While working through this module, continue as you did during baseline to put a check in the small box labelled *YES* in Column 8 when all of your children (age 3 to 13) behaved well away from home that day. On days when you are not away from home with your children, cross out the boxes in Column 8 to show that they do not apply. You will also want to keep track of timeouts and bedtime owed. Each time you call a timeout for misbehavior away from home, write down the child's initial in Column 8 of your assessment chart in the box labelled *Timeouts called, completed.* When the child does not go to timeout, leaves timeout early, or when you cannot call an immediate timeout, write the child's initial and *-½ hr.* in Column 3, "Bedtime problems," under the box labelled *Earned, owed bedtime for all modules.* When no timeouts are called for any child for any reason during the day, mark down each child's initial and *+1hr.* in Column 3.

Many children like to save up later bedtime hours for a special occasion. This is a very good idea. Keep track of later bedtime hours that children have used up by drawing a line through the extra time you've entered in Column 3.

The following example shows how Columns 3 and 8 might look on a family's assessment chart after they have begun using Module 8. In this family there are two children, Andy and Bridget. On the first day of

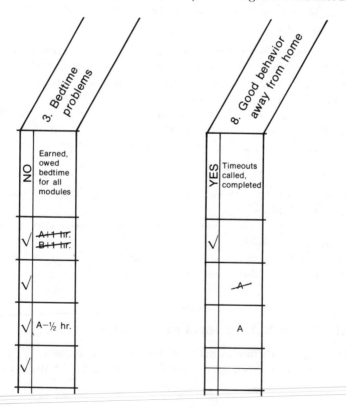

charting good behavior away from home, neither Andy nor Bridget misbehaved away from home. This was indicated by a check in the small box in Column 8. Since no timeouts were called during the day for misbehavior away from home or other problems, each child earned a 1 hour later bedtime. This was marked in Column 3 with the children's initials and *+1hr. (A+1hr., B+1hr.).* Each child used the hour of later bedtime that night, so a line was drawn through the notations to show that the bedtime had been used.

On the second day, Andy was sent to timeout and he went. His initial was written in the second box in Column 8 to show that a timeout was called for him, and his initial was crossed out to indicate that he went to timeout.

On the third day, another timeout was called for Andy. This time, he did not go to timeout. His initial was entered in Column 8 when the timeout was called, and *-½ hr.* was entered for him in the bedtime column when he did not go to timeout. Andy did not go to bed ½ hour early that night so the notation was not crossed out, and he will have to make up the bedtime that he owes some other time. Note that a child may owe more than ½ hour of bedtime for a particular day. Each time that a timeout is called and ignored or a delayed timeout is called, another ½ hour of bedtime is owed. On the other hand, only 1 hour of later bedtime can be earned by each child, as this is given to each child only when no timeouts have been called for any children for any reason during the day.

On the fourth day of charting, neither child was away from home with the parents. The box in Column 8 was marked through to show that it did not apply.

∞∞∞

1. How will you record timeout for good behavior away from home?
2. How will you keep track of the extra bedtime that children earn?
3. What will you do when children use their extra bedtime to stay up late or when they make up bedtime that they owe?

∞∞∞

7. Moving On to Module 9

You can move on to Module 9 when you have consistently followed the procedures in this module for at least 1 week. If behavior away from home is a very troublesome problem, don't move on until there are twice as many checks in Column 8 as there were during baseline. If you are overly concerned about other people's opinions or if people around you express their opinions about your children too freely, it may take several weeks for you to get used to the procedures described in this module. Make sure to continue using these procedures and charting for this module when you move on to Module 9.

If you start using the procedures described in this module and then stop, if you think you aren't using the procedures correctly, or if you aren't consistently using these procedures, return to the beginning of the module.

∞∞∞

1. How will you know when you are ready to move on to Module 9?
2. When is it a good idea to begin Module 8 again?

∞∞∞

Module 9: School Attendance

Once children have learned to get to bed on their own, they are ready to learn how to get up and prepare for play or for school on their own. Such self-sufficiency makes life with children more enjoyable for parents.

The treatment of some childhood behavior problems requires that children learn to be more independent in the morning. Children who refuse to go to school or frequently get stomachaches or asthma or allergy attacks in the morning that make prompt school attendance difficult are often overly dependent upon parents.

This module explains how you can encourage children to start the day in a self-sufficient and pleasant way and have a good record of school attendance. It includes instructions for parents faced with the difficult problem of school refusal, since many families whose children always attend school on time still have serious difficulties in the morning. More than earlier modules, this module requires that parents stop directing every step their children take and allow them to make choices and to take reasonable, age-appropriate risks. It helps children to establish a morning routine and deal with problems that make them want to avoid school. This module also requires that parents provide continuing examples of self-sufficient, organized, and cheerful morning behavior. The module is appropriate for children from age 4 through age 17.

School attendance as a problem in a competent family. A 35-year-old mother, employed since her marriage as a secretary-bookkeeper, a 32-year-old father, who is a mechanical engineer, and daughters, ages 10 and 13, make up this family. The girls are good students and popular. They fight a lot but are very loyal to each other. The older girl loves horses and wants to be a veterinarian. The younger girl wants to be an engineer like her father. Father works long hours at his office and at home after dinner. He is devoted to his family and has always shared housework and child care equally with his wife. Both parents recall being shy and fearful as children. For this reason, they are worried about their older daughter; since she began the fifth grade, she has feared school and avoided it whenever she can. Mother and Father wake up early each weekday morning and discuss who will get the older girl off to school and how. Despite their planning, each school morning ends with angry arguments involving the whole family.

School attendance as a problem in a less competent family. Mother, a 38-year-old homemaker who keeps the books for the grocery store she and Father own, Father, age 40, who runs the store, two boys, ages 7 and 9, and one 13-year-old girl make up this family. None of the children like school. The boys enjoy helping Father at work. The girl spends much of her time in her room listening to music and applying makeup. Mother has been depressed and unhappy about the amount of time Father spends at work since they were married. Now that they can afford to take vacations together and Father wants to get away, Mother is too depressed and fearful about traveling to leave home. The daughter's school attendance has always been spotty and, since she began the fifth grade, she has frequently refused to go to school. On weekday mornings, Mother wakes her daughter up early and from then on the two argue about whether the daughter will go to school. Once her daughter leaves for school or goes back to her room, Mother is usually so tired from the battle that she goes back to bed.

1. Deciding if You Need to Work Through This Module

Look at your baseline record in Column 9. You need not work through Module 9 if: *(a)* your baseline record included at least 5 school days and you are sure your baseline was fairly typical for your family, *(b)* there was a check in Column 9 for 5 out of 5 baseline days, *(c)* children were not punished for or threatened about school tardiness or absence, *(d)* no family member is unhappy about the morning routine, *(e)* during baseline, neither parent's activities were disrupted because of problems during the family's morning routine, and *(f)* during baseline, no family member took responsibility for getting another family member off to school or work.

If you decide to work through Module 9, draw a horizontal line across Column 9 underneath your last baseline day. The line will separate your baseline record from the record of your progress during Module 9. If you decide not to work through Module 9, continue filling in all columns of your chart and move on to Module 10. If at any time fewer than 5 of 5 days in Column 9 have checks, complete Module 9.

∞∞∞

1. Do you need to work through Module 9? If not, why not?

∞∞∞

2. Establishing a Morning Routine

Many problems with school attendance can be prevented if you establish a morning routine for yourself and your children. Suggestions for a morning routine follow.

a. Set out clothes in the evening for the next day

Each night set out the clothes that you will wear the next day. Encourage your school-aged children to do the same. If they ask, help children select clothes at night, not the next morning. If they haven't set their own clothes out the night before, they must select clothes by themselves the next morning. Select clothes in the morning only for the preschool child or for the severely handicapped child. If selecting clothes is a problem for your children, sit down with them one at a time and discuss which combinations of clothes will look good on them. Draw picture menus of good clothes combinations with young children and hang these near their closets.

Children who are allowed to select what they wear from an appropriate array of clothing learn to make minor decisions quickly and to bear the consequences of their decisions. The decisiveness and confidence they gain from this minor routine will help them as they grow older and face bigger decisions. You may not like what your children choose to wear, but it is important for your children to learn that it is all right for them to have preferences different from yours. And, it is important for you to learn that other people's opinions about how your children look and dress are less important than an opportunity for each child to develop a unique and independent sense of self.

∽∽∽

1. How can you encourage your children to set out clothes in the evening that they will wear the next day?
2. Should you select clothes in the morning for any of your children?
3. How can you help children who have problems picking combinations of clothes that will look good on them?
4. If you allow your children more independence in regard to the selection of their clothing, what will they learn? Will you be embarrassed by their appearance? How can you get over your embarrassment?
5. Will this procedure work if you don't set your own clothes out the night before? Why not?

   Each morning, Mrs. Smith tells all of her children what to wear that day. She does the same for her husband. Even though everyone in the family resents her bossiness, Mrs. Smith refuses to allow her husband and children to pick out their own clothing in the morning. She says that she is the only one in the family with any sense of style; if she lets her family decide what to wear, they'll all look like slobs. What problems do you think this family will have in the future? What would you advise Mrs. Smith to do?

∞∞∞∞

b. Use an alarm clock to wake up

Use an alarm clock to wake you up and expect every other family member to do the same. Take the following two steps to encourage family members to wake up on their own. First, every weekday, get out of bed when your alarm clock rings, wash, dress, eat breakfast, and prepare to start your day. Do the same on weekends when activities are planned for the early morning. If you don't develop a consistent morning routine, your children are very unlikely to do so either. Second, put an alarm clock in each bedroom. Make all household members responsible for waking up and getting to school or work on time. Set alarm clocks for children who can't yet tell time and teach young children how to turn their alarms off. If a child is a heavy sleeper, make sure the alarm is loud and position the clock across the room from the bed. Allow the alarm to ring in the morning until the child turns it off. Discourage the child's older sisters and brothers from turning the child's alarm clock off.

∞∞∞∞

1. What two steps can you take to encourage children to get up on their own every morning?
2. Why does the first step involve change on the part of the parents?
3. If a child prefers to have his mother wake him up and Mother has the time, why must she let an alarm clock wake up her child?

∞∞∞∞

c. Eat a healthy, relaxed breakfast

Take the following two steps to encourage healthy morning eating habits in your family. First, eat a healthy breakfast even if it is a small one. Make every effort to eat your breakfast in a relaxed manner, even if this means that you must get up 15 minutes earlier than you do now.

Second, set out a variety of foods for breakfast and allow family members to serve themselves, deciding what they want to eat and how much they want to eat. Children's appetites, like adults', vary with the weather, what they ate the night before, and what they expect to do that day. Children need to figure out for themselves how much food, and what kind of healthy food, gives them the best start in the morning. If a child decides not to eat breakfast and his parents don't nag him, he'll learn to eat when and as much as his body demands. If his parents nag, he may well develop eating problems, eating too little or eating too much.

Although the choices for breakfast will be determined by your budget and by family members' preferences, many good choices include leftover salads and sandwiches, fresh or dried fruit, unsugared cereal, milk, and bread. In cold weather, it is a good idea for family members, including older children, to take turns preparing hot cereal, pancakes, or eggs for the family's breakfast.

You can save money and improve your family's health by not buying sugared cereals or breakfast drinks. The first time that your children complain that all of the other kids eat Brand X for breakfast, look sympathetic and say something like, "I hear your point of view" or "I understand that other parents buy cereals that I won't buy." From then on when children repeat that complaint, you need only listen and look sympathetic. Eye contact, a smile, and a nod of your head will convey that you hear the complaint but don't have anything more to say on the topic.

If you respond when a child repeats an old complaint, you can be sure that you'll hear a lot more of that complaint—and of others—in the future. Parents who get upset and defensive when their children complain tend to produce perpetually dissatisfied children.

∞∞∞

1. How hard will it be for you to provide a good example by eating a healthy breakfast? What can you do to make this easier for you to do every morning?
2. Why is it important to provide children with choices about what they eat for breakfast and how much they eat?
3. What will happen if a child decides not to eat breakfast and his parents don't nag him about eating breakfast?
4. Will your budget suffer if you give children a choice at breakfast? If it will, in what ways could you provide children with choices at breakfast without ruining your budget?
5. What can you say the first time a child complains about the food you provide for breakfast?
6. Why is it important to say nothing when the child repeats this complaint?
7. What will happen if each time your children repeat a complaint, you discuss their dissatisfaction with them? Will they become less dissatisfied?

∞∞∞

d. Keep the television off in the morning

Get your morning news from the newspaper and the radio. Many families enjoy sharing a newspaper as they eat breakfast together. Young children can look at picture books while older children and their parents look at parts of the newspaper.

Television tends to distract family members and interfere with their morning routines, causing people to be late for school and work or to leave partly prepared. This may be because it is much harder to walk away from the television than it is to walk away from the radio or put down a newspaper or book. Television can also be used as a potent reward for studying as described in Module 11, Homework, Reading, and Television, but its usefulness is diluted if it is freely available in the morning. If you fear that children will turn the television on despite your requests, consult Module 11.

∽∽∽

1. How does television sometimes interfere with a family's morning routine?
2. Does television ever interfere with your family's morning routine?
3. Will you have problems keeping the television off in the morning? How can you solve those problems?
4. If you follow the suggestions in this section on establishing a morning routine, how will your routine change?

∽∽∽

3. Encouraging Young Children to Get Dressed and Eat Breakfast on Their Own

Take the following steps to encourage young children who can dress themselves to dress independently and eat breakfast without reminder. For each young child capable of dressing independently, set aside an outfit appropriate for school or daycare that the child does not like. Save this outfit for days when the child does not get dressed independently. Do not remind young children to get dressed and eat breakfast. Wait until 15 minutes before they need to be out the door, on the bus, or in your car. Then quickly and gently wash them and dress them in the outfits you have set aside. Allow them, if they wish, to take food to eat on their trip and see to it that they get to their destination for the day. If children are crying when you bring them to school, deliver them to a favorite teacher, say good-bye, and leave.

Young children want to be independent. The child who is slow dressing and whom you dress in disliked clothes and get out the door will gradually learn to get dressed quickly and independently. Since learning to dress quickly is something all children must master, there is no need to be harsh with the slow child. This will only hurt your relationship with the child and the child's self-esteem.

ထာထာထာ

1. What will you do if your young children do not dress and eat breakfast on their own?
2. If you do dress them and get them out the door, why is it important to do this in a quiet, gentle manner?

ထာထာထာ

4. What to Do When Children Are Late for School

Children should be responsible for getting themselves to school on time. Have children who ride a bus to school walk when they miss it, as long as they are at least 9 years old, the distance to school is 1 mile or less, and there is a sidewalk or walkway between home and school. Children who miss the bus but cannot walk to school for one of the previous reasons or because of a physical handicap should take whatever transportation can be arranged.

If you must drive children to school when they are late and this makes you late for work, subtract the amount of time you were late for work from the children's bedtimes that night. If you were an hour late to work, the children's bedtime will be an hour earlier. During the ride to school, make sure there is no discussion of lateness.

Have children who are late getting to school face the usual school penalties, including visits to the principal and detentions. If lateness to school is a frequent problem in your family, tell your children's teachers and the principal that you expect them to penalize your children and any other children who are late for school. Find out what the usual penalty for lateness is. If you are dissatisfied with the penalty, negotiate a penalty that seems meaningful and fair.

Do not write excuse notes when your children are late unless you really believe that they were late because of your actions. It is a good idea to write an excuse note when your daughter was late due to an emergency doctor's appointment. It is a bad idea to write an excuse note when your son was late because he overslept.

ထာထာထာ

1. From now on, who is responsible for making sure each child in your family gets to school on time?

2. If your children ride a bus, what will you do if they miss the bus?
3. What will you do if driving your children to school makes you late for work?
4. What will happen at school when each of your children is late for school, and how will this encourage each child to get ready quickly for school?

∞∞∞

5. Explaining the Morning Routine to Your Children

Before you begin the new morning routine, explain once to your children what you will do. You might say something like this:

> "Daniel and Robin, I think that it is important for you to learn to get yourselves up in the morning and off to school without my help. This will help you learn to be adults and depend upon yourselves. You both have alarm clocks in your rooms. From now on, I'm not going to call you to wake up; it's up to you to get up when your alarm goes off, wash, dress, and come down for breakfast. As always, you can eat as little or as much as you want for breakfast. It's your job to watch the clock so that you are ready to go out of the door at 7:45 to catch the school bus. If you miss the bus, you'll have to walk, no matter how bad the weather is."

Make sure that you include in your explanation:

1. Why you are beginning a new morning routine,
2. How children are to wake up,
3. Who is responsible for washing, dressing, and feeding the children,
4. If appropriate, what you will do if a young child is not dressed on time,
5. Who will see to it that the children are ready to leave for school on time,
6. What will happen if the children leave for school late.

Have your children repeat your explanation of the morning routine to make sure they understand what you've told them. Even if they don't seem to understand, follow through with your plan. They will understand after they've experienced the morning routine a few times. If children show an interest in planning the morning routine with you, get their ideas about breakfast foods and a schedule for the use of the bathroom.

∞∞∞

1. How many times will you explain the morning routine to your children?
2. What six things will you tell your children about the morning routine?
3. How will you find out if they understand you? What if they don't seem to understand?
4. How can you involve your children in planning the morning routine?

∞∞∞

6. What to Do When Children Refuse to Go to School

The first time that a child refuses to go to school, arrange for the child to stay home with supervision as you would if the child were sick. That evening, in a comfortable place at home, talk to your child about the problems at school.

Ask why the child does not want to go to school and listen carefully to what the child says. Do not suggest any reasons for not wanting to go to school to the child. Just ask open-ended questions until you are sure you understand the child's complaint. You could say, for example: "Do things happen at school that you don't like? What kinds of things? Where do those things happen? Who does it? Does it happen to other kids, too? Which kids? What do you do when this happens? What do other kids do when this happens? What do teachers do about this? What could I do to make things better at school? What could you do? What could the teachers do? Does anybody tell you not to talk about these things with me? Who tells you that?"

If your children have been told by an adult not to talk about school problems with you, reassure them that they are right to tell you about all of their problems. Tell them that you will never punish them for what they tell you or for things they are forced to do by adults.

If you suspect that something is wrong at the school or daycare center, question the child's teacher, childcare worker, the school administrator, parents of other children in the school, and local school officials until you know for sure that the school or center is a safe place for your child.

Although the majority of teachers and childcare workers are qualified, caring people, a few are not. These adults may frighten or harm children through physical or verbal abuse or through sexual molestation. If you suspect that an adult at your child's school or daycare center is incompetent or is abusing children, demand that your child be assigned to another classroom or group. If problems continue in the new classroom or group, carefully and quickly look for another school or daycare center for your child. Register complaints with the authorities who license or oversee the school as well as with the police if the problems involve sexual molestation.

When a child makes an accusation about someone at a school or daycare center, protect the child from further abuse while you investigate the complaint. At the same time, make every effort to be fair and reasonable with school and daycare authorities. If you are absolutely positive that the child's accusations are unfounded, continue with this module.

If you suspect that other children are threatening or causing your child physical harm, determine if the school is taking reasonable steps to ensure children's safety at school, on the school grounds, and on the school bus; if school authorities penalize bullies; and if all school personnel encourage verbal problem solving rather than physical confrontations. If you decide that the school is doing less than it might to protect your child, do what you can to protect your child from injury, including changing schools or way of transportation to and from school. Register complaints about the problem with the authorities who license or oversee the school and work with parents and teachers to remedy the situation. If you decide that the school is doing a good job, continue with this module.

If you suspect that your child is unhappy or nervous about school because of teasing by other children, a strange school, lack of familiar friends, oversensitivity, or poor social skills, continue with this module. Do the same if your child frequently has physical complaints on school mornings that your doctor says are due to anxiety.

∞∞∞

1. Do you have children who refuse to go to school or who are often too sick to go to school?
2. What will you do the first time that a child refuses to go to school?
3. What type of questions should you ask children about why they don't want to go to school?
4. What are three possible reasons for a child refusing to go to school?
5. What will you do if you suspect an adult is abusing your child?
6. What will you do if a gang of older bullies often victimizes younger children in the school yard?

∞∞∞

7. Helping School-Refusing and School-Phobic Children

When a child refuses to go to school three times or more in 1 month and when you are sure that school refusal is due to your child's personal problems rather than to abuse by adults or other children, your child should be considered a school refuser. If your child is visibly worried or anxious about going to school, your child should be considered a school phobic. All of this module will help your child, particularly the suggestions that follow.

On a day when your child has gone to school without reminder and stayed there for the full day, schedule 1 hour of special time in the evening to listen to your child's complaints about school if the child frequently complains about school. If there are two parents in your family, it is a good idea to let the child decide with which parent to spend the special time. Listen carefully and sympathetically to what your child says during the special time. When appropriate, share similar experiences that you have had to show you understand the child's hurt feelings and anger. Show particular interest in any steps the child has taken to make things better at school or, at least, to not be so hurt by what happens at school. Give no advice unless the child specifically asks you for advice. Even then, give as little advice as possible. If the child has no complaints, spend the special time doing something enjoyable together. Let the child choose the activity.

Do not talk with the child about school-related complaints except during the special time. Give no special time on days when the child did not attend without reminder. Arrange for sisters and brothers to earn special time by achieving goals important for them. Continue special time until the school-refusal problem has been forgotten by everyone. It is a good idea to continue special time for other children in the family too until they enter high school.

You also should arrange with your child a "reward menu," from which the child can choose two or three items on days when the child has gone to school without reminder and stayed for the full day. Choose rewards that you will be able to give repeatedly, that are age appropriate, that the child values, and that you feel comfortable giving only when earned and withholding when not earned. If you like, include one or more choices on the reward menu that require 5 days of school attendance. Give these as bonuses beyond the daily rewards.

Include some items that the child will be able to share with siblings so that they will benefit when the child goes to school without reminder and stays there for the full day. Siblings have enormous influence, for better or for worse, over one another's behavior. When siblings can benefit from one child's success, they work hard to contribute to that success. For example, if the child puts ice cream after dinner on the menu, keep ice cream on hand, only provide ice cream when it is earned, and provide ice cream to other family members also when the child earns and selects this reward.

Decide how many choices from the menu the child will be able to make for going to school without reminder and staying there the full day. The more serious the problem, the more important it is to give the child several choices from the menu for school attendance. Develop a lengthy written reward menu, so that the child will not tire of available rewards over the next few months. Post the reward menu where the child can see it. Physical affection and praise need not be listed on the menu, since you should praise your child after the child goes to school without reminder and stays there for the full day whether the child asks or not. Figure 3 shows a sample reward menu for going to school.

Figure 3. Sample Reward Menu for Going to School

Kurt's Reward Menu
(Choose three items on days that you go to school without reminder and stay there for a full day.)

Watch favorite television show at 4:00 p.m.

Invite two friends over for dinner

Play cards for ½ hour with Grandma

Get $1.00

Get 1 hour help with homework from Mom

Use the telephone for ½ hour

Have brownies for dessert after dinner for the whole family

Go to a movie of my choice with the whole family after 5 good days in a row

---

Continue daily rewards until 3 months have passed without school refusal. Then provide only a big reward, such as a movie or roller skating, for a week without school refusal, until another 3 months have passed without school refusal. Discontinue rewards for school attendance only when the child is clearly happy about going to school each day. Begin rewards for school attendance again at the first sign of school refusal. At the beginning of the next school year, be prepared for school refusal and the need to begin daily rewards again.

On mornings when the child does not get ready for school, take reasonable, practical steps to get the child out the door. These might include carrying younger children or propelling reluctant older children, no matter how they are dressed, to the car or school bus. If the child goes to school because of your efforts, there should be no special time or rewards that evening.

Don't worry if there is nothing you can do to get the child to school. Just make sure that on a day when the child refuses to attend school special time and rewards are unavailable and the child spends the day in bed or in the bedroom with no television or telephone privileges or visits from friends for the entire day. The child should take meals in the bedroom on such days. Children who refuse to go to school should be supervised by a responsible adult at home. Do not scold the school-refusing child on a day when the child does not go to school. Scolding will make it harder, not easier, for the child to get back to school, harm your relationship with the child, and damage the child's self-esteem.

Find out if your child wants to learn to be more relaxed on school mornings and at school. If so, purchase an audiotape and practice muscular relaxation with your child in the evenings at the end of your special time and before the child goes to bed. Or, if the child prefers, let the child listen to the tape alone at bedtime.

∞∞∞

1. When is the time to talk about school-related complaints with a child who often refuses to go to school?
2. On what days should such special time be available?
3. Will the child lose the special time if the child has no complaints?
4. What good things should happen when a school-refusing child goes to school without reminder and returns home at the end of the school day? Who else should share in these rewards?
5. What type of rewards should you include on the reward menu?
6. At what point should rewards for school attendance shift from daily to weekly? When should they be discontinued? When should they be reinstated?
7. What will you do when a child refuses to go to school?

8. Can you leave the child alone on such a day?
9. Is it wise to scold the school-refusing child on a day when the child does not go to school? Why not?

> Laurie, an 11-year-old, has been refusing to go to school lately. She gets up and gets dressed and then sits on her bed and cries for the rest of the morning until she has missed the school bus. Laurie's father drives past Laurie's school on his way to work. What reasonable steps could Laurie's father take to get Laurie to school? What steps would you consider unreasonable for him to take?

∞∞∞∞∞

8. Explaining School-Day Procedures to Your School-Refusing Child

Before you begin new school-day procedures, explain once to your school-refusing child what you will be doing. You might say something like this:

> "Kurt, both of us have been arguing and making each other miserable on mornings when you wake up with a stomachache and don't want to go to school. From now on, it's up to you to get up and ready for school on your own and to be out the door by 7:30. At 7:15, if I see you aren't close to being ready, Dad and I will dress you and get you out the door and into the car and to school. On days when you go to school without reminder and stay there all day, Dad and I will make life really great for you. You will get an hour of special time with us to talk about school and you will get to choose several rewards from a reward menu. On days when we can't get you off to school, Dad or I will stay home with you and make sure that you spend the day in your bedroom with no television, telephone, or visits from friends. Now, let's start making up a reward menu for your good school days. Should we put *fried chicken dinner* on it?"

Make sure that you include in your explanation:

1. Why you will use new school-day procedures,
2. What will happen on days when the child goes to school without reminder and stays there all day,
3. What will happen on days when the child refuses to go to school.

Have your child repeat your explanation of school-day procedures to make sure he understands you. Even if your child doesn't seem to understand, follow through with your plan. He will understand after he has experienced the procedures a few times.

∞∞∞

1. How many times will you explain school-day procedures to your school-refusing child?
2. What three things will you tell your school-refusing child about the school-day procedures?
3. How will you find out if the child understands? What if the child doesn't seem to understand?

∞∞∞

9. Keeping a Record for This Module

While working through this module, continue as you did during baseline to put a check in the small box labelled *YES* in Column 9 when all of your children (age 4 to 17) got to school on time that day. On days when there is no school, cross out the boxes in Column 9 to show that they do not apply. You should also keep track of the times that your school-refusing or school-phobic children who are being rewarded for school attendance got to school on time with no reminders, stayed for the full day, and were rewarded. Do this by marking the child's initial and a star in Column 9 in the box labelled *Good behavior, rewards given* whenever the child is on time to school. This will remind you to reward your child. Lightly cross out the child's initial and the star when you have rewarded the child.

The example on the next page shows how Column 9 might look on a family's assessment chart after they have begun using Module 9. In this family there are two children, Andy and Bridget. Bridget has been refusing to go to school and a reward menu has been constructed for the days on which she does go to school. On the first day of charting, Bridget was late for school, so nothing was marked in Column 9. On the second day, both Bridget and Andy were on time for school. This was indicated by a check in the small box in Column 9. Bridget's good behavior was also marked *(B*)*. When she received her reward for this behavior, the notation was lightly crossed out. On the third day, there was no school, so the box in Column 9 was crossed out.

∞∞∞

1. How will you record your children's school attendance?
2. How will you keep a record of the times you reward your children?

∞∞∞

10. Moving On to Module 10

You can move on to Module 10 when you have consistently followed the procedures described in this module for at least 5 school days. If school-refusal is a very troublesome problem, don't move on until there are twice as many checks in Column 9 as during baseline. If you have trouble getting up in the morning and off to work on time, it may take several weeks for you to get used to the procedures described in this module. If you have a child who is a school-refuser, it may take you a month to get used to the procedures described in this module. Make sure to continue using these procedures and charting for this module when you move on to Module 10.

If you start using the procedures described in this module and then stop, if you think you aren't using the procedures correctly, or if you aren't consistently using the procedures, return to the beginning of this module. If you are unable to put these procedures into effect or if after a month your child is not going to school twice as often as during baseline, consult a mental-health professional who has worked successfully with school-phobic children.

∞∞∞

1. How will you know when you are ready to move on to Module 10?
2. When is it a good idea to begin Module 9 again?

∞∞∞

Module 10: Chores and Allowances

Almost all parents complain that their children don't do their assigned chores without constant nagging. Parents worry about children's reluctance to do chores for two reasons. Many parents believe that children who don't take responsibility for work around the house are poorly prepared for the demands of adult life. In addition, working parents who spend their free time taking care of the house and the children feel resentful when their children don't help.

Dependent and overindulged children never have enough money to satisfy their needs, and they manage their money very poorly. Conflict with parents about money and difficulty separating from them during adolescence due to a lack of survival skills is a frequent result.

This module explains how you can encourage children to do their share of household work and learn to manage money by establishing a system of chores and allowances. It is appropriate for children from age 4 through 17.

Chores and allowances as a problem in a competent family. A 42-year-old mother, who is a hotel maid, an unemployed father, age 53, who was disabled by a factory accident, three teenaged girls, and a 10-year-old son make up this family. The two oldest girls work after school and give half their salaries to their parents. Since his accident, Father has kept house, prepared meals, and supervised the children. To earn money, he carves dollhouse furniture, which he sells to local gift shops. He would like to spend more time on his carving, but it takes him most of the day to get through the routines of cleaning and cooking.

Chores and allowances as a problem in a less competent family. A 33-year-old mother, who is a hair stylist, a 32-year-old father, who owns a chain of sports-equipment stores, a 13-year-old daughter, and a 10-year-old son make up this family. Since their children were born, Mother and Father both have bought things for the children whenever the children were bored or sad. For the last 3 years, there have been constant arguments between Mother and her daughter. These repetitive arguments center on the daughter's demands for more and more clothing, cosmetics, and privileges and the mother's anger at her daughter's rude and lazy behavior. Both parents are worried about their daughter's neglect of her school work and her preoccupation with boys.

1. Deciding if You Need to Work Through This Module

Look at your baseline record in Column 10. You need not work through Module 10 if: *(a)* you are sure your baseline was fairly typical for your family, *(b)* there was a check in Column 10 for 6 out of 7 baseline days, *(c)* children were not punished if they did not do their chores, *(d)* children were expected to do their fair share of household work, *(e)* no family member feels unhappy about the distribution of household chores among family members, and *(f)* during baseline, no family member was expected to do another person's chores.

If you decide to work through Module 10, draw a horizontal line across Column 10, underneath your last baseline day. The line will separate your baseline record from the record of your progress during Module 10. If you decide not to work through Module 10, continue filling in all columns of your chart and move on to Module 11. If at any time fewer than 6 of 7 days in Column 10 have checks, complete Module 10.

∞∞∞

1. Do you need to work through Module 10? If not, why not?

∞∞∞

2. Making Family Members Responsible for Their Own Laundry

Taking care of the laundry for a whole family can be a full-time job. If one parent does this job for the rest of the family, none of the children will be prepared to take care of their laundry when they leave home. When the person who usually does the family's laundry stops doing it, family members will have no choice but to take care of their own clothes.

Give adult and child family members as much responsibility as their skills, age, and height permit for taking care of their own laundry. Begin by giving each one a plastic basket to be placed in his closet. In these baskets, family members can store their dirty laundry and bring it to and from the washer and dryer or laundromat.

If you have a washer and dryer in your house, show family members how to operate them. Expect family members to do everything connected with their laundry, including putting it away in their rooms. Teach young children how to hang up wet clothing so that ironing is not necessary, and teach older children how to iron their own clothes, sew on buttons, hem skirts and pants, and make other minor repairs to clothing. Most children can put their clean clothes away by age 6, operate a washer and dryer by age 9, and make minor clothing repairs by age 13.

If laundry is washed at a laundromat, make family members responsible for putting dirty clothes in the laundry basket on laundry day, and ironing, folding, and putting away clean clothes that evening.

∽∽∽

1. Who does your family's laundry now?
2. How could responsibility for laundry be shared in the family?

> Mrs. Perkins does everyone's laundry on Mondays. She spends the whole day collecting dirty laundry, washing, drying, folding, ironing, and putting clothes away. Every morning her husband and children ask her to find their socks and shirts. They change their clothes several times a day without thinking of the extra work they are creating. Mrs. Perkin's children are doing poorly at school. None of them are willing to expend the effort needed to get good grades. Why might her children have problems at school? Mrs. Perkins thinks the solution to her children's school problems is for her to make life easier for them at home, so they will have more time to study. Is she right?

∽∽∽

3. Dividing the Household Chores Among Family Members

After you and your spouse (in a two-parent family) have divided responsibilities for the laundry among family members and for the laundry of infants and young children between yourselves, you can divide other chores among family members. Talk with your children about the chores they prefer to do. Think about each child's size, strength, skills, and daily schedule of activities. Try hard not to assign chores to children based on their sex. Remember that grown men need to know how to clean up after themselves in the kitchen, and grown women need to know how to take care of the outside of a house. Now, assign each child between one to four daily or weekly chores.

When assigning daily chores to children you might choose from a list like this: feed the pets, prepare a meal, set the dinner table, clear the dinner table, load the dishwasher or wash the dishes, wash the pots and pans, dry the dishes, put the dishes away, sweep the kitchen floor, collect the trash from each room in a large trash bag and put the bag in the collection or storage spot, bring wood in from the woodpile. All children should be expected to make their beds daily.

Weekly chores assigned to children could include some of those on the following list: clean the bathroom, vacuum the living room, dust the furniture, change the sheets on the beds, take the trash cans outside, bring the trash cans inside, sweep or shovel the steps or driveway, rake leaves, cut the grass, weed the garden, get groceries from a neighborhood store, bring laundry to and from the laundromat.

For each chore you assign, set a day and time for completion according to your standards. The ideal time for children's chores to be done is early in the morning before school or before or after dinner.

The following examples show how your chore lists could look for each child in your family.

Chores for Philip (10 years old)

Make bed by 8:00 a.m. every day.

Clear dishes from table, load dishwasher by 8:00 p.m. every day.

Take trash cans to curb by 8:00 a.m. every Tuesday.

Bring trash cans from curb to house by 8:00 p.m. every Tuesday.

Chores for Ann (8 years old)

Make bed by 8:00 a.m. every day.

Empty dishwasher and set table by 6:00 p.m. every day.

Feed and water dog and cat by 8:00 a.m. every day.

Your expectations may vary with the child's age or experience. For example, you might expect a 4-year-old to pull the covers up over the bed and straighten the pillow, while you might expect a 12-year-old to make the bed with hospital corners.

∞∞∞∞

1. What chores will you assign to each child in your family?
2. For each chore, what day and time must it be completed by?

∞∞∞∞

4. Deciding on a Daily Allowance for Each Child

List each child's current weekly expenses and total them. From now on, each child will be responsible for paying for all minor purchases. Included in a child's expenses will be lunch money, snack money, money for school supplies and books, money for charity, money for transportation, money for birthday and holiday presents, money for cosmetics, money for weekend recreation such as movies, money for sports equipment and supplies, and money for saving up for big items such as a school trip to Washington, D.C.

Philip's weekly expenses, for example, look like this:

$2.00 for two hot lunches a week
 2.00 for snack and milk money
 5.00 for a piano lesson
 2.50 for bus transportation
 2.00 for books, school supplies, charity, and savings

13.50 Total

Round off the total weekly expenses for each child so that it can be divided by 7 to give a daily allowance. For example, Philip's total was raised to $14.00 so that, divided by 7, it gives a $2.00 daily allowance.

Label a jar with each child's name and place the jars in the kitchen. From now on at the end of the day, place the child's daily allowance in the jar if, and only if, all the child's chores for that day were done on time and up to your standards. It is very important for you to pay the allowance at the end of the day when chores have been done. Do not pay the child's daily allowance if all chores were not done, if all chores were done but not on time, or if all chores were done but not the way you want them to be done.

Do not remind children to do their chores or comment if their chores were not done well. Talk to children about chores only when they've done well and you want to compliment them or when they ask you questions (that you have not answered before) about their chores. If chores were not done, do them yourself if necessary. Do not ask children to do their chores after the deadline or to do other children's chores. Children may swap chores among themselves though. When they swap chores, continue to pay each child's daily allowance for the chores you've assigned to that child.

When children's expenses increase considerably, add another chore, increase the weekly allowance, and pay one-seventh for the daily allowance. When children's expenses decrease temporarily, pay the same daily allowance and allow the child to try to save the difference. Young children can leave their money in their jars as a means of saving. Help older children open bank accounts for their savings. Do not lend your children money so that they will be encouraged to save.

If children have another source of income other than their daily allowances, make them responsible for paying for more things each week so that they will need the daily allowances you pay. If a relative provides money to the children whenever they ask, you will have to convince the relative to stop, explaining that the relative is hurting the children, not helping them.

∽∽∽∽∽∽

1. What are each of your children's total weekly expenses?
2. What daily allowance will you give to each child?
3. What will each child have to do to earn this daily allowance?
4. How and when will you pay the daily allowance?
5. Who will do chores that children leave undone?
6. Do your children get money each week from any source but you? If so, how will you adjust their expenses to take this extra source of income into account?

7. What could go wrong with this allowance system? How can you solve these problems?

Eddie has a newspaper route from which he earns $15 a week, which is more than enough spending money for him. His parents want Eddie to continue with his job, but they also want him to bear his share of household chores. Mention two things that Eddie's parents could do so that an allowance from them would be a meaningful incentive for Eddie.

ഇരുഗ്

5. Explaining Chores and Allowances to Your Children

Before you begin using a system of chores and allowances, explain it once to your children. You might say something like this:

"Patrick and Kevin, Mom and I are beginning a system of chores and allowances so that we can stop nagging you boys to do things around the house. Here is a list of the chores we expect each of you to do: Patrick—make your bed every day by 8:00 a.m.; feed the animals by 8:00 a.m.; take out the trash by 7:00 p.m.; and clear the dinner table and load the dishwasher by 7:00 p.m. Kevin—make your bed every day by 8:00 a.m.; set the dinner table, unload the dishwasher, and put away the dishes by 5:30 p.m.; and take care of your brother Brian after school every day from 3–5 p.m. Each of you will get $2.00 in a jar in the kitchen at the end of a day when you've done all your chores well, on time, and with no reminder. From this money, each of you must pay for all your school lunches, snacks, bus trips, gifts for friends' birthdays, books, and toys. If you spend your money too fast and run out, I may give you a loan, but I'll take the loan out of your future earnings for chores. You can swap chores, but I'll still pay each of you only if all the chores I assigned to you are done."

Make sure that you include in your explanation:

1. Why you are beginning a system of chores and allowances,
2. What chores each child is expected to do,
3. When and how these chores are to be completed,
4. What each child's allowance will be,
5. When and how you will pay these daily allowances,
6. What expenses each child pays for from the daily allowance,
7. Why saving will be important,
8. What will happen when children swap chores.

Have your children repeat your explanation of chores and allowances to make sure they understand what you've told them. Even if they don't seem to understand, follow through with your plan. They will understand once they've experienced the system of chores and allowances a few times.

∞∞∞

1. How many times will you explain chores and allowances to your children?
2. What eight things will you tell your children about chores and allowances?
3. How will you make sure they understand what you have told them? What if they don't seem to understand?

∞∞∞

6. Keeping a Record for This Module

While working through this module, continue as you did during baseline to put a check in the small box labelled *YES* in Column 10 when all of your children (age 4 to 17) did their assigned chores that day on time, up to your standards, and with no reminders. You should also keep track of the times that individual children did their chores and received their allowances. Do this by marking the child's initial and a star in Column 10 in the box labelled *Good behavior, rewards given* whenever the child does his chores. This will remind you to pay the child's allowance. Write down the amount of allowance given when the allowance is paid.

The example on the facing page shows how Column 10 might look on a family's assessment chart after they have begun using Module 10. In this family there are two children, Andy and Bridget. On the first day of charting, neither Bridget nor Andy did chores, so nothing is marked in Column 10. On the second day, both Bridget and Andy did their chores. This was indicated by a check in the small box in Column 10. Bridget's and Andy's good behavior was also marked *(B*, A*)*. When they received their allowances, the amount paid was written by their initials. On the third day, only Andy did his chores and received his allowance.

∞∞∞

1. How will you keep a record of chores done and allowances paid?

∞∞∞

7. Moving On to Module 11

You can move on to Module 11 when you have used the chores and allowances system consistently for at least 1 week. If compliance with a

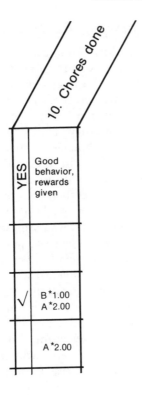

system of chores and allowances is an extremely troublesome problem, don't move on until there are twice as many checks in Column 10 as there were during baseline. If you have trouble managing money yourself, if you have a hard time saying no when children ask you to buy things for them, or if your children have another source of money than you, it may take several weeks for you to use the procedures in this module consistently.

If you start using the chores and allowances system and then stop, if you think you aren't using the system correctly, or if you aren't consistently using the system, return to the beginning of this module.

༚༚༚

1. How will you know when you are ready to move on to Module 11?
2. When is it a good idea to begin Module 10 again?

༚༚༚

Module 11: Homework, Reading, and Television

Most parents realize that children who read for enjoyment and do their homework independently are likely to succeed at school. Perhaps this is why homework is so often a battleground for parents and children. Some parents become too involved in their children's homework, forgetting that the children, not they, are going to school. They pester children about what homework they have and nag them to do it. They help children do part of their homework and then get angry when asked for more help. They plead with their children not to do homework in front of the television or with loud music playing but get no results. Other parents angrily reject their children's reasonable requests for help, because they fear they won't know the right answers.

The more time children spend watching television, the less time they have left for reading and homework. Many parents understand this but don't control children's television watching. Parents who are addicted to television, who leave the television on all the time, or who feel lonely if they can't hear the sound of the television have no hope of controlling their children's television use until they are willing to control their own use of television.

Children who watch a lot of television and many programs meant for adults are prone to nightmares and irrational fears and worries. They may think that violence is the best, or only, way to solve conflicts between people.

This module explains how you can increase the amount of time children spend on homework and reading every day and reduce the amount of time they watch television. It does this by establishing a homework hour and limiting television use. It is appropriate for children from age 6 through age 17.

Homework, reading, and television as a problem in a competent family. A divorced 44-year-old mother, employed as a secretary, and her five children make up this family. The two oldest children are in college, the middle child is in high school, the youngest two children are in middle school. Mother is particularly concerned about her 12-year-old son who, until he entered middle school, was an outstanding student like his older sisters and brothers. This year teachers have called several times to complain that the boy is not handing assignments in on time and sometimes not doing homework at all.

Homework, reading, and television as a problem in a less competent family. A 35-year-old father, who is a salesman, a 35-year-old mother, who is a waitress, the mother's 13-year-old daughter by her first marriage, and the couple's 2-year-old daughter make up this family.

The 13-year-old girl was an excellent student until shortly after her mother remarried. Since then she has lost interest in school and become preoccupied with her boyfriend and his family. From time to time she comes home late, acting as if she is drunk or on drugs. Her stepfather watches television and drinks beer from the time he comes home from work until he goes to bed. The more he drinks, the more likely he is to tell his 13-year-old stepdaughter that she is a stupid girl with loose morals who will never amount to anything. The 13-year-old watches television in her room to avoid her stepfather.

1. Deciding if You Need to Work Through this Module

Look at your baseline record in Column 11. You need not work through Module 11 if: *(a)* your baseline record included at least 5 school days and you are sure your baseline was fairly typical for your family, *(b)* there was a check in Column 11 for 4 out of 5 school days charted, *(c)* on days you checked, children did their homework without reminder, *(d)* teachers are completely satisfied with your children's homework, *(e)* no child watches more than 2 hours of television and no adult watches more than 3 hours of television a day, *(f)* no child watches television programs that feature violence or adult sexual behavior, and *(g)* children and adults use reading as a way to relax and to find solutions to important problems.

If you decide to work through Module 11, draw a horizontal line across Column 11 underneath your last baseline day. The line will separate your baseline record from the record of your progress during Module 11. If you decide not to work through Module 11, continue filling in all columns of your chart. If at any time fewer than 4 out of 5 school days are checked in Column 11, return to Module 11.

∞∞∞

1. Do you need to work through Module 11? If not, why not?

∞∞∞

2. Reducing the Number of Televisions in Your House

No family needs more than two televisions. Most families can manage nicely with one television. Remove televisions from bedrooms, the kitchen, and eating areas, even if the televisions support video games. Place them in a play room or family room. Leave personal computers in bedrooms if they are used for purposes other than playing noneducational games.

Donate extra televisions to a local school or hospital. Or sell them and use the cash to buy games and sports equipment that the family can use together.

∞∞∞

1. In what rooms in your house do you have television sets?
2. What is your plan for getting television sets out of bedrooms and eating areas? When will you carry out this plan? What help will you need in carrying out this plan? Who can you ask for help?

∞∞∞

3. Limiting the Use of Television in Your House

Take the following steps to limit the use of television in your house. First, stop watching television during family meals. Watching television at mealtimes encourages overeating and discourages important family conversations. When you eat alone, read instead of watching television.

Second, limit children's television watching to programs without aggressive, frightening, sexual, or dehumanizing content. While it is true that such content is central to fairy tales and the classics of literature, children who read books, or who are read to by others, can control the storytelling process. They can stop the story at any time it becomes distressing. It is for this reason that there is no need to censor what children read, as long as it is not explicitly pornographic. Television has such a hypnotic effect that some children will keep watching even when they are frightened or confused.

Third, keep the television turned off in the morning and for most of the afternoon. Later in this module you will learn to use television to reward children for reading and doing homework and must limit its use to make that reward meaningful. Whenever you can, replace your own television watching with reading, listening to the radio, working at a craft, exercising, or talking with friends and family. If you are a television addict, expect the same from your children. Most children do what adults do, not what they say.

Say no to children's requests to watch television in the morning or afternoon and to their requests to watch inappropriate programs. The first time you say no to a particular program, explain why. The next time, just say no. When children complain that "Everyone watches all the TV they want," explain that you are limiting television viewing to help them get into the habit of studying and reading. Say nothing the next time they complain.

Fourth, stop using the television as a babysitter. The next time that you wake up and realize that your children are up, begin teaching them to play quietly or read while you sleep. Explain to them that you will call this time "Quiet Time" and what they are to do during Quiet Time. Using a clock, show them how long Quiet Time will last. Tell them what you will do after a good Quiet Time. After a successful Quiet Time, reward all children who took part by telling them what they did that you liked and by an activity of their choice. Begin by expecting Quiet Time to last for as little as 5 minutes. After a few successful 5-minute Quiet Times, expect Quiet Time to last 10 minutes. Extend the length of Quiet Time until children can amuse themselves for at least 2 hours. Quiet Time prepares children for school by getting them used to amusing themselves, playing and working without adult attention or instructions. Very young children, in addition to children already in school, benefit from Quiet Time and the other procedures for limiting television use discussed in this section.

If children turn the television on when you want it off, buy a small padlock that fits through the hole in the prongs of the television's plug, so that the set can't be plugged into the wall (available through the Sears catalog). Many cable television services offer lock-out devices for some or all channels.

ကာကာကာ

1. Why will you and your family stop watching television while eating?
2. Why is it important to screen what children watch on television?
3. Why is it unnecessary to censor what children read (unless it is pornographic)?
4. What problems do you anticipate in keeping the television off in the morning and afternoon? How will you solve these problems?
5. What will you say when children complain about not being allowed to watch television as much as they want?
6. How can adults in your family limit their television use?
7. Why is it so important that adults provide a good example of television use to their children?
8. If you now use television as a babysitter, what will you do instead?
9. How will you get your children used to Quiet Time?
10. How does Quiet Time prepare children for school?

ကာကာကာ

4. Making Reading More Important Than Television Watching

Make reading more important in your family than television watching. Take your children to a public library once a week. Introduce them to the children's librarian and to activities for children their ages. Encourage them to roam around, finding books, magazines, and records that arouse their curiosity. Have children take out books and take out books for yourself. Instead of watching television together, make reading together in the evening a family tradition.

∞∞∞

1. What will you do to encourage more reading in your house?

Paul and Vicky want to devote the time from dinner until their two girls are in bed to the family. After dinner, while the girls are getting ready for bed, Paul and Vicky try to read and catch up with bills and paperwork. When the girls are ready for bed, the whole family likes to read a book together. The only problem is that the phone keeps ringing, disrupting the family's time together and their reading. Vicky feels obligated to answer the phone because she worries that her mother might be calling about an emergency. How could Paul and Vicky solve this problem?

∞∞∞

5. Establishing a Homework Hour

To be successful in school, your children need to develop daily reading and study habits. You can help them do this by establishing a homework hour for each of them.

a. Pick a time to do homework

Together with each child age 6 or older, decide on an hour each weekday (Monday through Friday) when the child will do homework or read. It is a good idea for the homework hour to be the same time each day. It is also easier for you if all children in the family have the same homework hour.

Children need time to eat a snack, play, and rest when they get home from school. Immediately after that is the best time for the homework hour. Although children often prefer to put homework off until after dinner, they are often very tired by then.

Some children would rather have the homework hour on Sunday than on Friday, yet they often forget what they were supposed to do by Sunday or discover, too late, that they don't have the supplies and books they need to complete the assignment. Setting the homework hour on Friday means one less supervisory task for parents on Sunday.

∞∞∞

1. At what time will the homework hour be for each of your children on each weekday?

∞∞∞

b. Pick a place to do homework
Decide with each child where homework is to be done. If the child has a bedroom of his own or shares a room with another child, homework should be done in the bedroom. For each child, arrange a desk with good lighting and a comfortable desk chair, as well as a reading light over the bed. After you have helped children arrange work areas in their rooms, it is up to them to keep the work areas tidy.

If there is no room for a table or desk in the child's bedroom, set aside a work area for the child's homework hour in another part of the house. The best work area is one that will only be used for the child's homework hour and that is located in a quiet, comfortable, isolated spot.

Use the kitchen or dining room table for children's homework hours if necessary. Make sure that no one is in the kitchen or dining room during the homework hour except the children who are studying. If there is no quiet work space in your house, arrange for your children to do their homework in a nearby public library or community center.

∞∞∞

1. Where will each of your children do homework?

∞∞∞

c. Provide supplies for homework
Most children will need some basic supplies (crayons, paper, scissors, tape, pencils, pens, erasers, notebooks, assignment pads, book bags or back packs, lunch boxes) and some special supplies that the teacher requires. At the beginning of the school year give children a generous stock of basic supplies. Have them supplement their basic supplies and buy special supplies with their allowances. For children who use the kitchen table or other common work areas, arrange a shelf or provide a large box where each child can store his supplies.

If you don't have one now, arrange a bookshelf in your house and make sure that it includes at least one good dictionary. An abridged or full-length encyclopedia is a good idea if you can afford one; have your local librarian or your child's teacher help you choose the encyclopedia. An atlas of world maps is another good addition to your family's bookshelf. Subscribe to a good daily newspaper if you can afford to.

∞∞∞

1. What homework supplies will you provide for each child? When will you provide them?
2. For what supplies will the child be responsible?

∞∞∞

6. Defining a Good Homework Hour

Children have a good homework hour if they do three things during the homework hour. First, they remain quiet in their homework spots for an entire hour. No noise can be heard from their homework spots in other parts of the house. This means that a child who has the radio on keeps the volume down without being asked so that you cannot hear it from another room. Second, children work on homework, or if they have no homework, they read books or work on quiet projects, such as scrapbooks, diaries, or stamp or photo albums. Third, at the end of the hour, they show you what they have accomplished and correctly answer three questions about their work or reading, convincing you that they have worked hard for the entire hour.

∞∞∞

1. What three things must happen for children to have a good homework hour?
2. What can children do during the homework hour if the teacher has assigned no homework?
3. At the end of the homework hour, is it your job to find your children and ask your children to tell you what they've done? Is it your job to correct your children's work or to find out if they've done the work the teacher assigned?
4. What do children have to convince you about at the end of the homework hour? How can they do this?
5. What problems do you anticipate with the homework hour? How will you solve these problems?

∞∞∞

7. What Parents Do During the Homework Hour

Stay out of children's rooms and away from common work spaces when children are doing their homework. The best thing for you to do at that time is to read the newspaper or a book.

Do not talk to your children during their homework hours except to answer three questions per child about homework or reading. Answer the questions they ask fully and carefully. If you do not know an answer, simply tell the child that you don't know.

∞∞∞

1. Where will you be during your children's homework hours?
2. What is a good thing for you to be doing at that time?
3. How will you handle your children's questions during the homework hour?

Don often knocks on his son's door during the homework hour to find out if Pete is working. Pete resents this so much that he usually gives a sarcastic answer, starting a fight with his father that lasts for the rest of the hour. What should Don be doing differently? How can Don manage his impatience and curiosity during Pete's study hour?

∞∞∞

8. Earning Television Time

Reward children who have had a good homework hour by allowing them to watch as much as 2 hours of television per day before and after dinner. When several children have good homework hours and you have only one television, let the children figure out how to resolve their disagreements.

For sisters and brothers to grow up together happily and to be good friends when they have left home, they must learn while they are young to resolve all sorts of disagreements without parental interference. The problem of sharing television time is one that children can easily resolve among themselves in a number of ways. Working on this problem will prepare them for more serious ones. If they all ask for your advice, you might suggest (only one time) that they roll dice or flip a coin when there is a disagreement about which program to watch or that they divide up the days in the week so that one child always chooses programs on certain days.

∞∞∞

1. How can children earn television time before and after dinner?
2. Why is it important to give children something good to look forward to after a good homework hour?
3. Why is it important to let children develop a system for sharing television time?

∞∞∞

9. Explaining the Homework Hour to Your Children

Before you establish homework hours, explain them once to your children. You might say something like:

"Vince, Kay, and Sheila, I think that if you get into the habit of doing your homework on your own every day and of reading on days when you don't have homework, you'll enjoy school and do well there. From now on, I'll expect each of you to spend an hour on school days in your room doing homework or reading. If you go to your room without reminder, stay there for an hour, and answer three questions at the end of the hour about the work you've done or the book you've read, that's a good homework hour. After a good homework hour you will get to watch television for 2 hours. The television will stay off in the morning and before 4:00 p.m. Now let's discuss what time your homework hours will be."

Make sure that you include in your explanation:

1. Why you are establishing homework hours,
2. What a good homework hour is,
3. What children get after good homework hours.

Have your children repeat your explanation of homework hours to make sure they understand what you've told them. Even if they don't seem to understand, follow through with your plan. They will understand once they've experienced the homework hour procedures a few times.

∞∞∞

1. How many times will you explain the homework hour to your children?
2. What three things will you tell your children about the homework hour?
3. How will you make sure they understand what you have told them? What if they don't seem to understand?

∞∞∞

10. Keeping a Record for This Module

While working through this module, continue as you did during baseline to put a check in the small box labelled *YES* in Column 11 when all of your children (age 6 to 17) did homework or read for 1 hour on that day. You should also keep track of good homework hours for individual children and when they are rewarded for these hours. Do this by marking the child's initial and a star in Column 11 in the box labelled *Good behavior, rewards given* whenever the child has a good homework hour. This will remind you that the child has earned television time. Lightly cross out the child's initial and the star when you have rewarded the child with television time.

The following example shows how Column 11 might look on a family's assessment chart after they have begun using Module 11. In this family there are two children, Andy and Bridget. On the first day of charting, neither Bridget nor Andy had a good homework hour, so nothing was marked in Column 11. On the second day, both Bridget and Andy had good homework hours. This was indicated by a check in the small box in Column 11. Their good behavior was also marked *(B*, A*).*When they received their rewards for this behavior, the notations were lightly crossed out. On the third day, only Andy had a good homework hour and was rewarded with television time.

ꝏꝏꝏ

1. How will you keep a record of your children's good homework hours?

ꝏꝏꝏ

11. Moving On to Module 12

You can move on to Module 12 when you have consistently followed the procedures in this module for at least 5 school days. If the school has complained about your child's homework, don't move on until there are twice as many checks in Column 11 as during baseline. If you are a television addict, if you rarely read, or if you often put off important tasks, it may take several weeks for you to work through this module. Make sure to continue using these procedures and charting for this module when you move on to Module 12.

If you start using the homework system and then stop, if you think you aren't using the system correctly, or if you aren't consistently using the system, return to the beginning of this module.

∞∞∞

1. How will you know when you are ready to move on to Module 12?
2. When is it a good idea to begin Module 11 again?

∞∞∞

Module 12: Loneliness, Unhappiness, Fearfulness, and Self-Injury

Children may have problems with loneliness, unhappiness, fearfulness, or self-injury for several reasons. They may be physically and verbally abused, have parents who suffer from emotional problems and present poor examples of necessary skills, or they may be too protected and inexperienced at dealing with problems. Like adults, children inflict injury on themselves when they can think of no other way to solve their problems. Through suicide attempts or fantasies about death, they may try to resolve abuse, neglect, and rejection by parents, teachers, and peers. Children who have very inadequate problem-solving skills or children who have observed adults using self-injury to solve problems are most likely to resort to self-injury themselves, even when the problems they face seem trivial to others.

If children are to avoid loneliness, unhappiness, fearfulness, and minor self-injury and avoidable accident, they must know how to: make and keep friends, solve problems instead of complain, handle fearful situations, express unhappy feelings through words, and take actions to produce happy feelings.

This module explains how you can help children who have problems with loneliness, unhappiness, fearfulness, and self-injury by encouraging happy and skillful behavior and rewarding children when they exhibit these behaviors or take actions to help themselves with these problems. It is appropriate for use with children from age 3 through age 17.

Self-injury as a problem in a competent family. This family includes a 26-year-old father, who is an insurance salesman, a 33-year-old mother, who is a homemaker, a 6-year-old daughter, and a 3-year-old son. The 6-year-old is a talkative, generally happy little girl. She is chubby, wears glasses, and looks and acts a lot like her mother. She is an excellent student at school, although she is quite a perfectionist. She is sometimes terrorized by the boys in her first-grade class, but she has many girlfriends. Her grandfather, to whom she was very close, died last year. At about the same time, her favorite aunt was diagnosed as having a malignant, inoperable tumor and began a series of hospitalizations. Since that time, she pulls out her eyelashes so that her lids are always without lashes.

Self-injury as a problem in a less competent family. This family includes a 28-year-old father, who is a housepainter, a 28-year-old mother, who is a secretary, and 11- and 2-year-old boys. This is both parents' second marriage. The older boy is the mother's by her first marriage. When he was 2, his natural father was jailed for armed robbery. When he was 6, his mother married his stepfather. Shortly after his mother married his stepfather, his natural father committed suicide. His stepfather gets drunk often and blames the boy for hurting his mother just as his "crazy father" did. At about age 4, the boy began having explosive temper tantrums and mutilating small animals. When he was 9, he joined a group of children who periodically vandalize local schools and shops. Although he only harms other people's property, he makes many self-destructive gestures and constantly talks about how he deserves to die for his bad deeds. He often runs away from home, always returning with an injury—a broken arm or leg, a burn, a deep cut. He has superior intelligence and shows talent in his drawing and creative writing. Many of his illustrated stories involve violent adventure fantasies. Although he does no homework and often disrupts the class, his grades and test scores are outstanding.

1. Deciding if You Need to Work Through This Module

Look at Column 12 of your chart. You need not work through Module 12 if: (a) you are sure your baseline was fairly typical for your family, (b) there was a check in Column 12 for 7 out of 7 baseline days, and (c) you put a check in Column 12 only when none of your children reported loneliness, unhappiness, or fearfulness, and there was no evidence of needless self-injury. If your children's problems are with the behaviors covered in Module 13—swearing, lying, stealing, fire setting, or violence—go through this module to learn techniques needed for Module 13 and then move on. As you work through this module, read all sections of the module even if your child only has trouble with one of the problems it covers.

If you decide to work through Module 12, draw a horizontal line across Column 12 underneath your last baseline day. The line will separate your baseline record from the record of your progress during Module 12. If you decide not to work through Module 12, continue filling in all columns of your chart. If at any time fewer than 7 out of 7 days in Column 12 have checks, complete Module 12.

When children's behavior is life-threatening or repeatedly results in self-injury, parents should seek professional help rather than work through this module on their own. Application of the procedures in this module to seriously disturbed children and families requires professional training and experience.

∞∞∞

1. Do you need to work through Module 12? If not, why not?

∞∞∞

2. Helping Lonely Children

Lonely children need to learn how to reach out to other children and make friends. They can be helped with this by seeing good examples of friendliness from their parents and having the opportunity to meet, choose, be similar to, and entertain friends.

a. Provide a good example of friendliness

It is important for you to provide a good example of friendliness for lonely children. If you provide this example, your children will learn to make and enjoy friends. If you don't, they will not learn this skill. If you have few good friends, or if you rarely spend time with people other than family and co-workers, develop a plan for making adult friends who can give you support in hard times, provide useful information, and have good times with you. Decide how you can become better friends with people you know and how and where you can meet new people. Look for people with a family like yours (the same number of parents head the family, the children are of about the same ages) whose lives are running fairly smoothly, who seem to be looking for friends themselves, and who live close by.

Making friends requires that you behave in a friendly way. Your behavior is friendly if you have eye contact when you are speaking to someone or listening to them; use facial gestures to show your pleasure in being with other people, for example, smiling at appropriate times during conversations; and show your interest in other people's interests, attitudes, and backgrounds by listening to other people carefully, asking questions for information, and repeating what was said to make sure you understand the other person's point of view.

One of the best ways to be friendly is by being a good listener. Try practicing being a friendly listener with another adult. First, you be the listener and have the other adult be the speaker. Begin by asking an open-ended question of the speaker, such as "How has your job been going lately?" or "What kind of vacation plans do you have for this summer?" For the next 3 minutes try to keep the speaker talking. Nod your head and say "mm-hm" when you understand the speaker and ask brief questions when you need more information. Every once in a while summarize what you've heard and find out if you've understood the speaker correctly. The second time you do this exercise, you be the speaker and let the other adult be the listener.

∞∞∞

1. How do children benefit from having friendly parents?
2. What does friendly behavior look and sound like?

3. What do you need to do more often when you talk with adults and children?
4. How can you be a friendly listener?

Nettie was hospitalized for depression twice in the last year. Now that she is feeling more like her old self, she's noticed that her 5-year-old son is a loner. He rarely plays outside with other children and when he does he usually ends up crying and running home. Nettie has friends, but all of them are unhappy people whose lives are in constant turmoil. She has decided to make friends with people who are successful at solving problems and who enjoy life. Nettie, divorced and on welfare, lives in a large Midwestern city. Suggest some economical ways that Nettie could meet new people. What could she do to make friends with the new people she meets? What problems will she encounter? How can she solve them?

∞∞∞

b. Respect children's desires to be like other children
When children first learn to become members of a group and to follow the group's rules, they become concerned about fitting in. Once children learn how to fit in, they are free to be more independent. Very often fitting in requires special clothes, shoes, haircuts, toys, or equipment. Allow children to spend the allowance they have earned to buy these special status symbols. When you plan to buy a child clothing, set aside an amount of money that you plan to spend on the clothing and ask the child to bring along allowance money. Then if the child feels that a more expensive, high-status brand is necessary, the child will be able to pay for the difference from allowance money.

∞∞∞

1. Why is it important to allow children to act like and look like other children their ages?
2. When will you next take your children shopping for clothes? How much money will be set aside for each child? How much choice about selection of clothes will you give each child?
3. What problems would occur if you gave a child more choice, within your budget, for clothing selection? How could you solve these problems while giving your child more freedom of choice?

Consuela immigrated to the United States 6 years ago. She has frequent arguments with her 16-year-old daughter, usually because she feels Maria dresses too seductively. Consuela is distressed because the arguing has had no effect on Maria's style of dressing. Maria has a job after school and pays for her own clothes and makeup. What should Consuela do to reduce the number of arguments she has with Maria? Why is it not a good idea for Consuela to try to influence the way Maria dresses?

coocoocoo

c. Don't choose your children's friends

All parents hope their children will choose good companions. The skill of choosing good friends is learned by experimentation, sometimes by making an error and suffering the consequences. When parents of young children screen their children's friends, they prevent their children from learning how to select friends for themselves. They also create an oppressive family atmosphere. Since friendships among school-aged children are relatively unstable, say and do as little as possible about these friendships. If you find a particular child objectionable, just explain and enforce your family's rules when that child visits, rather than forbidding the friendship. Remember that forbidden fruits are especially sweet. When young adolescents consistently choose friends who are in trouble with the police, failing school, and using drugs or alcohol, this is a signal of a serious problem and indicates that the whole family should consult with a mental-health professional.

coocoocoo

1. Name each of your children's three best friends.
2. Do you object to any of your children's friends? What have you done in the past about objectionable friends? Has this approach worked? If not, what could you do in the future that will work?

coocoocoo

d. Provide children with opportunities to entertain friends at home

Encourage school-aged children to take responsibility for inviting and entertaining their friends at home. Once the child has decided who to invite, it is the child's responsibility to speak to the potential guest and parents. After the child has extended the invitation, talk directly with the parents about transportation and how the children will be supervised while at your house. Most parents want to know that their children will be well cared for when away from home.

In some busy families, children can easily be cut off from friends because parents have little time to provide transportation and supervise play, and because children who don't reciprocate invitations are rarely invited back. The problem of limited weekend time can be solved by carefully planning weekend chores to involve children and their guests.

Be sure to inform the guests' parents that their children will be involved in grocery shopping, house cleaning, or lawn mowing. Provide each child with a small and reasonable task. Plan a special group activity when each child (and adult) has finished her task. Make sure that your guest does not do work assigned to your child (for example, cleaning the child's room while the child observes and directs).

∞∞∞∞

1. Who should invite a friend to visit your child at home?
2. What part should parents play in inviting and entertaining children's guests?
3. Is it fair to involve guests in household chores? What is the best way to involve them?

∞∞∞∞

e. Help your children participate in organized after-school activities
Organized after-school activities provide opportunities for children to meet new friends, as well as to learn new skills. Scouting, sports teams, ballet, music and art lessons, karate instruction, and films and story hour at the library are some examples. While some after-school activities are expensive, the cost of other activities depends upon the family's ability to pay. Your local public library as well as the public school should be able to help you locate affordable and appropriate activities for your children. Decide what activities are feasible and then ask children to choose one or more activities.

Some very shy children will say that they don't want to be involved in an activity. Explain that after-school activities are, like school, an important part of growing up and restate their options. When children choose their after-school activities, explain that you expect them to stay with the activity for the year; at the beginning of the next school year, they can make another choice. Act quickly and withdraw your child from an activity if you have good evidence that the activity is poorly supervised or that the adult supervisors are abusive to children. You can avoid such problems by carefully screening activities before you give your children a choice and by volunteering some time to supervise the activity. During the year, when children express reluctance to continue with the activity, quietly remind them that they will have another choice next year.

∞∞∞∞

1. What after-school activities are your children involved in?
2. How can you help them become involved if they are not involved?

3. What should you do when a child wants to discontinue an activity before the year is over?

∞∞∞

f. Help special-education children make friends through mainstreaming
Children with special educational needs are often educated in small classes with other special-education children. This limits their opportunities for making friends and their opportunities for learning to socialize with regular-education children. Discuss this problem with school administrators if your child is often segregated in special classes. Determine with the school administration what opportunities can be provided to the child to attend nonacademic classes, such as physical education, art, music, or practical arts, with regular-education students. It is possible that your child may have become dependent upon the special-education teacher and display age-inappropriate behavior in new situations. Without mainstreaming opportunities, the child has little chance to outgrow this "immaturity." Ask the school administrators to provide the regular-education teacher with counseling on behavior problems related to mainstreaming so that the teacher will be prepared for mainstreaming your child in nonacademic classes.

∞∞∞

1. Are any of your children special-education students? If they are, what steps have you taken to mainstream them at school? How successful were you? What steps could you take that might be more successful?

∞∞∞

3. Helping Unhappy Children

Unhappy children often are not skilled in problem solving. Instead of seeking solutions to their problems, they complain. Arguing, reasoning, or sympathizing with an unhappy speaker only produces more complaints. To discourage complaining and encourage problem solving, you need to learn the difference between complaining and problem solving, discourage complaining with inattention, learn to understand the child's point of view, and encourage problem solving with praise and attention. The skills that you learn in this section will also help you with children who have the other types of problems listed in this module and Module 13.

a. Learn the difference between complaining and problem solving
Children are complaining when they repeatedly talk about a bad

situation without considering realistic solutions, blame others for the problem, act helpless, ask others to solve the problem, or cry and whine. Children are problem solving when they talk about different ways to improve a bad situation and when they come up with their own advice and solutions.

The following exercise will help you learn the difference between complaining and problem solving. Decide which statements from the list show complaining (marked with a *C* in the answer key) and which statements are attempts at problem solving (marked with a *P* in the answer key). The correct answers are at the end of the statements.

1. "I don't have any friends."
2. "If only I had curly hair."
3. "Dad, this isn't the way Mom makes waffles. Here, I'll show you how to do it."
4. "Maybe I left my doll clothes at Ellen's house."
5. "Should I walk over to Jim's house and see if he's home?"
6. "If you loved me, you'd let me stay up later tonight."
7. "I've got an idea. I'll watch the baby while you take a nap, Mom. Then you'll feel more like watching me do my gymnastics routine."
8. "Mitch asked me to cut lawns with him this summer. Maybe I should give up my paper route to do that."
9. "All the other kids' parents let them watch all the TV they want."
10. "Should I cut swim team today so I can finish my homework?"
11. "Dad, can I take the bus downtown? I want to check out a new store in the mall. I've done my chores and homework, I've got enough money, and I'll be home in time to help you make dinner."
12. "I'm so bored. There's nothing to do around here. Please drive me downtown."
13. "Just show me how to do this science experiment, and I'll stop bothering you."
14. "Look how I fixed my braids by myself. Aren't they great?"
15. "Tell John to leave me alone. He keeps bugging me. He's such a jerk."
16. "Can I play outside while you and Aunt Susan are talking?"

Answers: 1. *C*, 2. *C*, 3. *P*, 4. *P*, 5. *P*, 6. *C*, 7. *P*, 8. *P*, 9. *C*, 10. *P*, 11. *P*, 12. *C*, 13. *C*, 14. *P*, 15. *C*, 16. *P*.

∞∞∞

1. When are children complaining?
2. When are children problem solving?

∞∞∞

b. Discourage complaining with ignoring

Any behavior that you pay attention to (in either a positive or negative way) will be more likely in the future. You will have reinforced this behavior. When inappropriate behaviors are consistently ignored, they become weaker. When inappropriate behaviors are sometimes ignored and sometimes rewarded with attention (either positive or negative), they grow stronger.

Take one of these five steps to discourage complaining. Each step must be taken as soon as complaining begins.

1. Silently walk away or turn away. Go to a quiet place and relax with an interesting book. Don't announce to the child "Now I'm going to ignore you, because you are complaining." Such a statement signals to the child that if complaining continues for long enough, you will pay attention. This is a good response to angry, abusive, and insulting words.

2. Change the subject. This is a good response when complaining occurs in the middle of an otherwise productive discussion.

3. Look at the child and listen quietly for as long as the child is complaining. Begin to speak only when the child changes the subject. This is a good response when a child has asked you to listen to a problem, and you've agreed to listen.

4. Show the child you understand his point by repeating the central idea of the child's statement and checking with the child to ensure that you've really understood. This is a good response when a child shows considerable concern about a problem and really seems to want you to understand his point of view.

5. When something is requested that you don't want to do, say no, and nothing else. Wait silently for the child to continue to speak. Each time the request is made, repeat your first answer. This is a good response when the child asks you to solve a problem that the child could resolve.

The following exercise lists different complaints. Keeping in mind that your goal is to pay little or no attention to the complaint and at the same time to encourage your child to trust you, what would be the best way for you to respond to each of the complaints? Select a number from 1 to 5, corresponding to the five ways to discourage complaining listed previously. The answers are at the end of the exercise.

1. "I hate the rotten stuff we have to do in math. Please write the teacher a note saying I was too sick to do my homework."
2. **Dad:** "Did you have a good time at Rob's house?"

Mike: "Oh, it was OK. I really wish we lived in a house like his. You ought to see the basketball net Rob's dad put up. It's neat."

3. "You are a cheapskate. No one is as mean as you."

4. **Sally:** "Mom, something really heavy happened today."

Mom: "What's up?"

Sally: "Well, during gym I heard Kathy and Lynn talking about me. They were saying terrible things, calling me all sorts of bad names. What's wrong with me? Why don't I have any friends? I hate myself."

5. "OK, here's what I want to tell you. My bike is falling apart. Daddy is always too busy to help me. It's a cheap bike. I just hope it rusts and then you'll have to buy me a new one for Christmas."

Answers: 1. *5,* 2. *2,* 3. *1,* 4. *4,* 5. *3.*

∽∽∽

1. What happens when parents yell at a child each time he complains? Will he complain more often or less often in the future?
2. What happens when inappropriate behaviors are consistently ignored?
3. What happens when parents sometimes ignore complaining and sometimes attend to complaining? Will it grow stronger or weaker in the future?
4. What are five ways to discourage complaining?

∽∽∽

c. Learn to understand the child's point of view
Unhappy children often seem to see the world only from their own perspectives. Your example can help children be more sensitive to others' feelings and needs. When children seek you out to listen to their problems, be a good listener. Listen carefully to what is being said, restate the central idea of what they've said in simple words, and check with them to ensure that you've really understood the main idea. Give no advice. This approach avoids repetitive arguments while promoting children's self-disclosure.

The following exercise begins with an example of a child's complaint and a parent's restatement. After studying the example, restate the main idea in the other complaints listed below.

Child: "Mom, I've got to talk to you. I can't stand my teacher. She is so mean you wouldn't believe it. She yells all the time. We never have fun like we did last year in third grade. I don't know what to do; I just feel like crying."

Mother: "What I hear is that Mrs. Schultz is pretty unpleasant. It sounds as though she has a quick temper and is easily upset. You don't look forward to school like you did with Miss Johnson and you haven't figured out how to make things any better. Is that what you are saying?"

Child: "Yeah, that's it."

1. "Dad, we've got to talk about soccer. I just can't compete with the other kids. They are much better than I am. Sometimes, I just want to hide when it's time to go to practice."
2. "Mom, Billy is always interfering when I have friends over, and you never do anything about it. A lot of the time I think you like him better than me."
3. "Dad, Mom is always nagging me to do my homework. She doesn't believe me when I tell her I don't have any. Then when I tell her to stop nagging, she grounds me. Can't you make her be fair to me?"

∞∞∞

1. How can you understand your child's point of view better?

∞∞∞

d. Encourage problem solving with praise and attention

To be emotionally healthy adults, children must gradually become their own good parents. Emotionally healthy adults do for themselves what their parents once did for them and with them. They think problems through and search for the best solutions, they praise themselves when they've made their best efforts to deal with difficult situations, and they accept their own human shortcomings. Encourage your children to problem solve and to give themselves advice by generously praising and approving whenever you notice that a child is problem solving. Even the slightest hint of interest in solving a problem on your child's part should be met with interest, attention, praise, and encouragement. The best way to discourage problem solving is by giving unwanted advice, making children take your advice, and criticizing their ideas. Give advice only when children ask for it.

For each problem-solving statement in the exercise that follows, think of a statement that shows your pleasure in the effort the child is making to solve his own problem. Remember that you can show pleasure in problem solving and at the same time say no when appropriate. Use the following example as a guide through the exercise.

Child: "Dad, you know how mad I've been at my social studies teacher for making fun of me? I've decided to write her a letter telling her just how I feel about what she's done."

Father: "I'm very pleased that you've thought of a way to solve your problems at school. If you feel like it, show me the letter when you're finished."

1. "I figured out a way to fix my bike. Can you take me to the bike shop right now so that I can get the part I need?"
2. "Well, my class didn't come in first in the paper drive. I guess you win some and you lose some."
3. "Can I skip dinner so that I can get my homework finished in time to watch the football game?"
4. "I know you want me to wear my sweater today. But the temperature is 72 degrees. After all, if I don't wear a sweater, I'll get sick, not you. What do you say, Mom?"
5. "Pete told me I'm a jerk. I'm not a jerk. It's just that Pete likes insulting people."

ထသထသထသ

1. How can children be encouraged to problem solve?
2. Why is it a good idea for children to learn to solve their problems without unrequested adult advice?
3. What's the best way to discourage problem solving?
4. When is the best time to give children advice?

Mick was a poor student in school, but a natural athlete. When his 14-year-old son asks him for advice about how to improve his soccer game, Mick gives very specific advice and answers all of his son's questions. Lately, his son has started asking Mick questions about how to improve his grades in math. Suggest how Mick could respond.

ထသထသထသ

4. Helping Fearful Children

You can help fearful children by encouraging them to plan how to handle their fears. You can also help them by teaching them to relax and explaining distressing family events to them.

a. Encourage children to say how they will handle frightening situations

Fears common among children include fear of the dark, of small animals, and of separation from parents. These fears go away as children grow older as long as parents don't worry about these fears or allow children to avoid difficult situations because of their fears. Fears about school were addressed in Module 9.

The first time that a child describes an irrational but common childhood fear, explain that many children have the same fear and that the fear will go away as the child gets older. The next time the child reports the same fear, ask the child to say what she will do about the fear, for example, "I'll think of something happy," "I'll tell myself, 'Everybody is afraid of something,'" or "I'll tell my mother I acted brave and she'll give me a kiss." From then on each time the child mentions the fear, have the child say what she will do about the fear. This kind of repetition is boring for adults but very helpful for children. Whenever you see evidence that the child is doing what she has said about the fear, give lots of praise and affection. Never suggest a fear to a child or read the child's mind. For example, do not say "You probably don't want to go to bed because you are afraid of the dark."

Many children have realistic fears—fears of nuclear disaster, of pain or death if they are chronically ill, of the death of a seriously ill parent, or of physical violence if they live in a dangerous neighborhood or have an abusive parent.

When children's fears are realistic, prepare them for dealing with or preventing what they fear. For example, children could write letters to elected officials expressing their fears and asking what the officials propose to do about the threat of nuclear war. Help children feel strong by encouraging them to tell you the worst thing they fear will happen and what they will do about it. Allow them to repeat this to you as often as they like. Do not pretend that a real threat does not exist or tell a child to stop thinking about the problem. Let children make this decision on their own.

Explain that all of our lives are enriched by the examples of children who face difficult challenges with courage. Find real-life stories about brave children and read them over and over with your child.

When children describe unrealistic fears, say something like "Thank you for sharing that with me" and change the topic of conversation immediately. An example of an unrealistic fear might involve getting cancer from touching a child who is sick.

∞∞∞

1. What fears do your children have?
2. Which of these are reasonable fears and which are unrealistic?
3. What have you done about these fears? How successful have you been? What could you do in order to be more successful?

Susan has had several operations on her left leg. She is 5 years old now, and her doctor has decided he must amputate her leg.

Should the doctor tell her what he is going to do? What should her parents do to prepare her?

Ten-year-old Martin is afraid of cripples and people with physical deformities. How should his parents respond when Martin talks about these fears?

∞∞∞

b. Explain that moderate anxiety is exciting and useful

When children first complain of anxiety or describe signs of tension (sweaty hands, racing heart, dry mouth), explain that anxiety is a signal from the brain to your body that says, "Get ready for a challenge." Encourage your children to invent good ways to get ready for important challenges, including relaxing, practicing skills, and gathering information. If your children do not know how to be relaxed and alert, obtain a relaxation-training audiotape and practice relaxing with them for a half-hour every day until they can get relaxed whenever they want to.

Getting more comfortable with your own anxiety also helps your children to be less anxious. From now on when you are anxious ask yourself two questions: "What difficult experience is challenging me?" and "How can I successfully respond to the challenge and reduce my anxiety?" You may also want to use an audiotape to practice relaxation.

∞∞∞

1. How can you explain anxiety to your children?
2. What can anxious children do to cope with anxiety?
3. How can you and your children learn to relax?

∞∞∞

c. Expose children to distressing family events

Discuss impending divorces or serious illnesses with children, answer their questions honestly, avoid blaming them for the problems, and give them a chance to feel helpful. Talk frankly about what happens during death, burial, and mourning. Be honest when your children ask questions for which you have no good answers. Make certain that children do not feel blamed for the family crisis, death, or illness and that they do not associate death or sickness with bad behavior.

∞∞∞

1. Do you expect any family crises in the near future? How will you prepare your children for these events?

2. Have you prepared your children for illnesses and deaths of family members? What more could you do?

∞∞∞∞

5. Helping Children Who Injure Themselves

If a child or anyone in your family has threatened or carried out self-destructive actions in the past, explain to the whole family that in the future you will take every threat or hint of self-injury very seriously. Explain that if, for example, a boy runs away from home and says that he is going to drown himself, or a teenage girl locks herself in the bathroom and says she is going to slash her wrists, you will immediately call the police and tell them of your emergency.

If an emergency does occur, call the police and take whatever measures you can to protect the family member. Ask the police to take the family member to the emergency room of the closest hospital. For children, make sure that the hospital has a child and adolescent inpatient psychiatric unit. If you've already made contact with a mental-health professional, have the professional meet you at the emergency room. Otherwise consult with emergency-room personnel as to whether brief hospitalization is required.

Make self-injury difficult in your home by removing guns and hunting knives from the house; storing poisons in a locked shed or cabinet or getting rid of them safely; storing sleeping pills, tranquilizers, and aspirins in a locked medicine cabinet; and substituting electric or disposable plastic razors for razor blades.

Avoid self-destructive talk or behavior. Self-destructive talk includes statements such as "I'll kill myself if I don't get the new job" or "If you kids do that again, I'll stick my head in the oven." Self-destructive behavior includes smoking in bed, driving when drunk, driving too fast, and not wearing seat belts. If you often think about suicide yourself, immediately make contact with a qualified mental-health professional and discuss your thoughts.

∞∞∞∞

1. Is anyone in your family likely to injure herself? Who?
2. Why do you think this person might injure herself?
3. What will you do to prevent family members from injuring themselves?
4. Have you explained this plan to all family members? What were their reactions?

5. How do you plan to provide your children with a safe and happy home and example? What changes will this plan require? How difficult will these changes be?

Virginia's uncle, Bob, who was injured in Vietnam and who had increasing pain since that time, died from an overdose of pills last week. Virginia was very close to her Uncle Bob. She doesn't know how he died but she is very curious. Should Virginia's parents explain what happened? How could they help her cope with this tragedy?

∞∞∞

6. Deciding What a Good Day Will Involve

Children who are lonely, unhappy, fearful, or injure themselves need to be rewarded for good days when they reach out to other children, enjoy themselves, confront challenges, and remain free from injury. Begin by deciding what a good day will involve for your child. If your child is lonely, a good day might involve inviting another child over to play, talking to a friend on the phone, writing a letter to a friend, or writing a story or drawing pictures about friends having fun together. If your child is unhappy, a good day might involve the child planning and enjoying one hour-long activity. If your child is fearful, a good day might involve going into a frightening setting (such as a Girl Scout meeting) and staying there for a reasonable period of time (for example, for the entire 2-hour meeting). If self-injury or needless accidents are your child's problem, a good day might be one involving no injuries or accidents.

Make sure that you are not expecting too much or too little of the child. If the child has never had such a good day, you are expecting too much. If the child has had such a good day 5 days a week, you are expecting too little.

If your child has more than one of these problems, work on one problem at a time, beginning with the problem of self-injury or needless accidents. When days that are good because of no self-injury occur every day for 2 months, move on to the next most troublesome problem. You can do this by broadening your definition of a good day. For example, a good day for a child who injures herself and is lonely might be defined as a day in which no self-injury occurs and in which the child is involved in 1 hour of friendly activity with other children. Again, work for 2 months of continuous good days. Continue to broaden your definition of a good day to include of all your child's problems with loneliness, unhappiness, fearfulness, and self-injury.

No child (or adult) is completely without lonely, unhappy, frightening, or accident-filled days. Nevertheless, when parents work to help a child overcome chronic problems in these areas, it is wise for them to help the child develop an immunity to unpleasant daily life events. In this way, formerly vulnerable children can learn to feel good about themselves and about prospects for the future, no matter how life treats them. For this reason it is a good idea to reward children for good days until just about every day is a good day.

∞∞∞

1. What will a good day be for each of your lonely, unhappy, fearful, or self-injuring children?
2. Sara is both lonely and accident prone. Which problem should her parents deal with first? What should they do when Sara has no accidents for 2 months?
3. Are normal children happy every single day?
4. Ten-year-old Julian has had many fears during the last 4 years. Why is it necessary for him to get to the point where he can go 2 months without a fearful day? How will that help him?

∞∞∞

7. Rewarding Children for Good Days

Together with your child, construct a "reward menu" from which the child will be able to select one or more items at the end of a good day. Choose rewards that you will be able to give repeatedly, that are age appropriate, that the child values, and that you feel comfortable giving only when earned and withholding when not earned. If you like, include one or more choices on the reward menu that require 7 good days. Give these as bonuses beyond the daily rewards.

Include some items that the child will be able to share with siblings so that they will benefit when the child has a good day. Siblings have enormous influence, for better or for worse, over one another's behavior. When siblings can benefit from one child's success, they work hard to contribute to that success. For example, if the child puts french fries for dinner on the menu, keep supplies for making french fries on hand, only provide french fries when they are earned, and provide french fries to other family members also when the child earns and selects this reward.

Decide how many choices from the menu the child will be able to make for good days. The more serious the problem, the more important it is to give the child several choices from the menu for every good day. Develop a lengthy written reward menu, so that the child will not tire of available rewards over the next few months. Post the reward menu where the child will see it. Physical affection and praise need not be listed on the menu, since you should praise your child after every good day whether the child asks or not. Figure 4 shows a sample reward menu for good days.

Once the child has had 2 months during which every day was a good one (using a definition of a good day that takes into account all of the child's problems with loneliness, unhappiness, fearfulness, and self-injury), gradually begin to lengthen the time interval required for a menu choice. At first, require 2 good days instead of 1 for a menu choice. After 2 months' success, require 3 good days in a row for a menu choice. In this way, gradually help the child have more and more good days in a row, until 7 good days in a row are needed for choices from the menu. When this happens and the child tells you (without being asked) that rewards are no longer needed to encourage working for good days, discontinue the reward system.

If good days become infrequent at any time, once again introduce rewards for a good day, and once again gradually help the child have more and more good days in a row. Illness or changes at school or in the family can reduce the number of good days. You will find that each time you have to reinstate the reward system, success comes more quickly.

∞∞∞

Figure 4. Sample Reward Menu for Good Days

Bennie's Reward Menu
(Choose two items on days in which you don't injure yourself or have needless accidents.)

An hour of special play time with Mom or Dad to play games I choose

An hour of time on the home computer

A dinner at a fast-food restaurant for the family

A ticket worth 50¢ towards a toy

Peanut butter cookies as a snack for the family

An hour of time to play with cousin Ken's dog

A movie for the entire family after 7 good days

1. What type of rewards should you include on the reward menu?
2. Why don't you need to include physical affection and praise on the reward menu?
3. When should you give your child rewards?
4. What will you do after 2 months during which every day was a good one?
5. When will you discontinue rewards for good days?

∞∞∞

8. Explaining Good Days to Your Child

Before you establish a good-day system, explain good days once to your child. You might say something like this:

> "Arthur, we are going to use a good-day system to help you with your problem of self-injury and accidents. A good day will be a day in which you do not hurt yourself or have a needless accident no matter how bad things are. As long as you don't hurt yourself or have an accident, I'll consider the day a good day, no matter what else you do. At the end of a good day, you'll get a choice of special privileges that you don't usually have. In a minute you and I will make up a menu of rewards from which you can choose at the end of every good day. Since you and your brothers always want fast food for dinner, one reward on the menu might be a fast-food dinner for all three of you at the end of a good day."

Make sure that you include in your explanation:

1. Why you will use a good-day system,
2. What a good day is,
3. What will happen at the end of a good day.

Have your child repeat your explanation to make sure he understands what you've told him. Even if he doesn't seem to understand, follow through with your plan. He will understand once he has experienced the good-day system a few times.

∞∞∞

1. How many times will you explain good days to your child?
2. What three things will you tell your child about good days?
3. How will you make sure he understands what you have told him? What if he doesn't seem to understand?

∞∞∞

9. Keeping a Record for This Module

While working through this module, continue as you did during baseline to put a check in the small box labelled *NO* in Column 12 when none of your children (age 3 to 17) had problems with loneliness, unhappiness, fearfulness, and self-injury. Mark the problems your children do have with their initials and the codes (L = loneliness, U = unhappiness, F = fearfulness, I = self-injury) that you used during baseline. You should also keep track of the good days that your children have and when they are rewarded. Do this by marking the child's initial and a star in Column 12 in the box labelled *Problems, good behavior, rewards given* whenever the child has a good day. This will remind you to reward the child. Lightly cross out the child's initial and the star when you have rewarded the child. The following example shows how Column 12 might look on a family's assessment chart after they have begun using Module 12. In this family there are two children, Andy and Bridget. Bridget is being rewarded for good days with no loneliness and Andy is being rewarded for good days with no fearfulness. On the first day of charting, neither Bridget nor Andy had a good day, and

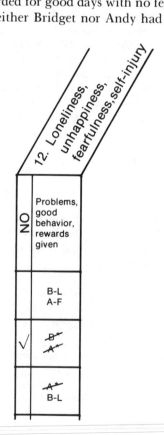

their problem behaviors are marked in Column 12 (*B-L, A-F*). On the second day, both Bridget and Andy had good days. This was indicated by a check in the small box in Column 12. Their good days were also marked (*B*, A**). When they received their rewards for their good days, the notations were lightly crossed out. On the third day, only Andy had a good day and was rewarded.

∞∞∞

1. How will you keep a record of the times when your children are lonely, unhappy, fearful, or injure themselves needlessly?
2. How will you record your children's good days?
3. How will you keep a record of the times that you reward your children?

∞∞∞

10. Moving On to Module 13

You can move on to Module 13 after you have worked through this module for all of your children's problems with loneliness, fearfulness, unhappiness, and self-injury and you have achieved 2 continuous months of good days. This module appears near the end of the chapter because it requires more changes in parents' lifestyles than earlier modules. Most families will master discouraging complaining and rewarding for good days in one family meeting and 1 to 3 weeks of practice. Families headed by parents who have many friends, are not fearful, are happy, and rarely think or talk about self-injury will find the rest of the module easy and will work through it in one family meeting and 1 to 3 weeks of practice. Families who lack some or all of these skills will find the sections on loneliness, fearfulness, unhappiness, and self-injury more difficult; they may need a few months to master the module. Little or no success with this module indicates the need for professional guidance.

If you start using the good-day reward system or other procedures in this module and then stop, if you think you aren't using the procedures correctly, or if you aren't consistently using the procedures, return to the beginning of this module and work through it more slowly. If you are troubled yourself by the problems this module covers, the module will be difficult, but rewarding.

∞∞∞

1. How will you know when you are ready to move on to Module 13?
2. When is it a good idea to begin Module 12 again?

∞∞∞

Module 13: Swearing, Lying, Cheating, Stealing, Fire Setting, and Violence

It is important to distinguish between normal children who engage in trivial antisocial behavior as they are learning the rules of adult society and children with poor moral judgment and antisocial values. All children experiment with swearing, lying, cheating, rule breaking, playing with fire, and aggression. Young children are not able to distinguish truth from fantasy, to understand how rules work, or to understand the impact of their actions on others. Older children are often unsure about how other people view them and their behavior; they usually test adults to see how much they observe and how consistently they reward prosocial and punish antisocial behavior. When adults are observant and fair, children gradually learn to follow society's rules and to understand the need for reasonable limits on individual action. Fair-minded adults expect of children no more than they expect of themselves; they clearly and simply describe and explain rules and the consequences for rule following and for rule breaking.

When parents are inconsistent, overly harsh, and unfair children become preoccupied with punishment. They follow rules to avoid punishment, not because they understand the reason for the rules or because they want to do the right thing.

A few children are often dishonest and frequently do things that harm or endanger other people. These children lack skills necessary for participation in a free and democratic society. They do not know how to get affection and attention in ways that have long-range benefits for themselves and for others. Although they may know the difference between right and wrong, they think that people do what is right only to avoid getting caught and punished. They don't understand that without honesty, fairness, and kindness people can't govern themselves. These children also tend to underestimate the likelihood that they will get caught and punished.

The parents of dishonest and violent children must make major lifestyle changes before they can expect similar changes from their children. Some parents believe that dishonesty and violence are necessary in this "dog-eat-dog" world and that morality is for "sissies." They teach their children to value money above all else, frequently use harsh punishment and threats of disinheritance when their children act independent, and are astonished when their children either disagree with their attitudes or are dishonest and violent at home.

Some morally decent but overly permissive parents do not enforce age-appropriate moral standards. They sympathize too much with their children's complaints and excuses and tend to believe that their children are the innocent victims of an unfair world.

Some unhappily married couples include one strict and one permissive parent. The permissive parent struggles to protect the child from the other parent's supposed cruelty, allowing the child to avoid or escape punishment for misbehavior and preventing the child from internalizing reasonable moral standards.

This module explains how you can help your children to reduce swearing, lying, cheating, stealing, fire setting, and violence and improve their moral judgment by encouraging prosocial behavior and rewarding them for this behavior. It is appropriate for children from age 3 through age 17.

Violence as a problem in a competent family. This family is made up of a 35-year-old mother, who is a secretary, a 50-year-old father, who is a truckdriver, and their 8- and 9-year-old sons. Both parents work overtime whenever possible, because they are saving for a larger house in a better neighborhood. While their parents are at work, the two boys are cared for by grandparents, who live upstairs. The grandparents indulge their grandchildren, never setting any limits on their behavior and buying them whatever they ask for. The 8-year-old is a good student at school and fairly well liked by adults (although some find him a bit demanding). With children his own age, he is becoming increasingly aggressive; a few times this year he has hit another child on the playground at school or in the neighborhood. Each time this happened, the victim had refused to do something his way. Children have begun avoiding him and refusing to play with him. When this happens, he screams at them, cries, and runs home.

Dishonesty and violence as a problem in a less competent family. A 40-year-old mother, who is a real-estate agent, a 39-year-old father, who is a lawyer, and their teenagers, two sons and two daughters, make up this family. The parents have made a lot of money in business along with inheriting a considerable amount of money. They feel that they have a right to use alcohol and drugs to relax from the pressures of the business world. The boys, one 13 and one 15, have been repeatedly arrested by the police for driving in stolen cars, for beating up and extorting money from young children, and for selling drugs to students at their school. Each time they were arrested, their father advocated for them and persuaded the judge to be lenient. The boys have also stolen jewelry and money from their parents and from other relatives. The parents' main concern is that the boys are not doing well in school and that rumors about their behavior may hurt business.

1. Deciding if You Need to Work Through This Module

Look at Column 13 of your chart. You need not work through Module 13 if: (*a*) you are sure your baseline was fairly typical for your family, (*b*) there was a check in Column 13 for 5 out of 7 baseline days, (*c*) you put a check in Column 13 only when no children in the family were involved in swearing, lying, cheating, stealing, fire setting, and violence, and (*d*) there were no occurrences of serious injury to other people or their property.

If you decide to work through Module 13, you should have already gone through Module 12. Begin Module 13 by drawing a horizontal line under your last day in Column 13. This will separate your baseline record from the record of your progress during Module 13. If at any time fewer than 5 out of 7 days in Column 13 have checks, complete Module 13.

When children's behavior is repeatedly very violent or dangerous, parents should seek professional help rather than work through this module on their own. Application of the procedures in this module to seriously disturbed children and families requires professional training and experience.

∞∞∞

1. Do you need to work through Module 13? If not, why not?

∞∞∞

2. Discouraging Swearing

Most children swear because they have heard others do it and because swearing gets them a lot of attention from adults. A very small number of children swear in a way that suggests a nervous habit. Sometimes these children are diagnosed as having Tourette's syndrome. In either case, take the following steps to eliminate the occurrence of swearing.

a. Stop swearing
Don't expect children to stop swearing if you still do. Don't proceed beyond this step until you have found a substitute for all the words you expect your children not to use.

∞∞∞

1. What must you do first if you expect your child to stop swearing?

∞∞∞

b. Help your child find a substitute for swearing
After a child has used a swear word, explain one time the meaning of the word he has used and why you object to its use (many parents object to swearing because of the words' violent and dehumanizing meanings); that when angry, it is a good thing to say "I'm angry" or "I don't

like what you've done" or "Don't ever do that again"; and that it is natural to talk in a very loud voice, cry, or walk away when angry.

Help the child think of satisfying, socially acceptable ways of expressing anger. For example, one child may want to run around the block and yell whenever he is angry. Another child may want to stomp around the house with a mean look on his face. A child who swears repetitively when anxious may want to say something bold like "Don't push me around" and then walk away and get completely relaxed. Help the anxious child learn to relax with relaxation training tapes.

Find out what your children want you to do when they are expressing anger without swearing. Some children want to be left alone. Others want to be told they are doing a good job. Still others want someone to listen to their angry feelings for a while, without judging or giving advice.

∞∞∞

1. What substitutes for swearing do you think your child will choose?
2. How will you find out what your child wants you to do when he is expressing anger without swearing?

∞∞∞

c. Call timeout when you hear a child swear
Immediately call timeout each time you hear your children swear. Do not threaten them, just call timeout when you hear them swear. If you warn or threaten, children won't learn to warn themselves not to swear. If you do not hear the swearing with your own ears, do not call timeout. Use earlier bedtime as explained in previous modules for delayed timeouts and when children don't go to timeout. Keep track of timeout and bedtime as you did in previous modules.

∞∞∞

1. What will you do the next time your child swears?
2. Is it a good idea to warn children that you will call timeout if you hear them swear one more time?

∞∞∞

3. Explaining Timeout for Swearing to Your Children

Before you begin using timeout for swearing, explain once what you will do. You might say something like this:

"Barb, from now on when you are angry or upset, I'd like you to say how you feel and show how you feel instead of swearing. I think we will both feel better if you express your angry or upset feelings in a different way. Tell me you are angry, throw some pillows around in your room, or run around the block a few times to get the angry feelings out, instead of swearing. If I do hear you swear, I'll send you to timeout right away. If I don't have to call timeout for you during the day, your bedtime will be 1 hour later that night.''

Make sure that you include in your explanation:

1. Why you will use timeout for swearing,
2. How children can express bad feelings through words and actions other than swearing,
3. What you will do when you hear a child swear,
4. What will happen on a day when a child is not sent to timeout.

Have your children repeat your explanation of timeout for swearing to make sure they understand what you've told them. Even if they don't seem to understand, follow through with your plan. They will understand once they've experienced timeout for swearing.

ထောထောထော

1. How many times will you explain timeout for swearing to your children?
2. What four things will you include in your explanation?
3. How will you make sure they understand what you have told them? What if they don't seem to understand?

ထောထောထော

4. Encouraging Honesty

Some children learn to lie in the following way. The first time they do something wrong, they admit their misbehavior to their parents; their parents punish them severely for the misbehavior and ignore their honesty. The second time they do something wrong they lie to cover up the misbehavior; the misbehavior goes undetected and the lying pays off. The third time they do something wrong, they lie about it again; this time, the parents detect the lie and punish them severely for lying. By the fourth time they do something wrong, they are very afraid of punishment and work hard at being good liars so they won't get caught.

How can you punish a child for misbehavior and reward a child for honesty about misbehavior? Make sure that honesty has a bigger payoff than dishonesty. If your child is honest about misbehavior, praise your child's honesty, while still letting the child suffer the consequences of his behavior. A child who steals candy from a store and when confronted admits stealing should be praised for honesty but must still pay for the candy and apologize to the shopkeeper. A child who lies about stealing the candy but was seen by the shopkeeper must still make amends and apologize and should also suffer a stronger consequence, such as donating the cost of the candy from his allowance to a charity for sick children. The consequence for dishonesty should be tied to the behavior in a reasonable way and be something that can be enforced. It should also be a healthy consequence for the child.

∞∞∞∞

1. How do some children learn to lie?
2. What will you do when your child tells you the truth about misbehavior?
3. What will you do when your child lies to you about misbehavior?

   Jack is an overbearing, hot-tempered father who bullies his children into doing what he wants. His 7-year-old son, Tony, lies constantly even though he's been punished severely for lying on a few occasions. Why does Tony lie so much? What will Jack have to do differently to help Tony?

∞∞∞∞

5. Explaining the Payoff for Honesty to Your Children

Before you begin giving a bigger payoff for honesty than for dishonesty, explain once what you will do. You might say something like this:

> "Kyle and Brent, I would like you to be honest with me about the things that you do. From now on when I discover that you have done something wrong, the punishment will be more severe than when you tell me about what you have done wrong. When you tell the truth about something you have done, I will be very proud of you and will be sure to compliment you for your honesty. For example, if you break a neighbor's window while playing ball and you come to me right away and tell the truth, I'll compliment you for your honesty and expect you to apologize to the neighbor and pay for the window replacement from your allowances. If our neighbor sees you do the damage and you deny responsibility, I'll expect you to pay for the window replacement and I'll take your bat and ball away for 2 weeks. In either case, I'll pay for the window replacement myself and then subtract what you owe me from your allowances."

Make sure that you include in your explanation:

1. Why you will give a bigger payoff for honesty than for dishonesty,
2. What you will do if your children are honest about their misbehavior,
3. How the consequences for misbehavior will be more severe if children are dishonest.

Have your children repeat your explanation of the payoff for honesty to make sure they understand what you've told them. Even if they don't seem to understand, follow through with your plan. They will understand once they've experienced the payoff for honesty a few times.

∞∞∞

1. How many times will you explain the payoff for honesty to your children?
2. What three things will you include in your explanation?
3. How will you make sure they understand what you have told them? What if they don't seem to understand?

∞∞∞

6. Dealing with Cheating, Stealing, Fire Setting, and Violence

Take the following steps if your child engages in cheating, stealing, fire setting, and violence. Avoid doing anything more than what follows, for example, do not add harsh punishment or a sermon.

a. Provide an example of prosocial behavior

If you engage in criminal behavior (including white-collar crime such as cheating on your income tax and padding your expense account) your children will find out no matter how hard you try to conceal your actions. Before you go any further, find legal and ethical ways to get what you want, or scale your needs down, so that antisocial behavior is no longer necessary.

When children make excuses for their antisocial behavior, listen to the excuses and then help them think of how they could have achieved their goals without antisocial behavior. For example, suppose you hear the following story from your son Jim. Your son Bob was attacked by a bully at school. When his brother Jim ran to his defense, Jim accidentally ran into a teacher, knocking her to the ground, bruising her, and breaking her glasses. The teachers tell you a different story. They report that Bob was not attacked, that Bob and Jim terrorize children on the playground, and that this is not the first time that someone has been hurt by Bob or Jim. Ask Jim to tell you how he could have helped his brother and avoided hurting the teacher. After thinking a bit, Jim may admit that Bob really didn't need any help defending himself, and that there was no need for a fight or to hurt a teacher. When children hurt someone they are responsible for the consequences, regardless of why they believe they inflicted the injury. Don't force a child into agreeing with your point of view about this or into admitting guilt.

∞∞∞

1. Do you need to change any antisocial or criminal behavior to give a good example of prosocial behavior to your children?
2. What should you do when your children make excuses for their antisocial behavior?

∞∞∞

b. Have your child apologize and make restitution

Have your child apologize to the injured party, work out a reasonable method of restitution, and follow through with this plan under your supervision. Apology and restitution are necessary regardless of the supposed cause of the event, and even under very difficult circumstances. Children who do things that cause others harm or that they know to be wrong and who don't apologize or make restitution often suffer from terrible guilt. Help the child rehearse making an apology and arranging for restitution. The purpose of restitution is not to make your child suffer but to help the people whom your child injured through antisocial behavior. Once the child has apologized and made restitution, do not talk about the incident again, unless the child brings up the topic. Examples of apology and restitution for cheating, stealing, fire setting, and violence follow.

Apology and restitution for cheating. If your 13-year-old son cheats on a math quiz, and the teacher calls you to complain, arrange for your son to apologize to the math teacher and to the children who took the exam without cheating and to make restitution in a manner agreeable to the teacher. Restitution might involve a commitment to spend 10 after-school or before-school hours doing boring but important classroom tasks.

Apology and restitution for stealing. If your 8-year-old daughter steals a coloring book from a toy store, take her back to the store, locate the store manager, and ask her to return the book and say that she is sorry. If she has damaged the book, help her work out a plan for repaying the store from her allowance and have her agree to an extra fine if she does not repay the store on time. If necessary, pay the store for the damages and subtract them from your daughter's allowance.

Apology and restitution for fire setting. Your 15-year-old son and some friends of his decide to express their anger at a math teacher by starting a fire in her classroom after school. The fire spreads, causing considerable damage to several classrooms. Have your son apologize in person to each of the people in the school who've been affected by this event. Have your son talk to the school's principal and to the math teacher who was the target of the fire setting to work out restitution that is agreeable to the school and possible for your son.

Apology and restitution for violence. Suppose that you have a 13-year-old daughter, one of a group of girls who gang up on an unpopular classmate and jokingly threaten to beat her with a hanger. While fooling around, another member of the gang slips and pokes the hanger in the girl's eye, damaging her vision. Certainly no apology or restitution can restore the girl's vision. Yet it is very important that each girl involved apologize to the victim and her parents and work out a way to show her remorse that satisfies the victim's family as well as you. For example, your daughter might spend every Saturday for the rest of the school year reading to the victim and helping her with her homework.

∞∞∞

1. What steps will you take if your child cheats, steals, sets a fire, or harms other people or their property?
2. An 8-year-old boy steals another boy's jacket. How could he make restitution?
3. A 10-year-old girl sets fire to her neighbor's tool shed. How could she make restitution?

> Six-year-old Bennie took the last piece of pie from the refrigerator without asking his mother. When his mother discovered what he had done, she screamed and called him a thief. Was Bennie's behavior antisocial? What will happen if Bennie's mother continues to call him a thief for taking food from the refrigerator?

∞∞∞

7. What to Do about Repeated or Dangerous Acts of Antisocial Behavior

The preceding steps are appropriate for occasional acts of cheating, stealing, fire setting, or violence. For children who have repeatedly engaged in cheating or stealing, such as a child who has stolen from other children and from stores two or three times, and for children who have committed very dangerous forms of antisocial behavior, such as setting more than one fire or causing serious bodily injury to another person, follow the steps for rewarding for good days outlined in Module 12. For example, if your child has been setting fires, you would decide on a menu of rewards from which your child could make choices at the end of every day when no fire was set.

You may already be rewarding your children for good days with no loneliness, unhappiness, fearfulness, or self-injury following the recommendations of Module 12. If so, continue rewarding for good days, but define a good day more broadly. For example, define a good day as one that includes no self-injury and no fire setting.

ﾟ∽ﾟ∽ﾟ∽ﾟ

1. Do any of your children engage in repeated cheating, stealing, or fire setting, or cause serious bodily injury to others?
2. How will you reward these children for good days?
3. How will good days be defined for each child?

ﾟ∽ﾟ∽ﾟ∽ﾟ

8. Keeping a Record for This Module

While working through this module, continue as you did during baseline to put a check in the small box marked *NO* in Column 13 when none of your children (3 through 17) had problems with swearing, lying, cheating, stealing, fire setting, or violence. Mark the problems your children do have with their initials and the codes (SW = swearing, LY = lying, C = cheating, S = stealing, FI = fire setting, V = violence) that you used during baseline. You should also keep track of timeouts and bedtime for swearing, of good days, and of when rewards are given. Keep track of timeouts for swearing as you kept track of timeouts in other modules: mark the child's initial for timeout, cross it out when the child goes to timeout, and mark the initial and -½ *hr.* in the bedtime column for timeouts that are ignored or delayed. As before, you can give children an hour later bedtime when no timeouts are called. When a child has a good day, mark the child's initial and a star in the box labelled *Timeouts called, completed. Problems, good behavior, rewards given.* This will remind you to reward the child. Lightly cross out the child's initial and the star when you have rewarded the child.

The example on the following page shows how Column 13 might look on a family's assessment chart after they have begun using Module 13. In this family there are two children, Andy and Bridget. Bridget is being rewarded for good days with no stealing and Andy has problems with swearing. On the first day of charting, Bridget stole and Andy

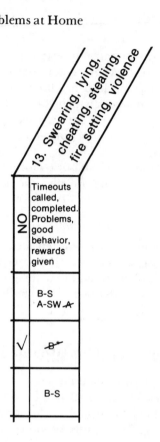

swore. Their behaviors were marked in Column 13 (*B-S, A-SW*), and it was also noted with his crossed out initial that a timeout was called for Andy and that he went. On the second day, Bridget had a good day and Andy did not swear. This is indicated by a check in the small box in Column 13. Bridget's good day was also marked (*B**). When she received her reward for this good day, the notation was lightly crossed out. On the third day, Bridget stole again, but Andy did not swear.

∽∾∽∾∽∾

1. How will you keep a record of the times when your children are involved in swearing, lying, cheating, stealing, fire setting, or violence?
2. How will you keep a record of your children's good days?
3. How will you keep a record of the times that you reward your children?

∽∾∽∾∽∾

9. Returning to the Beginning of the Module

If you start using the good-day reward system or other procedures in this module and then stop, if you think you aren't using the procedures correctly, or if you aren't following through consistently, return to the beginning of this module and work through it more slowly. If you frequently engage in any of the activities covered in this module, the module will be difficult but rewarding for you and your child. The procedures described in this module should become a permanent part of your childrearing style. You are finished with this module when you consistently and easily follow the module's procedures with little encouragement from others, when you have successfully used rewarding as described for all problems covered by this module, and when 7 out of 7 of your children's days are free from antisocial behavior.

∞∞∞

1. How will you know when you are finished with Module 13?
2. When is it a good idea to begin Module 13 again?

∞∞∞

5

Solving Problems at School

This chapter shows how to solve problems at school by working through the four School-Problem Modules: Module 1, Assembling a Home-School Team; Module 2, Assessment; Module 3, Improving Academic Performance; and Module 4, Improving School Behavior. The modules describe how to solve problems of underachievement, low achievement, disorderly behavior, and unhappiness at school through an alliance between mental-health professionals, teachers, other school personnel, and parents. The modules can be worked through in order to help one or more children with mild to severe academic or behavior problems, to prevent academic and behavior problems in a group of children who seem to be at high risk for later difficulties at school, or to train teachers in classroom behavior management. The procedures in the modules are appropriate regardless of the historical cause of inadequate achievement, disorderly behavior, or unhappiness.

The modules in this chapter can be used alone or together with the modules in Chapter 4. When a child has significant behavior problems at home as well as at school and parents have asked for help with home and school problems, it is a good idea to work through the modules presented in Chapter 4 until solutions for home problems are in place before beginning the modules in this chapter. Once the family has made progress at home, they are ready for the modules in this chapter. When the school has approached parents about problems at school, the School-Problem Modules should be put into place before home problems are addressed. The Home-Problem and School-Problem Modules can be instituted at the same time, but this requires the guidance of a skilled professional, trusted by both the family and the school.

Which Children Can Benefit from the Modules

The School-Problem modules are designed for children from nursery school (age 4) through the end of elementary school, or age 13. All of these modules are appropriate with minor changes for students in middle school and for high school special-education classes. The major focus of the modules is on the 4 to 13-year-old age group.

How Professionals Can Use the Modules

Mental-health professionals and paraprofessionals and educators can use the modules to help individual children with serious academic or behavior problems either in the regular classroom or in the resource room. They can use the modules to mainstream special-education students into the regular classrooms. Before extensive psychological or psychiatric testing is ordered, they can use the modules to arrange for an alternative plan to prevent a troubled student from entering the special-education stream. Professionals can also use these modules to implement economical classroom-wide or school-wide early intervention programs to help students who are struggling in the regular-education classroom, to prevent further deterioration, and to avoid expensive supplemental programming. The modules can also be used by teachers to improve their classroom management skills. All of the School-Problem Modules are appropriate for use in public and private day and residential schools. Transition from a residential or treatment school back to a child's own school is eased when the modules are used in both settings.

How Parents Can Use the Modules

Motivated parents can use the School-Problem Modules to forge an alliance between home and school and to prevent problems at school. Parents who want to play a positive role in their children's school careers and whose children do not have serious academic or behavior problems will be able to follow these modules without professional help and lead a "home-school team," a team of parents and professionals, so long as the school is willing and able to cooperate. Parents whose children have serious school problems or who face a school administration uninterested in collaborating with parents will benefit from consulting with a professional experienced in setting up behavioral programs for school children and familiar with the school in question. This professional can lead a home-school team.

The Home-School Team

The School-Problem Modules are usually worked through by a home-school team of professionals and parents in meetings and continuous assignments spread out over the school year. Each team includes adults responsible for the target child's welfare. The classroom teacher and the child's parents must participate. If the parents are unwilling or unable to participate, a teacher, counselor, or other child advocate can substitute for parents. The parent substitute needs a small weekly budget and free time to spend with the child each weekday afternoon or evening. Meetings may also include the school principal, school social worker, school psychologist, and the special-education teacher, as well as mental-health and medical professionals based in the community. The team leader may be any of the adult participants. Children rarely express a desire to be included in these meetings. Nonetheless, it is only fair to let them know what happens in these meetings and to allow them to attend if they are interested.

If the family has already worked through the Home-Problem Modules with a professional, that person should lead home-school meetings. If the modules in Chapters 4 and 5 are to be used simultaneously, a mental-health professional who is skilled in behavioral interventions both with families and in schools should lead the home-school meetings.

It is the team leader's responsibility to either carry out all the appropriate procedures or to delegate responsibility to team members for these procedures and to supervise team members' efforts. Novice team leaders benefit from carrying out or supervising most procedures in the modules by themselves; this prepares them to anticipate the difficulties that team members will later encounter. Novice home-school leaders are most successful when their teams first focus on individual children. Experienced team leaders can delegate more responsibility to team members and be effective supervisors.

In many schools, state law determines who must be the formal leader of the team of professionals responsible for special-education students (in some areas this is called the pupil-personnel team). The formal leader of the pupil-personnel team has definite legal responsibilities that no one else can discharge. The objectives of the pupil-personnel team and of the home-school team are usually identical. The modules in this chapter are one way to achieve these shared objectives. Thus the formal leader of the school's pupil-personnel team and of the home-school team could be, but does not have to be, the same person. When a pupil-personnel team leader and a home-school team leader work together, they need to divide responsibilities between them. The most logical division would require the pupil-personnel team leader to carry out the legal reporting responsibilities and to serve as a member of the home-school team for this purpose, while the home-school team leader is responsible for guiding the team through the modules.

Makeup of the Modules

Each module targets a goal, such as assembling a home-school team, and explains the relationships between the goal and children's problems at school. The modules begin by describing how the procedures in the module might apply to an individual child and to a group of children.

Sections in each module are meant to be read and worked through one at a time. They are designed so that achievement of the module's goal can be tailored to fit the needs and preferences of children, families, teachers, and educational administrators.

Questions follow most sections. The questions help readers think about the section, suit it to their needs, and plan and monitor appropriate assignments for team members. When readers cannot answer these questions, they should go over the section until they can answer the questions and then move on to the next section. At the end of Modules 3 and 4 are questions designed to be answered after the module has been read and its procedures have been tried. Answers to these questions provide a record of progress through the modules; they can be used to write detailed case notes and reports to supervisors.

Readers can work through modules as quickly or as slowly as circumstances require. The time that it takes to complete each module depends upon the experience of the team or teacher at using the modules, the number of children that the module is being used with, and the goals of the team or teacher. A team focusing on one child can, in general, work through a module in one meeting and begin applying the module's procedures. Sections at the end of the modules help families decide when to move on to new modules or when it is a good idea to return to the beginning of a module. The best time to start working through the modules is in the first month of the school year. It is a good idea to begin working through Module 4 no later than the end of the third month of school.

Deciding Which Modules to Work Through

Each module in this chapter builds upon the previous module and should be worked on in the order presented. Working through all of the modules, though, may not be necessary to achieve some of the goals of intervention. This section provides guidance in deciding which modules to work on. Additional guidance for choosing nonmandatory modules is found at the beginning of the modules.

In most cases, Module 1, Assembling a Home-School Team, will always be used. A home-school team is needed because it is much easier to quickly resolve a child's school problems with the cooperation of parents and of all the school personnel who are involved in the child's daily activities. While it is possible to make some progress at school without parents' cooperation, it is impossible to make any real progress at school without the cooperation of significant school personnel. Once the team is assembled, all subsequent work may be shared by team members, or implemented by one team member.

Module 2 is used by the team to assess academic or school behavior problems in one or more children. The foundation that is laid by following the procedures in Module 2 permits the team to assess the effectiveness of efforts to remedy academic problems in Module 3, and school behavior problems in Module 4. Module 2 must be worked through regardless of the child's problems or even if it is not clear what problems the child has. Answers to the latter question will result from working through the module.

Whether the child has academic problems alone, both academic and behavior problems, or just behavior problems, the team should complete the procedures in Module 3. It is obvious that underachieving and low-achieving children would benefit from improved academic performance. It is not immediately obvious why unhappy and behavior-disordered children would benefit from improved academic performance. Consider this: The more time and effort children of any ability level invest in their schoolwork, the less time they have to engage in inappropriate behavior, and the more chances they have to see themselves in a good light and to feel happy. Behavior problems sometimes disappear when a child is motivated to do more schoolwork and of higher quality.

Module 3 should be used even with children who have behavior problems but are high achievers and have excellent academic records. Even the best student can produce work of higher quality if appropriately challenged.

After putting in place the procedures in Module 3 so that they are being carried out consistently, the team can move on to Module 4. Procedures in Modules 3 and 4 are designed to become permanent elements in the classroom teacher's instructional style.

Of the four School-Problem Modules, Module 4 is the one most likely to be attractive to teachers. Nevertheless, the home-school team, working with children who have serious academic or behavior problems, should work through this module only after completing Modules 1 to 3; earlier procedures are often sufficient to decrease undesirable school behavior.

Teachers may elect to work through Module 4 to improve their classroom management skills (when none of their students have serious academic or behavior problems). In this case, they need not assemble home-school teams, but they should complete Module 2, gathering baseline data on some or all of their students' school behavior, before working through this module.

Module 1: Assembling a Home-School Team

When children have academic or behavior problems at school, a team composed of the classroom teacher, building principal, school social worker, school psychologist, and special-education teacher often meets to determine what the problem is and how the problem can be remedied. Federal law (Public Law 94-142) requires that this team involve the child's family in the planning process. Unfortunately, schools often have no precedent for involving families in educational planning. As a result, some parents who desire involvement are merely spectators to the planning and behavior-change process, and some educators find that parents are unwilling to attend meetings or to follow up on recommended changes.

This module shows you how to assemble an effective home-school team composed of the people directly involved in the children's welfare at home and at school.

Assembling a home-school team to help one child. A family sought treatment from a clinical psychologist because of violent conflicts between family members and because of the 8-year-old boy's aggressive and destructive behavior and poor achievement at school. For 4 months, the family worked through the Home-Problem Modules with the psychologist, resolving major problems at home. At that point, the clinical psychologist assembled a home-school team composed of the boy's parents, his school principal, his current and previous year's classroom teachers, and the school social worker. School personnel were pleased, because they were ready to refer the boy for psychiatric testing, even though they doubted that the results would help them decide what to do differently at school. They agreed to use the School-Problem Modules in order to improve school performance, reduce behavior problems, and prevent the boy from being diverted into the special-education stream.

Assembling a home-school team to help several children. A special-education teacher was responsible for six learning-disabled children, ranging in age from 10 to 12, whose classroom behavior was inattentive, inappropriate, and disruptive. The special-education teacher teamed up with the school psychologist 2 months into the school year. Together they assembled one home-school team for each child in the class that included parents, the building principal, the director of special education, and the school social worker. The school psychologist used the Home-Problem Modules to help each child's family resolve home problems, and the special-education teacher led the home-school team through the School-Problem Modules. The home-school team discussed all children at one time as they worked through School-

Problem Modules 1, 2, and 4. The team had separate meetings with each child's parents when they worked through School-Problem Module 3.

The home-school team agreed that their purpose was to help parents resolve behavior problems at home, make the classroom a vehicle for learning, and teach children the skills they would need to return to a regular-education classroom. Since members of the home-school and pupil-personnel teams overlapped, there was no duplication of team members' efforts. Data collected by the home-school team was used instead of standard psychoeducational batteries when testing and reporting was mandated by state law.

1. Deciding if You Need to Work Through This Module

You need not work through this module if (a) you have identified children to be helped by the School-Problem Modules, (b) for each identified child, there is a well-functioning home-school team committed to using the modules, and (c) each of the people on the home-school team believes he will benefit personally from the success of the modules or (d) you are a teacher using these modules to improve your classroom management skills and your students do not have serious academic or behavior problems.

∞∞∞∞∞

1. Do you need to work through Module 1? If not, why not?

∞∞∞∞∞

2. Selecting Children to Be Helped by the Modules

When you select individual children to work with, choose children who have had repeated, serious achievement or behavior problems. The offer of special services can harm children by labelling them as defective. For this reason, special services (even of a preventive nature) should only be offered to an individual child when there is compelling evidence that the child is troubled.

At times, someone tentatively identifies an individual child as a possible candidate for special remedial or therapeutic services at school. A classroom teacher may find a child particularly irritating and think that some sort of treatment will benefit the child, or the parent of an unhappy child may decide that special school services are the answer. Such tentative identification does not necessarily mean that the child is the source of the problem or that treating the child will remedy the problem. The teacher's classroom management skills may be deficient and the child's irritating behavior may best be treated by provision of training to the teacher, rather than by singling out the child for special help.

Confirmation of a child's need for special services must be established by thorough assessment of the sort described in Module 2. In order to gather baseline data as described in Module 2, a home-school team must be assembled. The effort of assembling the team is well justified when the team gathers baseline data ruling out the existence of serious problems and saving the child from unnecessary labeling as "special."

To avoid labelling children, School-Problem Modules can be offered to everyone in the child's class. Children at every ability and performance level can benefit from them. When all children in a class are involved in the School-Problem Modules, one team consisting of all parents and appropriate school personnel could be assembled and could meet periodically throughout the year. These meetings would be an admirable substitute for the perfunctory parent-teacher meetings that rarely accomplish much.

If you want to select a group of children for the modules in this chapter but do not want to offer the modules to an entire classroom, first decide which group of children will benefit most. For example, you might select all children identified by fifth-grade teachers as underachievers, referred to the building principal for disruptive classroom behavior, or taught by student teachers or teachers who wish to improve their behavior-management skills. When identifying individual children, select too few rather than too many children. Each individual child you involve in the modules will require at least 90 minutes per week of one or more team member's time. When working with an entire class, 5 hours per week per class is sufficient time.

∞∞∞

1. Will you select one child for the modules in this chapter? Who will you select and why?
2. Will you work with an entire class of children? Who will you select and why?
3. Will you select a group of children? Who will you select and why?
4. What steps will you take to avoid labelling as defective individual children using the modules? How will you know if these steps are successful?

∞∞∞

3. Assembling the Home-School Team

The membership of the home-school team will vary depending upon how you select children for the School-Problem Modules, how many children are identified, and why these children were identified. All of the adults involved in the child's welfare at school should be at each meeting. If a child is being medicated to control behavior problems at school, include relevant medical professionals in the first team meeting.

Parents could be involved in all home-school team meetings or they could be involved only when the team works through Modules 3 and 4. They could meet individually with the team or as a group, in place of conventional parent-teacher conferences. This is most appropriate when the home-school team was assembled for the purpose of working through Module 2 and identifying individual children in need of help or applying Modules 2, 3, and 4 to an entire classroom.

∞∞∞

1. Who will you invite to the first home-school team meeting? Why?

∞∞∞

4. Conducting Home-School Team Meetings

Schedule the first home-school team meeting at the school or in a mental-health professional's office at a time convenient for the entire home-school team. Read through the School-Problem Modules before the meeting, so that you are prepared to answer everyone's questions. Anticipate possible objections and plan how you will respond to each one. If you have never led a group before, invite some friends to play the parts of group members in a role play of the first meeting.

Get to the meeting place earlier than the rest of the team. Arrange chairs so that all group members will be able to see each other and you. Choose a seat for yourself that will allow you to be seen and heard easily by all group members. The ideal seat for you is at the head of the table, facing the door through which people enter and exit the room. Place writing materials and copies of this book at each seat. Arrange ways of preventing interruptions during the meeting. For example, take the phone off the hook, or ask someone to field calls and take messages during the meeting.

Begin every meeting on time even if only a few people have arrived. Compliment the few who arrived on time, and explain that you will begin the meeting on time to reward them for their promptness. When latecomers arrive, briefly summarize what they missed.

Introduce yourself at the first meeting and thank everyone for coming. Ask everyone to say who they are and how they are involved with the target child. Briefly explain that you have called the meeting in order to assemble a home-school team that can use the School-Problem Modules to help troubled children. Explain why you have invited each person to the meeting and what role you expect that person to play.

To heighten everyone's commitment to participation in the home-school team, it is especially important to encourage team members to talk about the costs and benefits of team participation at the first meeting. Look around the room and ask group members one at a time to discuss how success with the modules would benefit them and how it would hurt them. Encourage them to think of direct personal gains (e.g., reduced problems in the classroom, good evaluations by supervisors, better relationships with parents) and indirect personal gains (e.g., pride in helping troubled children). Encourage them to think of direct and indirect personal costs (e.g., extra work, conflict with disinterested co-workers). Do not disagree with anyone's objections. Take notes during this discussion.

After each person has described what he views as the costs and benefits of the School-Problem Modules for him, correct any misconceptions the group has about the mechanics of the modules. Invite the group to ask every question and raise every objection that comes to mind. Answer every question with a pleasant, brief, informative statement and repeat your answers as often as necessary.

Summarize the benefits of participation that have been mentioned by group members and congratulate group members for recognizing the value of participation. Summarize the costs of participation that have been mentioned and congratulate group members for their honesty. Explain to the group that each anticipated cost of participation represents a problem that the group needs to solve in order to succeed. Guide the group through a discussion of each potential cost of participation until the group has come up with what all believe to be a good solution for the problem. Keep notes during this discussion, summarize each solution the group seems to have agreed upon, and read this solution back to the group. Make sure that everyone in the group believes the solution will work and knows how it will work before you move the group on to a discussion of another cost of participation.

Each time objections are raised or less than useful ideas are put forth, restate the problem at hand (the personal costs of participation) and ask for more ideas. If this discussion becomes long and involved, invite the group back to finish this discussion in another meeting. Ask group members to prepare for the next meeting by devising clever solutions for unresolved problems.

The format for every meeting after the first includes the following elements:

1. Finding out what new things have happened to team members with the target child (or children) during the week,
2. Checking on assigned work by looking at charts and listening to everyone's reports about what was done,
3. Dealing with problems that emerged during the discussion of assignments, particularly failure to follow directions,
4. Explaining one new School-Problem Module, or part of a module, verbally and using role playing for further demonstration, if team members were successful with the last meeting's assignment,
5. Checking for comprehension of the new module on the part of team members by asking "What if" questions and by role playing,
6. Checking for objections to the new module and countering these objections,
7. Giving a specific assignment to team members and checking that everyone knows what he is expected to do before the next meeting and what he is expected to bring to the next meeting.

Success with the modules in this chapter requires that the team leader follow the steps listed in the Checklist for School-Problem Modules (found at the end of this chapter) each time the team meets. It is a good idea to make copies of the Checklist and to use one to keep track of progress during each home-school team meeting.

The frequency with which the home-school team meets depends upon how many children the team has identified, whether parents are involved in team meetings as individuals or as a group, and how faithfully team members discharge their responsibilities. Certainly the team must meet at least two times for Modules 1 and 2 and at least four times for Modules 3 and 4.

∞∞∞

1. When and where will the first home-school team meeting be held?
2. What objections to the use of the School-Problem Modules or to participation in the team do you anticipate?
3. How will you respond to these objections?
4. How confident are you in your group-leadership skills?

5. What group-leadership experience have you had? If you are inexperienced at group leadership, how will you prepare yourself for the home-school team meeting?
6. Why is it important to have team members talk about the costs and benefits of team participation?
7. How will you use the Checklist for School-Problem Modules?

∽∽∽

5. Moving On to Module 2

You can move on to Module 2 when you have selected individual children or groups of children to be assessed for academic and behavior problems and for possible intervention via Modules 3 and 4 and when you have assembled a home-school team for each child or group of children. If you feel that you have not successfully selected children or assembled a team, return to the beginning of this module.

∽∽∽

1. How will you know when you are ready to move on to Module 2?
2. When is it a good idea to begin Module 1 again?

∽∽∽

Answer these questions after your first home-school team meeting
1. How did you prepare for a productive and uninterrupted meeting? How successful were your preparations? Looking back on the meeting, how could you have improved your preparations?
2. What did you tell each person about his future role on the team?
3. What costs and benefits did each group member anticipate from participation?
4. What misunderstandings did the group have about the modules and how did you correct them?
5. What questions and objections were raised? How well did you handle the group's objections? Looking back on the meeting, how could you have improved your response to objections?
6. Who did you congratulate for recognizing the benefits of participation and how did they react?
7. Who did you congratulate for recognizing the costs of participation and how did they react?
8. What are the costs anticipated by the group, and how did the group agree to solve these problems?
9. Which problems were unresolved? What can you do to ensure that these problems are resolved?

10. Looking back on the meeting, how could you have heightened the group's commitment to using the School-Problem Modules? How could you have made the benefits of participation more salient to the group?

∞∞∞

CHECKLIST FOR SCHOOL-PROBLEM MODULES

Fill in this checklist each time you have a home-school team meeting.

Before the meeting begins, fill in this information:

Leader's name———————————— Meeting date ——————

People at the meeting and their reasons for participation ————

————————————————————————————————

————————————————————————————————

Which module, or which parts of a module, do you hope to cover in

this meeting? ——————————————————————————

————————————————————————————————

What problems do you anticipate during the meeting?——————

————————————————————————————————

————————————————————————————————

What can you do to avoid these problems? ——————————

————————————————————————————————

————————————————————————————————

At the beginning of the meeting, follow these steps:

1. Find out what new things have happened to the team members
   with the target child during the week. List here any events, good or
   bad, that either you or the team considers important.

   ————————————————————————————————

   ————————————————————————————————

   ————————————————————————————————

2. Look at the assessment chart and listen to everyone's reports about
   what assigned work was done. Congratulate those who did their
   work. List their names here and what they did.

   ————————————————————————————————

   ————————————————————————————————

   ————————————————————————————————

3. Talk with team members about work that was not done. Decide if it still needs to be done. If so, develop a plan to ensure that the work will be finished this week. Take into account the problems that prevented the work from being done thus far. Describe your plan here.

_____

_____

_____

4. If the work has been done, review the assessment chart and consult the module to decide if the team is ready to move on to the next module or if it is best to continue working on the current module. What have you decided to do? Why?

_____

_____

_____

During the team meeting, make sure to:

1. Explain the reason for the new module, including what it is likely to achieve in the short run and in the long run.

2. Tell the team what they need to accomplish, why it is important, and how much time will be required for accomplishment of the task.

3. Read or explain one section of a module at a time, sharing the reading with team members whenever possible. Have team members take turns answering questions about that section. Use role playing for further demonstration, if necessary.

4. Check for comprehension of the new module on the part of team members by asking "What if" questions and role playing.

5. Check for objections to the new module and counter these objections only after you have listened carefully to everyone's opinions, respected everyone's ideas, and let everyone know that his opinions are valued. Make sure that everyone knows what he is expected to do before the next meeting and what he is expected to bring to the next meeting.

6. Congratulate team members each time they help the group solve a difficult problem or show enthusiasm for the task.

After the team has finished going through the module and before the meeting ends make sure to:

1. Remind team members about what they need to do, pointing out to each team member what new things he will be doing from now on. Describe what each team member needs to do.

   _____

   _____

   _____

2. Ask each team member to tell you, in his own words, about what he needs to do, making sure that all team members understand and agree to their responsibilities.

3. Ask team members to think of things that could go wrong with what each person is assigned to do, and together with the group modify the assignments to solve these problems. Describe potential problems in the assignments and how the group has agreed to solve these problems.

   _____

   _____

   _____

4. Make sure that someone will complete the assessment chart and attend every meeting of the team. Who will this be?

   _____

5. Set a time and place for the next team meeting and remind the team to bring evidence of the work they've done to the meeting. When and where will the meeting be held?

   _____

   Will team members be reminded by phone or mail about this meeting? By whom?

   _____

Module 2: Assessment

Teams composed of educators, mental-health professionals, and parents are often hesitant and ineffective because each member of the team looks at the child's problem from a different vantage point not well understood by other team members. A breakdown in communication is to be expected if the data on which important team decisions are based are understood by only one or two team members. Well-meaning attempts to help schoolchildren also fail because unreasonable and vague goals are set, and because without clear evidence of progress everyone loses confidence.

Teams that insist on gathering evidence about children's problems before they intervene are in the best position to determine if the children's problems are serious enough to warrant intervention and to decide if intervention is successful. These teams will know for sure which problems have been resolved by intervention and which have not. They will know for how long solutions have worked and what unexpected new problems have emerged.

This module shows you how to gather evidence to determine if children's problems are serious enough to warrant intervention and how to measure the success of your efforts as you work through School-Problem Modules 3 and 4. Once you are feeling comfortable measuring children's academic achievement and classroom behavior with these measures, you will find ways to substitute them for expensive educational evaluations and to base report card grades and decisions about class placement on these measures.

Assessment to help one child. The parents of a 13-year-old boy with superior intelligence sought help from a clinical psychologist because of the boy's lack of friends, frequent crying, strange behavior at home and at school, and failure to do any school work. The boy had been beaten frequently by his father, who had been depressed for many years, and infantilized by his mother, who felt sorry for him. After the family worked through the Home-Problem Modules with success, the psychologist assembled a home-school team at the boy's school. With the help of a school psychologist, the team began collecting baseline data concerning the boy's daily accomplishments in math, language arts, social studies, and science and his behavior problems and unhappiness.

Assessment to help several children. A director of special education became concerned about the amount of money spent by the school district on out-of-district placements. When he looked closely at the reasons for these placements, he found that very often the children had behavior problems that neither parents nor teachers knew how to manage. The Special-Education Director convinced his superintendent and the school board that it would be fiscally responsible to fund a prevention program aimed at finding children with significant academic, behavior, and mood problems and providing classroom-based intervention to large numbers of these children. He argued that not only out-of-district placements, but also expensive and often useless testing could be bypassed with such programming. With the school board's blessings, the director had his special-education staff work together with classroom teachers to gather baseline data on performance in math, reading, spelling, and science and on behavior problems and happiness.

1. Keeping an Assessment Chart

Make a copy of the School-Problem Assessment Chart that follows. Enter daily dates (month, day, year) in the date column, beginning with the date of the next school day. Continue entering consecutive daily dates until you've filled the date column.

Column 1 after the date is labelled "Math" and Column 2 is labelled "Reading." Columns 3 and 4 are left blank for you to fill in school subjects. With these four columns, you will assess children's academic performance. Columns 5 and 6 are labelled "Good day" and "Happy day." They are used to assess children's behavior in school.

You will begin by getting a "baseline record" for each child. The baseline record is a record of children's achievements and behavior before a behavior-change plan is begun. The information gathered during baseline will tell you how severe each child's presenting problems are. Intervention is the period of time during which a behavior-change plan is in place. By comparing information gathered during baseline and during intervention, it is possible to measure a child's progress during intervention and to measure the effectiveness of the modules. You will also be able to determine how long effects last after you complete each module. By selecting a series of targets for intervention (e.g., four academic subjects, appropriate school behavior, happy school behavior) and working to achieve first one target and then a second until all intervention targets have been achieved, it is possible to make sure that it is intervention and not some other circumstance (such as the child's maturing) that is responsible for change. This approach to documenting and understanding behavior change is called a multiple-baseline, single-case experimental design.

Work through the sections in this module for each target child. Fill in the chart for at least 10 school days in a row to get a baseline record. If anything unusual happens during this baseline (e.g., the

School-Problem Assessment Chart

DATE	1 Math	2 Reading	3	4	5 Good day	6 Happy day

child is absent from school or sick during school or no instruction takes place because the day precedes a major holiday), extend baseline until you've charted for at least 10 typical days. If unusual events are typical of this child or of the classroom, keep a baseline record for 10 school days in a row. Figure 5, One Child's School-Problem Assessment Chart, shows what a chart might look like after 10 school days.

The baseline of the first academic subject you target for intervention (e.g., math) will be 10 school days long. Although you begin intervention in math on day 11, you continue charting the three other academic subjects, along with good days and happy days, as described later in this module. Once improvement in math is evident, perhaps on day 25, you continue intervention in math and begin intervention in another academic subject, perhaps reading, while continuing to chart the other academic subjects and good days and happy days. Follow this same procedure until intervention has been introduced for all academic subjects and for good days and happy days. As a result, you will have six baseline records of varying lengths. The shortest one will be in the first target of intervention, the longest one will be in the very last target of intervention.

During baseline, do nothing different other than charting. Do not remind the child or the family that you are charting. Once you have completed your baseline record for the first academic subject, begin working through Modules 3 and 4 and continue filling in every column of your chart. By continuing to keep a record for other academic subjects and the good and happy days as you begin working on one subject, you will produce what is called a multiple-baseline design. This design helps you determine if changes that you see in children's behavior are the result of intervention with the modules or if they may be caused by other random factors. If problems that you have not intervened with become much better, some other factor, such as the child's maturing, may be at work. A continued record can show when it is not necessary to use the modules for behavior that had been a problem at the beginning of the charting. For each child, choose the team member who will be responsible for charting from the beginning of baseline until the end of the year (the coder). The coder must attend all team meetings and bring the child's chart. The team leader meets with the coder once a week to supervise charting.

∞∞∞∞

1. Why is it important to gather baseline data on children chosen for intervention?
2. How long will the baseline period be?

Figure 5. One Child's School-Problem Assessment Chart

DATE	1 44 Math	2 91 Reading	3 55 Science	4 47 History	5 Good day	6 Happy day
3/4/85	89	76	50	40	X	X
3/5/85	80	40	52	44	✓	✓
3/6/85	0	98	92	54	✓	✓
3/7/85	90	72	92	90		X
3/8/85	82	70	30	19	X	X
3/11/85	36	93	55	44	✓	X
3/12/85	0	48	72	80	✓	✓
3/13/85	0	51	58	55	✓	X
3/14/85	30	70	55	20	X	✓
3/15/85	74	97	55	90	X	✓

3. What will you do if something unusual happens during baseline?
4. Will the child or family be reminded about the charting?
5. When will the coder begin and end charting?
6. When and where will the coder and the team leader meet each week?

∞∞∞

2. Getting a Baseline Record for Module 3

To assess children's skills for Module 3, begin by labelling Columns 3 and 4 with the names of two important academic subjects other than math and reading. When children are underachievers or low achievers, pick two subjects in which they perform below potential or below average for their age. When children are unhappy or show behavior problems, pick the two subjects, other than math or reading, in which their grades are lowest. The subjects in which they have the lowest grades are also probably the ones in which they exhibit the most behavior problems or unhappiness.

Beginning tomorrow and every day thereafter, collect all of the child's written assignments (quizzes, tests, seatwork, homework, work-book pages) in each of the four academic subjects identified in Columns 1 to 4. Make sure that each assignment you collect has the child's name on it, along with the date of collection.

Score each day's work in math in this way. First, assign a zero to any assignment due on the day of collection that was not handed in. Second, place a check beside each correct answer on an assignment. Divide the number of correct answers by the total number of questions in the assignment and multiply the result by 100 to derive a percentage. Third, add the percentages for all the assignments due on the day of collection (those handed in and those not handed in) and divide by the total number of assignments for that day. The resulting number is the daily math assignment score. Record the daily math assignment score in Column 1 beside the date.

Score each day's work in reading and the two other academic subjects in the way described for scoring math assignments. When you encounter difficulty in scoring assignments in reading or other subjects, base your scoring rules on the purpose of the assignment. For example, if the purpose of the assignment is to practice writing complete sentences and at least 10 complete sentences are expected in the child's story, divide the actual number of complete sentences the child composed by 10 and multiply the result by 100 to derive a percentage. It is a good idea to write out all of your scoring rules and provide them to teachers. This may encourage teachers to be more explicit about assignment expectations with students.

Some teachers use subjective and mixed methods of scoring assignments. For example, they take points off for what they consider to be poor penmanship on a spelling test. Use the rules for scoring described previously, rather than these subjective scoring rules. Scoring assignments objectively makes it easier for teachers to assign written work more often and gives children clear guidelines for assignment completion.

When children are given daily written seatwork or homework assignments, clear guidelines about how the assignments will be scored, encouragement to complete these assignments independently, and accurate feedback about performance, they benefit in several ways. They get ample opportunity to work through and review new concepts and skills. Since they know exactly what is expected of them, they are less likely to be frustrated and more likely to succeed. They get the chance to work on their own under reasonable conditions, so that independent thinking becomes a pleasure rather than torture. Finally, they try their hardest because they know their good work will always be acknowledged with praise and their failures will lead to helpful information about errors, rather than punishment.

After you have recorded at least 10 daily math assignment scores, calculate the child's baseline mean math score by dividing the sum of daily math assignment scores by the number of daily math assignment scores that you have recorded. The result rounded down to the nearest integer is the child's math intervention goal. Record the math goal at the top of Column 1. Derive and record goals for the other three subjects in the same way.

∞∞∞

1. For each child chosen for intervention, how will you label Columns 3 and 4?
2. How will you find each child's daily scores in the subjects?
3. How do children benefit when they are given daily written assignments, clear guidelines about how the assignments will be scored, encouragement to complete these assignments independently, and accurate feedback about performance?
4. How will you calculate the intervention goal for each child in each subject?

∞∞∞

3. Graphing Daily Assignment Scores

By graphing the daily assignment scores, you will be able to communicate effectively about what you are doing with other team members, family members, and children. Plot daily math assignment scores on a graph, with dates on the horizontal axis and percent correct on the vertical axis. Draw a line parallel to the horizontal axis to show the child's math intervention goal. Draw a vertical line before the day when academic intervention begins. The graph will show progress from baseline through intervention in a manner easily understood by children and adults. Graph progress in the other three subject areas in the same way. Figure 6, the Graph of Daily Math Scores, provides an example of graphing subject scores.

You can use the graph to learn about students' academic potential if you keep the following information in mind. Underachieving students of mid-range and high ability are easily detected from the graph.

Figure 6. Graph of Daily Math Scores

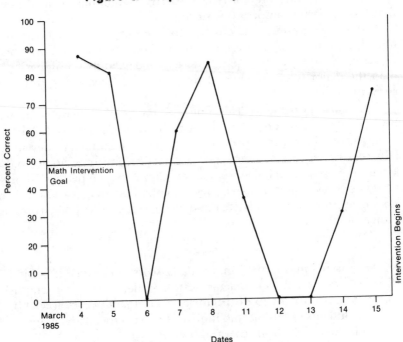

They tend to perform very inconsistently during baseline. Their baseline scores are often all over the graph, ranging from very high to very low scores. The underachieving student's baseline mean underestimates the child's ability. More consistent daily performance would raise the baseline mean.

It can be difficult to distinguish between a low-ability student and a student of mid-range or high ability with major social or emotional problems by relying solely on the graph. Both groups of students show a flat, low baseline profile, so that most of their scores fall close to a fairly low baseline mean. Low-ability students have simply not mastered the skills required for adequate performance. Socially and emotionally deficient students rarely succeed at independent work. Because these children often underestimate their own capabilities, it is easy for adults to assume their ability is low. Information about daily behavior problems and unhappiness, collected as described later in the module, and an intelligence test administered by an experienced psychologist will suggest whether a flat and low baseline profile indicates low ability. In most cases, a score from a group-administered intelligence test is already in the child's school records. Children who have few good days or happy days, an average or above-average IQ, and a flat, low baseline profile probably have social or emotional skill deficits that are hindering academic performance.

With the graphs, it is possible to determine whether disruptive, but high ability, students are benefiting from the curriculum. Their performance will be consistent from day to day, and at a higher level than the majority of the class, if they are in fact benefiting from the curriculum.

It is also possible to determine with the graphs whether children from single-parent, poor, or minority households are really underachievers or whether they perform poorly on standardized achievement tests because they were never exposed, either in class or at home, to the kinds of questions included in the tests. Children who perform consistently on daily assignments at a level comparable to at least half their classmates cannot be considered underachievers despite poor scores on standardized tests.

∞∞∞

1. Why is it important to graph daily scores in academic subjects?
2. How can you detect underachieving students from the graphs?
3. Why is it difficult to distinguish between students of low ability and students of middle and high ability with social and emotional problems solely from the graphs?

Connie's parents have just been divorced. From time to time, Connie seems unhappy at school. Why is more information needed to decide if Connie is in need of intervention? What kind of information is needed? How could Connie be hurt if intervention is unnecessarily provided?

∞∞∞

4. Rank Ordering Children's Scores

The following procedure applies when the home-school team wishes to use the School-Problem Modules with the high-risk children in one or more classrooms. Rank ordering children's academic scores can identify underachieving and inconsistent students and help to detect troubled students who have not yet come to any adult's attention. Rank ordering students' scores also prevents potential high-risk students from being labelled or isolated; the collecting and scoring of written assignments and the recording of scores necessary to rank order students should be a routine matter in every classroom.

After you have collected data from an entire classroom, rank order the baseline means of all students in a classroom in major subject areas and select as possible targets for intervention the children with the lowest means in all subjects. The number of children selected will depend upon the resources available for intervention. This approach to identification will only work if all students receive similar assignments (e.g., the same workbook pages in each academic subject) and work on them independently for the same amount of time each day (e.g., 15 minutes per workbook assignment per subject per day).

If the children are so different that they could not all be given the same assignments, you will not be able to rank order children in the manner just described. In this case, collect and score daily written assignments in a subject (e.g., math) from each child. Next, count the number of baseline daily math assignment scores that fall at least 25 percent below each child's baseline math mean (the child's math scatter index). The larger the child's math scatter index, the more inconsistent the child's daily math performance during baseline.

Rank order the children in the classroom in respect to the math scatter index to find out which children are most inconsistent in math. Follow the same rank ordering procedure in other major academic subjects. Select as possible targets for intervention the children who are most inconsistent during baseline in their major academic subjects. The number of children you select must depend upon your resources and upon the broad purpose of your prevention program.

The scatter index is a more useful index of underachievement than standardized achievement tests. Achievement tests are time consuming and expensive to administer. Since they are not criterion referenced, they rarely measure growth on material taught to the student. Their usefulness is limited, because they cannot be repeated throughout the year to gauge educational progress. In contrast, the scatter index is economical because it is an outgrowth of usual classroom activities. Calculating the scatter index does not take time away from classroom instruction. The scatter index is the ultimate criterion-referenced measure, and because it can be calculated repeatedly throughout the year, it is a superb measure of educational progress, sensitive even to minor changes in the classroom program.

တၵတၵတၵ

1. How will you select children for intervention if they receive similar assignments and work on them independently?
2. How will you select children for intervention if they receive very different assignments?
3. Why is the scatter index a more useful index of educational progress than standardized achievement tests?

တၵတၵတၵ

5. Getting a Baseline Record for Module 4

On the same day that you begin keeping track of children's academic scores, begin marking their charts for good days and happy days. For some children, behavior problems and unhappiness will be the main focus of intervention rather than academic improvement. It is important, however, to keep a baseline record of behavior problems and unhappiness for all identified children, even if these problems are not evident. The School-Problem Modules are designed so that they won't disrupt the normal flow of interaction between teachers and students or among classmates. Sometimes though, intervention with modules (or other unrelated events) might encourage behavior problems and unhappiness. The continued baseline record would reveal the need for help in these areas, using Module 4, and perhaps the need to implement Module 3 differently.

At the end of every school day, put a check in Column 5, "Good day," beside the date if no adult involved with the child at school had any complaints about the child's behavior. During the day as a memory aid, an X can be put in Column 5 when a behavior problem is evident. Remember that the child should never be reminded by anyone about this charting procedure or threatened about it.

At the end of every school day, put a check in Column 6, "Happy day," beside the date if no adult involved with the child at school reported that the child showed any evidence of unusual, excessive, or inappropriate sadness or moodiness. During the day as a memory aid, an X can be put in Column 6 when sadness or moodiness is evident. Refer to Figure 5 for an example of charting good days and happy days.

∞∞∞

1. When will you check Columns 5 and 6 on each child's chart?
2. Why is it important to keep a record of behavior problems and unhappiness for all identified children?

∞∞∞

6. Moving On to Module 3

Once you have a baseline record lasting at least 10 school days, check over the record and decide if it represents the way the child usually is at school. If it does, you can move on to Module 3. If it does not seem to give an accurate picture, continue until you have charted for 10 consecutive and reasonably accurate days. Then begin on Module 3.

∞∞∞

1. What will you do if a child's baseline record does not seem accurate?
2. If it does not seem accurate, what can you do to ensure that the rest of the baseline record will provide a more accurate picture?

∞∞∞

Answer these questions after you have a baseline record for each child

1. What intervention goals for each child in each academic subject have you found?
2. What special scoring rules have you devised? Why? How well have they worked? How could you improve upon these scoring rules?
3. What have you learned about the quantity of written assignments given to the children in each subject area?
4. What have you learned about how expectations for successful assignments are communicated to children?
5. What changes have you observed in these areas since you began scoring daily assignments? Are these changes positive? If not, how could you bring about improvement in the quality and quantity of assignments made to children?
6. Based on the graphs and other evidence about school behavior and school performance, why do you believe each child is a low

achiever, an underachiever, or a child with major social or emotional problems?

7. As a result of looking carefully at each child's chart and graphs, have you discovered any children who are not at high-risk and who do not need intervention? How did you make this decision?

8. Which high-risk children have you selected for intervention? Why?

9. How did you decide to provide intervention to this number of children?

10. Is your baseline record for each child reasonably accurate? If yes, what will you do next? If no, why do you think the baseline record wasn't accurate? What will you do to ensure that a new baseline record will provide a more accurate picture?

∞∞∞∞

Module 3: Improving Academic Performance

More time is spent diagnosing academic problems than remedying them. Too often parents and teachers decide that a child labelled as underachieving, learning-disabled, minimally brain-damaged, emotionally disturbed, developmentally delayed, or mentally retarded cannot learn, or that children who come from impoverished, minority backgrounds and have poorly educated parents cannot learn. Too often adults who would never work full time for no pay expect their children to study without any incentive.

All children can learn if the adults responsible for their schooling are willing to encourage achievement and productivity by taking the time to reward children for producing school work of high quality, quantity, and consistency. This module shows you how to improve the quality, quantity, and consistency of children's school work through a system of notes about academic performance from teachers and rewards from parents. It is appropriate for children from age 4 through 13.

Improving academic performance to help one child. A fifth-grade student in a special school program for talented and gifted children produced sloppy work in his regular classroom and rarely followed through on assignments in the special class. He spent much of his time reading science fiction stories. When called on to answer questions at school, he often seemed to be daydreaming. His parents, both doctors, were concerned about their son's school progress. They consulted with a clinical psychologist who helped them work through the Family-Problem Modules, clearing up problems of noncompliance and setting up a chore and allowance system. The psychologist then assembled a home-school team and gathered baseline data that showed highly inconsistent academic performance, particularly in math and science, and only one happy day out of 10 baseline days.

Improving academic performance in several children. The vice-principal in charge of discipline at a middle school spent most of her time lecturing children who were referred to her office for bad behavior by classroom teachers. To make her job more pleasant, she identified the children who had been sent to her office at least three times in the first month of school, and with the approval of the principal and the school's pupil-personnel team, she assembled a home-school team to help these high-risk children. After gathering baseline data on all the children, she found that each child was disruptive in only one or two academic subjects. She decided to reward the children for working harder in these subjects, believing that the harder they worked, the less time they would have for disruptive behavior.

1. Deciding if You Need to Work Through This Module

Look at each child's baseline record in Columns 1 to 6. You need not work through Module 3 if: (a) you are sure the baseline was fairly typical for the child, (b) compared to classmates, the child showed a relatively high mean and low scatter in each academic subject, (c) the scores in Columns 1 to 4 are the product of work the child did independently, rather than work that the child did with the help of a teacher, aide, or parent, (d) the scores in Columns 1 to 4 were the product of assignments appropriate for the child's age and grade, rather than assignments that were overly easy or overly familiar to the child, and (e) the child averaged more than 3 good days and 3 happy days a week, and neither the child nor any adult at school or home has complaints about the child's school behavior or happiness. If any of your answers suggest that your baseline data were invalid, continue baseline until it yields useful information, then return to this module.

If you decide to work through Module 3, select the academic subject of the four you charted in which the child's work was particularly deficient (with a very low mean or very high scatter compared to classmates). If the child is excellent academically but has behavior problems, select the subject in which the child has the lowest scores. Now, draw a line across this column underneath your last baseline day. This subject will be your first target subject. While targeting this subject for improvement, you will continue collecting baseline data in the other five columns on your chart.

∞∞∞

1. Will you work through Module 3? If not, why not?
2. Have you decided that your baseline data are invalid? Why? What will you do next?
3. If you will work through Module 3, what target academic subject will you select for each child? Why have you selected these subjects?

∞∞∞

2. Arranging a Family Conference

Depending upon how and why the home-school team was assembled, parents may have been involved as the team worked through Modules 1 and 2, or this family conference may be the parents' first exposure to the School-Problem Modules. The family conference must include at least one member of the home-school team other than parents. A good combination is the team leader (if this person is not the child's classroom teacher) and the classroom teacher.

Arrange an hour-long family conference at a time convenient for all participants. Include the target child, both parents, and the school-aged siblings of the target child as well as any adult residents of the household who share parenting duties. If the parents' English is poor, get help from someone who speaks the parents' native language. Invite parents to the conference and confirm the appointment before the meeting. Explain that the conference is the first step in a program designed to help the target child do better at school.

To increase the chances that parents will attend the meeting, have a home-school team member who is known and liked by the family invite the family to the conference and run the conference, provide transportation and babysitting for very young children, hold the conference at a convenient time and in a convenient location, and make a reminder call to the parents the night before the scheduled meeting.

Begin the meeting with a statement such as this:

"Thank you for coming here today to talk with me. I've invited you here because John's math work is very inconsistent from one day to the next even though the overall quality of his work is at the fourth-grade level. I propose that today you look at a graph of John's work, write an agreement with John to improve his work, and discuss how, together, we can make the agreement work. Before we begin, do you have any questions for me?"

Give brief, frank answers to the family's questions. Next, show the family graphs that display the child's baseline scores in the target academic subject and in the other academic subjects you've charted. Explain the graphs like this:

"As you can see from this graph, John's reading work has been fairly consistent. Notice how many scores are close to 75. Now look at this math graph. Notice how many scores fall far below and far above the average score of 60. Just think, if John had only a few more 60s and 70s instead of these zeros, his average score would be 70 and he would get a B in math rather than a D. I think it would be a good idea to help John get more 60s and 70s in math. What do you think? And what do you think about this, John?"

Parents may say that they would prefer to work on problems they are having with the target child at home. This is particularly likely if the family has not worked through the Home-Problem Modules in Chapter 4. If home problems do not interfere with the child getting to school and staying at school each day, arrange to help parents work through the Home-Problem Modules as soon as the School-Problem Modules' procedures are in place. If home problems do interfere with the target child getting to school and staying there, use the modules in

Chapter 4 to get the child back to school on a regular basis, then add the modules in this chapter.

∞∞∞

1. How will you increase the chances that parents will attend the family conference?
2. How will you present the child's academic performance to the family?

Bobby Joe's mother and stepfather were invited to a family conference after the home-school team at Bobby Joe's school identified him as an underachiever, particularly in math and reading. When his parents learned that the classroom teacher (the leader of the home-school team) proposed to help Bobby Joe do better classwork and homework, they began complaining about his temper tantrums and bedwetting. What could the teacher say to Bobby Joe's parents about these problems?

∞∞∞

3. Negotiating a Good-News Note Agreement

Once the family agrees to work on improving the child's performance in the target academic subject, help the family negotiate a "good-news note agreement." A good-news note agreement involves parents' rewarding children whenever they bring home "good-news notes" from school—notes saying a child did well academically that day.

When family members are illiterate, when conference time is very limited, or when you prefer to be directly involved in the negotiation process, help the family design a "reward menu," or list of rewards. Include items that can be given repeatedly, are age appropriate, are desirable to the child, and are acceptable to parents. Tell parents to give the child a choice from the menu only on days when the child brings home a good-news note. If the child and parents agree upon a large delayed reward, ask parents to decide how many good-news notes the long-term reward will cost the child. Stop the family from adding to the menu any long-term reward that costs more than 10 good-news notes. Remind the family to give the child a daily reward for each good-news note and to add long-term rewards as bonuses over and above the daily rewards. During the negotiation of a reward menu, make sure that all family members have a chance to state their opinions and that the group compromises on a solution acceptable to all family members.

The family should negotiate a lengthy written reward menu, so that the child will not tire of available rewards over the next few months. The reward menu should be posted where the child can see it. Physical affection and praise need not be listed on the menu, since parents should praise their child after good-news notes are received whether the child asks or not.

When parents are overbearing and they belittle the child and ignore the child's concerns, interrupt the negotiations to provide an example for these parents. Tell the parents that you would like them to watch and listen to you carefully. Role play the part of an honest and caring parent who is negotiating a reward menu with the child. As you role play, be direct about what rewards you are willing to give. At the same time, show understanding of the child's perspective. Object to any reward proposed by the child that is unethical, overly expensive, or impractical. Repeatedly make counteroffers of acceptable rewards linked to the child's initial request until the child wholeheartedly agrees to your proposal. Whenever necessary, gently coach the child and begin the role play again. For example, you might ask a whining shy child to sit up and look you in the eye when talking.

After you finish the role play, ask the parents to tell you what you did and said and how your behavior differed from theirs. If the parents did not notice what you did differently, role play one more time with the child. Parents might say that you listened more or that you offered acceptable options rather than merely rejecting the child's suggestions. Ask them why your approach might have a bigger payoff in the long run. They may say that compromises are more likely to result from such an approach and that the child might gradually learn to make more reasonable requests. Ask the parents to adopt your approach. Praise them for good negotiating and interrupt with more role playing and coaching of each parent until the parents are able to engage in fair give and take with their child. The process of coaching parents in fair negotiating can take the better part of an hour. With parents who are particularly unskilled, you may want to schedule another family conference in order to complete the good-news note agreement. Figure 7 shows a reward menu for good-news notes negotiated by an 11-year-old boy and his family.

Parents who object to providing material rewards for children's good behavior are often willing to reward children by spending special time with them. Special time with parents is an effective reward if it is provided at the same hour each evening, if children can choose the activities for the hour, if the children can choose to play with mother, father, or both parents, and if parents only provide special time in exchange for good-news notes.

Figure 7. Sample Reward Menu for Good-News Notes

Bart's Reward Menu
(Choose two items from this list in exchange for one good-news note.)

50¢

Lasagna for dinner

Dinner at a fast-food restaurant for the whole family

One hour later bedtime

Friend sleeps over

Mom's chocolate cake for dessert

One hour bike ride with dad

One hour hike in woods with mom and older brother

Both of these in exchange for five good-news notes

Saturday matinee movie with older brother and one friend

Pizza for Saturday night dinner

---

a. Using a game to teach the family to negotiate
Rather than guiding the family through the negotiation of a reward menu, you can use a board game to teach them negotiating skills. The game, called *Solutions,* can be obtained from the author at POB 389, Madison, CT 06443. After familiarizing yourself with the game, show the family how to play it.

When your goal is to teach the family to solve behavior problems by negotiating their own agreements without your participation, use *Solutions* to lead family members through a negotiation process that ends with a contract signed by all family members. The game's instructions prompt the family to agree about how and when to reward a desirable behavior, or the result of a desirable behavior, and to write contracts aimed at different target behaviors. *Solutions* ensures that family members have an opportunity to disagree and to resolve their disagreement.

∞∞∞

1. What is a good-news note agreement?
2. When should you help a family negotiate a reward menu?
3. What type of rewards should be included on the menu?
4. When is special time with parents an effective reward?
5. When, and only when, can the target child make choices from the reward menu?
6. When can you use the *Solutions* game to teach negotiating skills?

Every time the home-school team leader asked Lucy a question at the very beginning of their first family conference, her mother answered. The more this happened the quieter and more fidgety Lucy became. What could the team leader do to teach Mother how to listen?

ᩚᩚᩚ

b. Troubleshooting the good-news note agreement

After the family has arrived at a good-news agreement, check with all family members to determine whether they understand the agreement and whether they believe the agreement will work. Take objections seriously and explore each objection carefully. Help the family modify the agreement if any family member felt coerced into agreeing or agreed just to make another family member feel good. After you have answered all the family's questions, get a verbal commitment to the agreement from everybody. If the verbal commitments sound tentative, persist until all possible objections are resolved. Explain why it is necessary to remove obstacles to full commitment. Be patient, since this process can sometimes take the better part of an hour. If you think that parents will resent giving agreed upon rewards, cannot afford to give any material reward, or are unwilling to provide special time, provide the family with a goody bag consisting of a number of small desirable objects to be given to the child whenever a good-news note comes home.

ᩚᩚᩚ

1. What will you do if family members have objections to the good-news note agreement?
2. What will you do if you think that parents can't afford material rewards or won't provide special time to their children?

ᩚᩚᩚ

4. What to Do When Parents Believe Their Children Can't Change

When discussing the good-news note agreement's chances for success, some parents raise the question of hyperactivity or learning disabilities as the cause of the achievement deficit and wonder whether the good-news note agreement is too superficial a tool to resolve what they view as the real, underlying problem. These parents are generally reassured with words to this effect:

> "Many parents ask this question. What I tell them all is that even if the child is hyperactive or learning disabled, any good treatment program is going to bring about change in the child's academic performance and classroom behavior. Of the treatment options available to you, what I am proposing is the least radical or invasive. More extreme measures involve medication and segregation of the child from the regular classroom. If you had a headache I'm sure you would try an aspirin before you consented to brain surgery. I'm proposing that you take the same approach to your child's schooling. Let's try to make this agreement work. If it does, more serious measures will be unnecessary."

Of course, every child should be thoroughly screened for evidence of medical illness, physical handicap, and perceptual or cognitive deficits that may contribute to the child's poor performance. Positive evidence of these conditions should lead to appropriate medical treatment and follow-up. Since the child's academic performance is rarely improved by the tests or their findings, it is advisable to initiate the good-news note agreement even though a child has been referred for neurological or other medical tests. Academic performance may improve before the test results are available.

∞∞∞

1. What could you say to a parent who doesn't believe the good-news note agreement will help his learning-disabled child?

∞∞∞

5. Preparing the Family to Keep Track of Their Agreement

At the end of the conference, provide the family with a copy of the Good-News Note and Reward Chart that follows on which to record receipt of good-news notes and disbursement of rewards. Parents should fill in the date column with consecutive dates of school days, beginning with the first date on which the good-news note agreement will be used. Parents should put a check in the next column when they

Good-News Note and Reward Chart

DATE	Got note	Gave reward

DATE	Got note	Gave reward

DATE	Got note	Gave reward

receive a note. Whenever they give a reward from the menu, they should describe it in the final column. An example of how parents should fill out the chart is found in Figure 8, One Family's Good-News Note and Reward Chart. Some families prefer to save all good-news notes and to describe the reward for which each note was exchanged at the top of the note. Ask parents to bring the chart or their good-news notes to every meeting and to have them close by when talking to you by phone.

Before closing the family conference, repeat to the family all the details that have been established during the conference. Then, gently quiz family members about these details. Adopt a humorous manner, making up stories about what will happen at home and school from now on and having family members fill in the blanks or provide the ending to vignettes. At the slightest indication of poor comprehension or disagreement, review specific arrangements until comprehension and agreement are certain.

cඉcඉcඉ

1. How will parents keep track of good-news notes received and rewards given?

cඉcඉcඉ

6. Keeping in Touch with the Family

If you can, arrange to call the family each week to check on progress with the agreement. Ask them to tell you for each school day whether a note was received and what kind of reward they gave. If you cannot talk with the family once a week, encourage family members to call you when they have problems with the agreement or when they are ready to add a new target subject. Most problems can be resolved over the phone, but at times you may decide to arrange a face-to-face meeting.

cඉcඉcඉ

1. How will you keep in touch with the family?

cඉcඉcඉ

7. Giving Good-News Notes

Once the family has negotiated a good-news note agreement, the child's classroom teacher should give the child good-news notes on days when the child's daily assignment score in the target subject equals or exceeds that child's intervention goal. The simplest form of a good-news note reads: "John's math score today (9-15-85) is 55. The goal is 44. Good

Figure 8. One Family's Good-News Note and Reward Chart

DATE	Got note	Gave reward
9/23/85	✓	$ .50 LASAGNA
9/24/85	✓	1 HOUR LATER BED TIME CHOCOLATE CAKE
9/25/85		
9/26/85	✓	BIKE RIDE CHOCOLATE CAKE
9/27/85	✓	HIKE FAST-FOOD DINNER
9/30/85	✓	
10/1/85		HIKE FAST-FOOD DINNER
10/2/85		
10/3/85		
10/4/85	✓	BIKE RIDE $ .50

DATE	Got note	Gave reward

DATE	Got note	Gave reward

235

News!" Most teachers prepare many copies of a good-news note form that reads: "_____'s _____ score today (__-__-__) is __. The goal is __. Good News!"

So long as the child's daily score equals or exceeds the child's intervention goal, the good-news note goes home. The note goes home even if the child's performance in a nontarget subject area is poor that day or if the child's behavior was disruptive that day. The note goes home without comments on it, such as "Must improve conduct" or "More effort needed in social studies."

The good-news note system will not work if the teacher gives notes when they have not been earned or if the teacher withholds notes when they have been earned. The leader of the home-school team, or some other team member if the leader is the classroom teacher, should take responsibility for spot-checking the child's daily work and determining that notes are always (and only) given out when earned. The most common reason for lack of success with this system is noncontingent reinforcement. Children quickly learn that no matter how hard they work they won't always get a note when they've earned one (perhaps because of unrelated difficulties in class that day), or that whether or not they work hard, they will always get a note (perhaps because the teacher is short sightedly sympathetic).

When teachers give children good-news notes, they should take a few minutes to point out what the children did right, and encourage the children to praise themselves and to guess what they did that led to success. This approach focuses students' attention on what they need to do in order to succeed. It minimizes attention to useless strategies along with anxiety about errors. On days when no assignment is given, a note that says, "No work was assigned today" goes home with the child.

∞∞∞

1. On what days should good-news notes be given?
2. Why should children's daily work and receipt of good-news notes be spot-checked?
3. Why is it important for teachers to review work leading up to receipt of a good-news note with the target child, stressing what the child did correctly?
4. Why is it not a good idea for teachers to review mistakes that prevented a child from earning a good-news note?
5. What should teachers do on days when no work is assigned in the target academic subject?

   Violet earned a good-news note today in math, but at recess she slapped a classmate. Should Violet get a good-news note? Why?

∞∞∞

8. Determining if the Good-News Note Agreement Is Working

Once good-news notes in the target academic subject have started to be used, continue collecting data in all columns of the child's assessment chart just as you did before. Check the data in the target academic subject at least once a week to determine if the agreement is working.

On the child's graph for the target subject, draw a vertical line after the last baseline day. If you haven't done so thus far, connect the dots that represent baseline scores. Now connect the dots that represent all intervention scores. Compare the child's baseline and intervention progress after good-news notes have gone home for at least 2 weeks.

If the good-news note agreement is working, you will find a slow and steady improvement in one or more of these dimensions: *quality* (the child's mean score), *quantity* (the number of days when assignments are handed in for scoring), or *consistency* (the child's scatter score). Your graph will show visible changes in all three dimensions.

If there is an improvement in quality, as shown in Figure 9, the level of intervention scores will be visibly higher than the level of baseline scores, with scores later in intervention higher than scores earlier in intervention. If there is an improvement in quantity, as shown in Figure 10, you will have recorded scores above zero more often during intervention than you did during baseline. If there is greater consistency (and less scatter), as shown in Figure 11, the line connecting intervention scores will be straighter than the line connecting baseline scores. A child may improve along all of these dimensions; improvement along one or two dimensions is more likely, especially soon after intervention begins. Whenever you see improvement along any dimension, show the graph to everyone involved (including the child, of course), point out the success, and congratulate them for their contributions.

∞∞∞

1. In what three ways might a child's work improve?
2. What will you do when a child's work improves in any way?

∞∞∞

9. Adding Other Target Subjects

Once you have seen slow but steady improvement for at least 3 consecutive weeks in the target subject, continue intervention in the target subject and begin intervention in a second target subject. From now

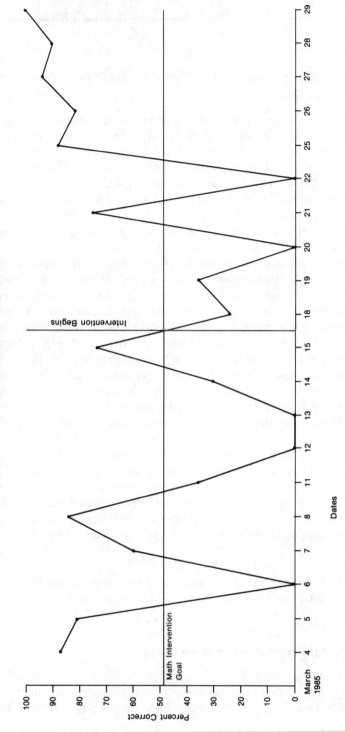

Figure 9. Graph Showing Improvement in Quality of Math Work

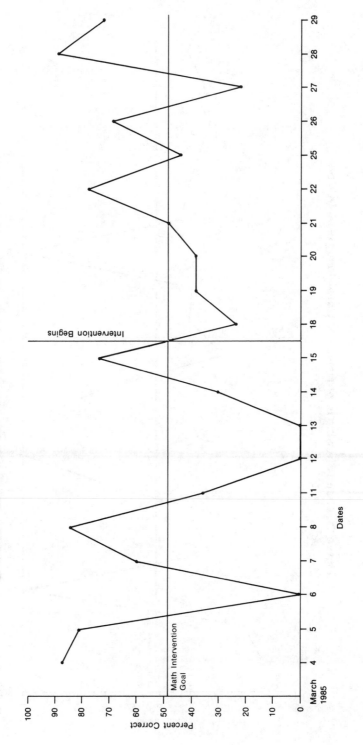

Figure 10. Graph Showing Improvement in Quantity of Math Work

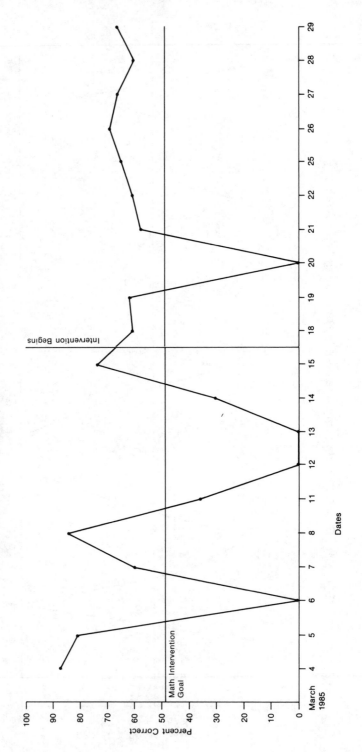

Figure 11. Graph Showing Improvement in Consistency of Math Work

on, send home a separate good-news note for daily goal attainment in each subject. Tell the parents to require a good-news note in both subjects for a menu choice. If the family included a long-term reward in their agreement, ask parents to provide the long-term reward in exchange for the agreed upon number of good-news notes; any number of these notes can come from either target subject. When you see continued improvement in both target subjects for 3 consecutive weeks, add a third and then a fourth target academic subject in the manner just described.

∞∞∞∞

1. When will you begin intervention in another target subject?
2. How will children earn rewards when other target subjects are added?

∞∞∞∞

10. Raising the Goal in a Target Subject

Once you have seen consistent improvement in all target subjects, raise the goal slightly in the target subject in which the child's intervention goal is lowest. The best way to choose a new intervention goal in the target subject is by averaging the child's scores from the beginning of intervention to the present date and using the average rounded down to the nearest integer as the new intervention goal. Good-news notes should be provided in the target academic subject whenever the child reaches or exceeds the new intervention goal. Look for consistent improvement in the target academic subject; this will consist of 3 weeks during which the quality, quantity, or consistency of school work is better than during baseline and better than during the first phase of intervention. Consult Figures 9, 10, and 11 for illustrations of improvements along these three dimensions. After improvement is evident, raise the goals in the other three academic subjects you've charted one by one. Always be prepared to lower a goal to its earlier level when the child's school work declines.

∞∞∞∞

1. How will you choose a new intervention goal in the target subject?
2. When will you choose a new intervention goal in the target subject?

∞∞∞∞

11. What to Do When People Attribute Improved School Work to Other Causes

If you see an improvement following the introduction of good-news notes, don't be surprised if other people don't credit intervention and your efforts for improvement. Each person involved is likely to see something he has been doing (other than intervention) as the real cause of improvement. For example, parents may say that the child has improved because they stopped feeding him foods with chemical additives. Once success is apparent, it really doesn't matter how other people explain its origins, just keep the agreement going.

∞∞∞

1. Does it matter if other people explain the child's academic success as due to their efforts instead of the intervention?
2. What would you say if a parent said to you, "I knew that those good-news notes wouldn't work, but when I asked that Kevin be seated away from that troublesome Jones boy, his classwork really improved"?

∞∞∞

12. What to Do When Progress with the Good-News Note Agreement Is Slow

If progress with the good-news note agreement is slow, the home-school team should consider plans to correct each possible cause of slow progress. Put all plans of action into effect, one at a time. If a plan works, the corresponding cause probably was to blame for slow progress. For example, you decide that an abrupt change in difficulty of schoolwork and a chaotic classroom atmosphere are two possible causes of slow progress. You ask the teacher to provide a more gradual transition from old to new work. After that, the child shows consistent evidence of success. Your plan (smoothing the transition from old to new work) supports your guess about the cause of poor progress (an abrupt change from old to new work).

One reason for slow progress with the good-news note agreement is if the child's baseline data do not accurately represent the child's independent work during baseline. If, for example, a teacher's aide helped the child do a lot of work during baseline, the first goal set for intervention will be too high, and no progress will occur despite the child's efforts. When this is the case, lower the goal to a more reasonable one and continue the good-news agreement.

Sometimes the beginning of the good-news note agreement coincides with an abrupt change in the curriculum from relatively easy review work to very difficult, unfamiliar work. When you discover that this has happened, you have two choices. The child could be provided with a mixture of easy and difficult work each day, with the work always weighted to the familiar. With this approach the child is always gradually moving from very familiar to somewhat less familiar work with ample opportunities for success each day. A second option you have is to lower the child's goal to the child's average performance level on the more difficult work and continue the agreement.

The child's intervention goal may be so high and the work so easy that raising the goal is not effective. When this is the case, making the work a bit more challenging is the answer.

Behavior problems, either the target child's or classmates', may impede improvement despite a sound good-news note agreement. When this is the case, as soon as evidence indicates that the good-news note agreement is being carried out correctly by parents and teachers, move on to Module 4, continuing the procedures in this module.

Sometimes after the good-news note agreement has been in effect with success for a while, the child suddenly begins to put out less effort and to succeed in reaching the goal less often. The child could be tired or satiated with the reward menu. Talk with the child and try to design a more appetizing menu of rewards, one that is consistent with guidelines for rewards presented earlier. After instituting the new menu, wait at least 10 school days to see if the child returns to earlier levels of success.

If the intervention goal is too low, reinforcement for achieving the goal may have produced a decline in the child's work. The child is unlikely to be aware that this has happened. If raising the child's goal by a small amount (e.g., 5 percent) produces a return to earlier levels of success, then the reason for decline is obvious. The problems presented that may interfere with progress of the good-news note agreement and their solutions are summarized in Table 1.

∞∞∞

1. What will you do if progress with the good-news note agreement is slow?
2. What are six possible causes of slow progress with the good-news note agreement?

∞∞∞

Table 1. Possible Problems with the
Good-News Note Agreement
and Their Solutions

The child's baseline data do not accurately represent independent work during baseline.	→ Lower the intervention goal and continue the agreement.
There has been an abrupt shift from relatively easy review work to very difficult work.	→ Provide a mixture of relatively easy and relatively difficult work or lower the intervention goal. Continue the agreement.
The intervention goal is high and the work the child is asked to do is too easy.	→ Make the work slightly more difficult and continue the agreement.
Behavior problems are slowing progress.	→ Make sure the agreement is correctly instituted by parents and teachers. Continue the agreement and move on to Module 4.
The child is tired of the reward menu.	→ Introduce new rewards into the menu and continue the agreement.
The intervention goal is too low.	→ Raise the intervention goal and continue the agreement.

13. Weaning Children Off Good-News Notes

After working through Modules 3 and 4 with success, if time remains in the school year, wean the children off good-news notes and work for long-term gains. Explain to parents and teachers that your aim is to encourage children to keep working productively for fewer and fewer material rewards. Instruct everyone to praise children when they do well in school and to be sure to take pleasure in any evidence of children's accomplishments.

Keep agreements going as established and begin scheduling "probe" days approximately every 5th day. On probe days, assignments are given without giving good-news notes if these are earned and notes that say "Probe today" are sent home. On these days, the child is told that today is a vacation from good-news notes and that it is hoped the child will work hard and feel good about succeeding, even though no good-news notes can be earned. The child can learn to do without good-news notes by being encouraged with talk about self-reward. (What will you say to yourself if you get all your work done today? What will the other kids say when they see you are working hard? How will your parents feel when you tell them that you worked hard today even though you couldn't get a good-news note?) No one but you should know in advance when probe days will occur. When 5 consecutive probe days reveal that the child is consistently achieving at or above criterion without the expectation of reward, schedule probe days about every 4th day. When 5 more consecutive probe days reveal that the child is consistently achieving the intervention goal without expectation of reward, schedule probe days about every 3rd day. Continue in this way until the good-news note agreement is no longer necessary to encourage high-quality academic performance. Always be prepared to reduce the frequency of probe days and to reinstate the agreement without probe days as soon as the child's achievement declines.

∞∞∞

1. When will you begin to wean children off good-news notes?
2. What are "probe" days?
3. What can children be told to encourage them to work hard without good-news notes?
4. How often will you schedule probe days as you begin to wean children from notes?
5. How will you increase the schedule of probe days?

∞∞∞

14. Getting Families Ready for the Next School Year

Meet with all the parents at the end of the school year to review children's progress and discuss plans for the summer and the following school year. Schedule a meeting with each family at the beginning of the next school year to collect new data and to determine which successful school and home procedures should be reinstated.

∞∞∞

1. How will you get families ready for the next school year?

∞∞∞

15. Moving On to Module 4

You can move on to Module 4 as soon as you have worked through the procedures in this module for the target child, are consistently using the procedures, and the target child has received three good-news notes a week for 3 consecutive weeks. You do not need to wait for success in all academic subjects before moving on. If there is any reason to believe that there has been spontaneous improvement in the child's school behavior or mood during this module, wait until there is substantial academic and spontaneous behavior improvement before moving on. It is important to continue using these procedures and charting for this module as you work through Module 4.

If you start using the procedures described in this module and then stop, if you think you or team members aren't using the procedures correctly, or if you or team members aren't consistently using the procedures, return to the beginning of this module. If members of the home-school team are not following through as you've requested, it may take several weeks to accomplish some of the procedures in this module and establish a sound good-news note agreement for target children.

∞∞∞

1. How will you know when you are ready to move on to Module 4?
2. When is it a good idea to begin Module 3 again?

∞∞∞

Answer these questions for each target child after the family conference is over

1. What unexpected problems arose during the family conference? How did you deal with those problems?
2. Thinking back on the meeting, how could you have made it more productive?
3. What reward menu has been agreed upon by the family?
4. How many daily choices will the child get in exchange for each good-news note?
5. What long-term rewards are included in the menu? How many good-news notes will these long-term rewards cost the child?
6. What problems arose during negotiation of the good-news note agreement, and how did you deal with those problems?
7. Looking back on the negotiation process, how could it have been improved?
8. How will the family keep track of the receipt of good-news notes and the giving of rewards?
9. How will the family get in touch with you?

**Answer these questions for each target child before
you begin the good-news note agreement**

1. In which academic subject will the child receive a good-news note?
2. What score must the child reach or exceed to receive the note?
3. Who will provide the good-news note?
4. How will you know if a teacher gives good-news notes when
   unearned, or withholds them when earned? What will you do if
   you detect poor follow-through? Is there any way that you can
   prevent problems in follow-through?

**Answer these questions for each target child after
3 weeks of intervention**

1. What have you learned from a comparison of the child's baseline
   and intervention scores in the target academic subject?
2. If the graph shows improvement, have you told anyone about the
   improvement?
3. Are you ready to begin intervention in another academic subject?
   When will you be ready?
4. Does the child's graph indicate that progress is slow or poor?
5. If progress is slow or poor, why might this be and what plans could
   you devise to correct the blocks to progress?

**Answer these questions for each target child after there
has been progress in each target subject**

1. What type of progress have you seen in each target goal?
2. Is the child ready to be weaned off good-news notes?
3. What is your plan for decreasing good-news notes? What will you
   do if the child's performance worsens after you institute this plan?
4. How will you continue this module into the next school year?

Module 4: Improving School Behavior

The successful student has versatile self-control skills, learns quickly from direct instruction, casual observation, and personal experience, and .takes pleasure in academic accomplishments and time spent with classmates and teachers. This student probably will do well in life despite occasional unproductive experiences at school. Families have more opportunity than schools to impart the problem-solving skills that ensure children's success at school. Unfortunately, few parents recognize the relationship between how they rear their children at home and how well their children behave in school. Parents who demand uncritical compliance and use punishment liberally or who set few limits on children's behavior and gratify even the most whimsical demands prevent children from becoming responsible, productive, and happy students.

The successful teacher is intelligent, patient, and warm and has superb management skills. This teacher will impart knowledge, skills, and helpful attitudes even to students from poorly functioning families. Although classroom management techniques seem essential to teaching at all levels, most good teachers stumble onto successful management practices. They rarely get more than superficial exposure to classroom management during their training. In their entire careers, they may see few demonstrations of good management practices by the school administration.

This module is designed to help children to learn self-control skills and teachers to improve management skills. It shows teachers how to encourage alert, productive, happy, and sociable school behavior and to discourage inattentive, disruptive, and antisocial behavior. This module concerns children whose school behavior is inappropriate and those who are often unhappy at school. The aim of this module is to create a benign classroom environment that will moderate children's behavior problems and unhappiness even if the source of the problem is outside of the classroom. Children who exhibit behavior problems and unhappiness often suffer punishment in many areas of their lives. Their behavior and mood may change when they are no longer punished, believe they have more control over rewarding experiences, and hear unqualified praise. When this module's procedures are in effect, children earn rewards for good school behavior and avoid harsh, inconsistent, and ineffective punishment. The procedures described in this module are intended to be used with entire classrooms, even if only one child in the classroom is the target of intervention.

Giving good instructions is the first method of improving school behavior presented in this module. A procedure called "timeout" is presented next. Timeout stands for "time out from positive reinforcement." In this procedure, children go to a "timeout area" for a fixed amount of time because of behavior problems. During timeout, a child has no chance for exciting social interaction. The "good-behavior game," also used in this module, is a procedure that encourages all children to be on their best behavior at school without constant reminders. The game builds cooperation between well-controlled and poorly controlled classmates. (More information about the game can be found in a 1969 article by its originators, Barrish, Saunders, and Wolf, in Volume 2 of the *Journal of Applied Behavior Analysis*). Ignoring and praising, and assertiveness, apologies, restitution, and good manners are also presented in this module. This module is appropriate for children age 4 through age 13.

Improving school behavior to help one child. Since kindergarten, a fourth-grade student had explosive, violent temper tantrums and fought with children and teachers, who disliked and feared him. The boy had a tragic family history; his mother was killed in a family fight and his alcoholic father was chronically depressed and suicidal. School consultants had recommended the introduction of behavior management procedures at home and at school for several years, but no one had taken responsibility for following through on these recommendations. The fourth-grade teacher, fearing that the school would recommend residential treatment if the boy's behavior didn't improve, assembled a home-school team, gathered baseline data, used good-news notes with rewards given by the school psychologist to improve the boy's academic achievement, and began to encourage him to control his explosive behavior and to promote self-control skills in all her students.

Improving school behavior to help several children. An elementary-school math consultant found that the math scores in 3 (out of 22) heterogenously grouped classrooms declined over the year. The consultant visited these 3 classes in late spring during math instruction and at other times. She found that two teachers liked and understood math, but were often sarcastic and irritable with the children. One new teacher was unfamiliar with the math curriculum and so poorly organized that very little instruction took place in her classroom. The math consultant discussed her observations with the building principal; with his support she organized an inservice workshop in classroom behavior management for the three teachers about whom she was concerned, and used this module as a text for the workshop and for follow-up supervision.

1. Deciding if You Need to Work Through This Module

Look at the baseline record in Columns 5 and 6 of the child's School-Behavior Assessment Chart. You need not work through Module 4 if: (*a*) you are sure your baseline was fairly typical for the child, (*b*) the child averaged more than 3 good days and more than 3 happy days a week, and (*c*) neither the child nor any adult at school or home has complaints about the child's school behavior or happiness.

∞∞∞

1. Do you need to work through this module? If not, why not?

∞∞∞

2. Giving Instructions That Children Can Follow

One of the first things that teachers can do to help children improve their school behavior is to learn to give instructions that children can follow. Take these steps when giving children instructions or making requests:

1. Give as few instructions as possible. Try to let children learn by experiencing, whenever safe, the natural consequences of their own behavior. Give a set of instructions only to children who can recall more than one instruction.

2. Give specific, brief instructions *one time*. When a teacher gives instructions over and over, this signals children that they need not listen carefully the first time instructions are given. As a result, the teacher who repeats instructions encourages inattentive behavior. Good instructions tell the child exactly what to do and when to do it. Some examples of good instructions are: "Leave your workbooks under your seats during the test," "Erase the board now," and "Hand in your ending to the story by 2:00." If you are sure that a child cannot comply with your request, don't make it.

3. Look at the child, smile, and use a pleasant tone of voice when giving instructions. Try not to give instructions when you are angry, since you may be too upset to follow through. Your anger may frighten or confuse children, making it hard for them to follow your instructions. Also, children rarely comply freely with sarcastic or humiliating instructions, and they tend to avoid listening to adults who issue instructions in these ways.

4. When you give instructions, always ask for positive action ("Read pages 2 to 4 and answer the questions on page 5 by 1:00").

Never request negative or "dead-man's" actions ("Stop fidgeting" "Be quiet" "Stop chattering" "Don't leave your seat"). Instead of telling a child to stop doing something, ask the child to engage in a substitute positive behavior. For example, instead of telling a child "Stop interrupting me when I tell the class something you already know," ask the child to "Make a list of each word I explain to the class that you already understand, and give me the list at 4:00."

5. Always set a time limit for instructions ("Now" or "At 2:15") and wait until the time limit is up to see if the child has followed through as requested. While waiting, do not remind the child of your request or use threats or bribes to get the child to follow through. If the instruction is to do something right away, wait silently for 1 minute to see if the child does as you ask. If the instruction is to do something by a specific time, wait until that time to see if the child does as you ask. Instructions that include no specific time limit are unclear. The child has no idea of when instruction following is required, and so procrastination and noncompliance often result. If the teacher asks when instructions will be followed, the child will often say "soon" or "not yet." When the teacher forgets to check on instruction following (this can very easily happen when there is no time limit), the child learns to ignore future instructions.

6. Give instructions only when you are willing and able to follow up on the child's compliance or noncompliance. If there is no way for you to find out if a child has followed your instructions, don't give them.

7. It is always a good idea after giving an instruction (or set of instructions) to gently determine if all children have understood. Find out by asking in a pleasant way different members of the class to repeat what you've said in their own words. Praise children who understood. Ask children who didn't understand to ask questions of you or of classmates until they show comprehension.

8. If children in your class cannot understand or retain verbal instructions, work on ways to provide instructions that will be effective. For example, you might tape record instructions for a child who is a poor reader and has a poor memory.

∞∞∞

1. Describe eight steps in giving children instructions and asking them to do things.
2. Which instructions will be eliminated by these steps?
3. How do children respond when a teacher repeats the same instructions over and over? Do they listen carefully to the teacher? Why don't they need to listen carefully?

4. Is there any point in asking children to do things they can't do?
5. Why is it important to provide a time limit for each request?
6. How long should you wait for compliance after giving instructions?
7. How can you determine if children understood your instructions?
8. What can you do if children in your class cannot understand or repeat verbal instructions?

∽∽∽

3. Deciding What Behaviors Deserve Timeouts

After you have learned to give instructions that students can follow, begin using timeout. Timeout, as described earlier in this chapter, is a method of behavior control that involves sending children to a timeout area away from the rest of the class when they exhibit behavior problems.

You need to decide what behavior problems you will call a timeout for in your classroom. You will probably want to call timeout for the following:

1. Noncompliance. Noncompliance occurs when a child does not follow a clear, reasonable instruction issued by an adult before a stated time limit. Noncompliant behavior is often described by parents as "not minding" or "not listening." Call timeout when the stated time limit has been reached and the child has not complied.

2. Temper Tantrums. A temper tantrum takes place when a child, who has not been mistreated, is out-of-control for at least 1 minute, screaming, crying, throwing things, or hitting. Timeout should be called as soon as a temper tantrum begins. The earlier timeout is called, the better.

3. Fighting. A fight always involves at least two children. Whenever you see one child hit another or hear one child call another a name or whenever one child complains about another child, a fight is taking place. Involved in the fight are the aggressor and the victim. Using this definition of a fight, you never have to decide which child started or provoked a fight. Timeout should be called for both children as soon as a fight is observed. Victims need to learn how to avoid aggressors as much as aggressors need to learn self-control.

It is important to call timeout as soon as a temper tantrum or a fight begins. This teaches children that even a small amount of misbehavior will not be tolerated. When a teacher calls timeout only after temper tantrums or fights get out of hand, children learn to escalate their misbehavior until the teacher can no longer tolerate the situation. In this way, the teacher who waits a while before calling timeout trains students to be poorly controlled.

∞∞∞

1. What, in your own words, are noncompliance, a temper tantrum, and a fight?
2. Why is it important to call timeout as soon as a temper tantrum or fight is spotted?
3. How does calling timeout for both the victim and aggressor in a fight benefit teachers and children?

   Carl keeps making faces after a teacher says, "Stop that." Is Carl noncompliant? Why not?

   Whenever students fidget in Mrs. Jones's class, Mrs. Jones tells the other students a joke about the fidgeting student. Is Mrs. Jones ignoring fidgeting? Why do you think so many children fidget in her class?

∞∞∞

4. Preparing a Timeout Spot in the Classroom

Set up a timeout spot in your classroom in a quiet but isolated area (a desk facing away from the class is one possibility) where children can distract themselves by working, reading, or sitting quietly. Leave books and quiet activities in the classroom timeout area and allow children to bring their work to the timeout area when you call timeout. If behavior problems are infrequent in your classroom, then a timeout area with two desks separated from each other and from the class by cardboard partitions will be enough. If you suspect that a number of children will need timeouts at the same time, arrange different colored timeout carrels around the classroom. For each carrel, get an inexpensive timer and label it with tape of the carrel's color. When you send a child to timeout, say "Jim, timeout in the blue carrel." If you are consistent about enforcing timeout by using a back-up timeout area for children who are noisy in classroom timeout as described later, you will find that without help you can maintain this system. A teacher's aide, part of whose job is to be a timekeeper for timeout, would increase your effectiveness as a teacher.

∞∞∞

1. What area will you use for timeout in your classroom?
2. What problems do you anticipate in use of this area? How can you solve these problems?

∞∞∞

5. Calling a Timeout

Call timeout as soon as inappropriate behavior begins. It is not kind to wait or warn or give the child a "second chance." Teachers who do this train students to be poorly controlled and expose them to needless troubles. Such warnings prevent children from learning to think before they act and from warning themselves: "If I do this, then I'll get timeout." Call timeout by saying "timeout" and waiting silently for the child to go to timeout. Call timeouts as often as necessary. Timeout is most effective when children know that no matter what they do that is inappropriate, you will call a timeout. When appropriately used, timeout is not a thrilling punishment; it is a boring consequence that takes children away from exciting interaction with peers and teachers. Once children learn that there are some things for which you will lecture them or about which you will call their parents or tell the principal rather than calling timeout, they will try to find out what else you will exempt from a timeout.

∞∞∞

1. How far along should inappropriate behavior be before you call timeout?
2. What will children learn to do if you delay calling timeout until the timeout behavior has gone on for a while?
3. How do you call timeout?
4. Why is it important to call timeout each and every time you spot a timeout behavior?

   Mr. Fogarty calls timeout properly when he is alone with his class. But when the class has visitors, he feels uncomfortable calling timeout. Predict how Mr. Fogarty's class acts when the building principal visits.

∞∞∞

6. What to Do When a Child Goes to Timeout as Requested

Expect children to go to the timeout area within 1 minute after you call timeout. Once a child is seated quietly in the timeout area, set a timer for 5 minutes. Five minutes is a good length for a timeout for any child since it minimally disrupts the flow of classroom activities. The longer timeout is, the fewer opportunities you have to call timeout and to teach children your expectations. If you prefer a longer timeout, make it uniform for all children, and no longer than 15 minutes. A good guideline is 5 minutes until grade 4, 10 minutes until grade 6, and 15 minutes until grade 8. Allow children to return to their seats without further discussion of the problem leading up to timeout after they have spent the appropriate amount of quiet time in the timeout area. The buzzer on the timer can be their signal for returning to their seats. You or a teacher's aide should set the timer, not the child. Do not talk to the child about what the child did before timeout or why you decided to call timeout. As soon as inappropriate behavior begins again, call another timeout, even if the child just finished a timeout.

It is a good idea to allow children to do classwork or to relax when in timeout, because the purpose of timeout is to teach children to remove themselves from situations either physically or mentally when they are on the verge of misbehavior. Guilt (especially externally produced guilt) often follows misbehavior, but rarely prevents misbehavior. Sending a child to timeout and instructing her to mull over her misdeeds teaches the child (at best) to feel guilty after poorly controlled behavior; it does not teach the child to control her impulses at the moment she is about to misbehave. When a child goes to timeout when told, stays there for the appropriate quiet time, and returns to her desk when the timer's buzzer goes off, praise the child for following through appropriately. Say, for example, "Good job, Lisa, you went into timeout on time and were quiet."

It is unwise to discuss why you called timeout once the timeout is over. There are likely to be disagreements between you and the child about exactly what happened. Such a discussion punishes the child for successful completion of timeout, makes the child mentally rehearse misbehavior, and encourages future misbehavior. Repeated appropriate use of timeout will teach the child how to discriminate between appropriate and inappropriate behavior, with no need for lectures or sermons.

∞∞∞

1. What do you expect children to do when you call timeout?
2. After you have called timeout, when will you set the timer?
3. How soon after a child comes out of timeout will you call timeout again?
4. What is the purpose of timeout? How does teaching children to feel guilty defeat this purpose?
5. What will you say when children go to timeout quickly and quietly and return to their seats when the timer's buzzer goes off?
6. Is it a good idea to discuss the cause of timeout after timeout is over? Why not?

∞∞∞

7. What to Do When a Child Doesn't Go to Timeout or Misbehaves in Timeout

When children don't go to timeout when told or are noisy or disruptive in the timeout area, immediately send them to a back-up timeout area, outside the classroom. Do not answer children's questions about why you have called timeout. After calling timeout, wait no more than 1 minute to see if the child is going to the classroom timeout area. If the child does not go quickly and quietly to timeout, take or send the child to a back-up timeout area and notify the back-up timeout supervisor.

Allow children to return to the classroom only after they have been in the back-up timeout area for 30 consecutive quiet minutes. Children vary in the length of time they spend attention seeking in the back-up timeout area before they quiet down for 30 consecutive minutes. The less response they get, the more quickly they quiet down. When back-up timeouts are used more than three times a day for a child, or when the child never successfully completes the first back-up timeout, a mental-health professional should be directly involved in work with the child.

The back-up timeout area should be quiet and isolated but safe. Allow the child to choose whether to read, do work, or sit quietly. The child should have safe, easy access to the toilet and should be provided with lunch and snacks at the regular times. The supervisor in the back-up timeout area should not talk to children in timeout; the supervisor's job is to send children back to the regular classroom after 30 consecutive quiet minutes in timeout.

Almost every school suffers from a lack of space and supervisory personnel. Nonetheless, any school in which children's behavior is at times disruptive needs a back-up timeout space and an appropriately trained supervisor. In a pinch, the school can install a carrel in the principal's outer office, in the nurse's room, or in the teachers' lounge and instruct the school secretary or nurse in supervising back-up timeouts. The success of timeouts in the classroom will depend upon how carefully you plan for and monitor back-up timeouts. If the school secretary always asks children in timeout why they were naughty or the school nurse always comforts children who cry in timeout, then timeout in the classroom will be ineffective.

∞∞∞

1. What will you do if a child doesn't go to timeout on time or behaves inappropriately in timeout?
2. Where will your back-up timeout area be and who will be the back-up timeout supervisor?

3. What problems do you anticipate with back-up timeouts and how can you solve these problems?
4. How long should you wait before sending children to the back-up timeout area?
5. When can children return from the back-up timeout area?
6. What is the supervisor's job in the back-up timeout area?
7. Should the supervisor talk to the children? Why' not?

∞∞∞

8. Using Timeout as the Only Consequence for Undesirable Behavior

Timeout is most effective when it is the only consequence for undesirable behavior. Use timeout instead of giving sermons. If you call timeout as soon as you see or hear inappropriate behavior, you will have no chance to lecture children about their errors. If they go to timeout properly and then return to take part in the class, you will once again have no chance to deliver a sermon about bad behavior. If you use timeout as described, you will see a rapid decline in inappropriate school behavior and there will be no need for sermons.

At times, children's behavior is so unacceptable to adults that they feel the need for a strong punishment instead of timeout. This is often the case when a child injures another child or an adult. At these times, administer an extended timeout in the back-up timeout area. The length of extended timeout will depend upon the age of the child and other circumstances best evaluated by the teacher. In no case should an extended timeout longer than 3 hours be administered. If a 10-year-old boy knocks down another boy, giving him a black eye, timeout for both boys would be appropriate. If, however, the aggressor has a long history of attacking other boys and has been warned that the next fight will result in an extended timeout, then 3 hours in a back-up timeout area might be required for the aggressor. Extended timeouts are not effective if the decision to administer them is made after the problem occurs. Develop a list of all the situations that might warrant an extended timeout, decide how long the extended timeout will last, and forewarn all children, school personnel, and parents about your plan to use extended timeouts.

If a child behaves inappropriately at a time or in a place when calling timeout in the classroom would be difficult, the child owes you a delayed, double timeout in the classroom whenever timeout in the classroom is possible.

∞∞∞

1. Why should you use timeout instead of giving sermons?
2. What should you do when a child injures another child or an adult?
3. When should you make an exception to the rule of having both the aggressor and the victim in a fight go to timeout?
4. What should you do if a child behaves inappropriately at a time or in a place when calling timeout in the classroom would be difficult?

∞∞∞

9. Explaining Timeout to Your Students

Before you begin using timeout in your classroom, explain it once to your students. Post lists of the behaviors you will call timeout for and the things that children should do when you call timeout. You can explain timeout by saying something like this:

> "I've decided to use something new called timeout, because I think it will help all of us. I think that timeout will help you children learn to think before you act and to keep yourselves busy when you might otherwise do things that would bother me and the other children.

> "When I call timeout, go quickly and quietly to the timeout area over there and read, work, or just relax until you hear the buzzer. I will set the timer so that the buzzer will go off after you have been in timeout for 5 minutes. When you hear the buzzer, return to your seat and take part in the class again. I've posted a sign listing the things that I will ask you to go to timeout for. I've also posted a sign that lists the things to do when I call timeout. I'll go over each of them in a minute and explain them.

> "If you go to timeout in the way that I've just explained, I'll tell you that you've done a good job when you return to your seat. If you don't go to timeout quickly and quietly when I call timeout or if you are noisy in timeout, I'll send you with your books to stay in the nurse's office until you have been there for 30 quiet minutes in a row. When you are there, the nurse will not talk with you. If I call timeout at a time when you can't go to timeout in the classroom, for example, when we are on a field trip, I'll say "double timeout later." That means that when you are next in the classroom, I'll tell you to go to the timeout area and stay there for 10 minutes. If anyone ever has a fight or hurts another person, the child who has done the harm will go to the nurse's office for a 3-hour timeout.

> "At first, I am sure that you will go to timeout only when I tell you to. When you go to timeout, you will get away from situations

that might cause you and the rest of us a lot of trouble. After a while, I bet that some of you will learn to avoid trouble at school by putting yourselves in timeout—either walking away or using your imagination to ignore difficult situations or situations that might get you in trouble. I think that timeout will help me, because I will no longer need to nag or threaten any of you.

"How many of you already take timeouts, by walking away or daydreaming, when you start to get angry or bored? Who can tell me when it is a good time to use imagination to take a timeout? When is it a good time to take a timeout by walking away?"

Make sure that you include in your explanation:

1. What going to timeout means,
2. Why you will use timeout,
3. When you will call a timeout,
4. What children can do during timeout,
5. What will happen if they go to timeout on time,
6. What will happen if they don't go to timeout or misbehave in timeout,
7. When you will call an extended timeout,
8. What you will do if you can't send them to timeout right away.

To make sure that your students understand timeout, see how many children can repeat your explanation. Give everyone a chance to do this.

You may want to prepare a description of timeout rules and an explanation of timeout suitable for your students and try this presentation out on a co-worker or supervisor. Ask how this person believes your students will react.

∞∞∞

1. How many times will you explain timeout to your students?
2. What eight things will you tell your students about timeout?
3. How will you make sure they understand what you have said?

∞∞∞

10. Training a Teacher's Aide to Administer Back-Up Timeouts

When a child is particularly disruptive in the regular classroom and unlikely to behave in classroom timeouts or when the school has many disruptive children but no supervisor for back-up timeouts, it often pays to hire a teacher's aide to administer back-up timeouts. If the aide is assigned to a particularly disruptive child, the teacher would call timeout for the child as usual. Only when the child did not go immediately to timeout would the aide escort the child outside the classroom to a back-up timeout area. As soon as the child consistently went to immediate timeout in the classroom, the aide's job would be finished. If the aide were assigned to administer back-up timeouts for several classrooms, teachers would call timeouts as usual and call the aide to the classroom to escort children to back-up timeouts. Since a reasonable goal is for the disruptive student to learn to go to timeout as instructed in the classroom, it is important to provide the child with an incentive for going to timeout in the classroom (a briefer timeout than in the back-up area) and an incentive for successfully completing timeout (praise and recognition).

∞∞∞

1. When is it a good idea to hire a teacher's aide to administer back-up timeouts?
2. What is the aide's job? When would the aide's job be finished?
3. If you have decided to train a teacher's aide to assist with timeouts, describe the plans that you have for involvement of the aide in timeout.
4. Why is it a good idea to plan from the beginning to encourage the child to take timeouts in the classroom? How can you accomplish this goal?

∞∞∞

11. Keeping Track of Timeouts

It is extremely important to keep a careful daily record of each timeout you call and of each time the child goes into timeout. Without such a record, all sorts of problems can arise. It will be impossible to estimate whether timeout is being used appropriately and whether it is effective. It will also be impossible to respond to complaints that timeout is being used in an abusive or capricious manner. In Column 5, "Good day," of the child's assessment chart, write *TO-5* when you call an immediate timeout in the classroom for 5 minutes; *TO-10* when you call a delayed timeout in the classroom for 10 minutes; *TO/BU-½ hr.* when you call a timeout in the back-up room for 30 minutes and *TO/BU-3 hrs.* when you call an extended timeout in the back-up room for 3 hours. When the child has gone to and stayed in timeout for the required amount of time, cross off the notation. Whenever you call an extended timeout indicate the reason.

ထာထာထာ

1. Why is a record of timeouts important?
2. How and where will you keep a record of timeouts for each child?

ထာထာထာ

12. Using the Good-Behavior Game

Timeout will help you decrease inappropriate behavior in children. Used consistently, it will help children learn skills of self-control and frustration tolerance. The good-behavior game, used together with timeout, will allow you to increase behaviors that benefit the individual child and the entire classroom. You can focus the good-behavior game on simple goal behaviors, such as quiet voices, or more complex goal behaviors, such as attentiveness or cooperation with classmates.

Prepare for the use of the good-behavior game by getting enough red ribbons with safety pins through them and red chips for half the class, enough blue ribbons with safety pins through them and blue chips for the other half, and one large transparent jar to situate prominently in the classroom. Make up a reward menu of highly rewarding activities and privileges to be won in the game. Because of limited budgets, putting together an effective reward menu can be a real challenge. Enlist the efforts of parents of your students, members of the parent-teacher association, even members of your school board. Perhaps local merchants can donate coupons for fast-food meals, small toys, or school supplies to add to the choices on your class's reward menu. Your observations of what students like and frequently ask for will also help you add good choices to the reward menu. One teacher put an old clawfoot bathtub in the back of her fourth-grade classroom and filled the tub halfway with colorful pillows. When she saw how eager students were to sit in the tub and read, she added 15 minutes reading time in the tub to her class's reward menu and found that this reward was chosen more often than any other.

Try to make up a long menu with many exciting choices. Let the children help you construct the menu and post it in the classroom. Figure 12 shows a sample reward menu for the good-behavior game.

To begin the good-behavior game, have children close their eyes and draw a red or blue ribbon from a bag each morning. They wear the ribbons throughout the day in order to identify their team membership.

Figure 12. Sample Reward Menu for the Good-Behavior Game

Reward Menu for Ms. Green's Third-Grade Class
(Each member of the winning team chooses two.)

Use the classroom computer for ½ hour

Get 15 minutes extra recess

Get a special sticker

Make brownies with the help of the teacher

Play the teacher's guitar for 10 minutes

Decorate your face with makeup like a clown and wear it all day

Read a story of your choice to the class

Have your name posted on the hall bulletin board

Get one funny animal eraser

Draw a picture on the blackboard that the teacher leaves up all day

---

Children can also be identified by buttons they pin to their clothes or colored shirts. One teacher bought 15 large red T-shirts and 15 large blue T-shirts. At the beginning of each school day, students drew a shirt from a bag and wore it over their clothes. At the end of each day, one student took the shirts home, washed and dried them, and brought them back to class the next day. Make sure that you collect the ribbons or other team markers at the end of the day.

Each day call timeout for behaviors posted on the list in your classroom. When you call timeout for a child, put a chip of the same color as his ribbon in the jar. Place the jar high up where all the children can see it throughout the day.

At the end of the day, count up the chips in the jar in front of the entire class. The team with the fewest chips in the jar is the winner. Compliment the winning team, but do not discuss the reasons for timeouts with the losing team. Encourage good sportsmanship by the winning and losing teams. One way to do this is by having the winners and losers line up and shake hands with everyone on the other team, just the way sports teams do after a game.

Each member of the team that has won the good-behavior game gets at least two choices from the reward menu. Give the child the reward (e.g., a chocolate-chip cookie) or an "IOU" describing the reward (e.g., a 7:00 p.m. congratulatory phone call to the student's parents). On the IOU, describe when the reward is available (e.g., 1/2 hour on the classroom computer, from 8:00 to 8:30 a.m.). Allow children to hold on to their IOU's and cash them in when they choose.

Have the winning team members make their two menu choices right away. If the team had no chips in the jar, give each member a third menu choice. When there is a tie, give both teams menu choices if neither team had more than one chip in the jar. Follow this procedure every school day and add to the menu as often as possible.

When you want to focus on specific desirable behaviors such as happiness, attentiveness, cooperation, sharing, or quiet voices, pick one desirable behavior (e.g., attentiveness) to work on. The behavior you choose might be a problem for one child in the class or for many children. List the opposite of the desirable behavior (e.g., inattentiveness) at the top of your posted list of behaviors that earn timeout. Explain to the children and demonstrate for them one time inattentiveness and attentiveness. Do not single out children who have problems with the target behavior. Give all children a chance to demonstrate how they act when they are inattentive and attentive. Tell them that you will be giving timeouts for inattentiveness and praising attentiveness whenever you see it. Continue focusing on attentiveness until this has become a habit for all your students. Then move on to another target behavior.

If children ever seem apathetic about being on the winning team, rethink your reward menu—it probably is not very exciting. If children can already get most of the choices on your menu either at school or at home without being on the winning team, they won't work hard to win.

∞∞∞

1. What is the purpose of the good-behavior game?
2. How will you prepare for the good-behavior game?
3. How will you concentrate on a specific behavior with the good-behavior game?
4. What will you do if your students seem apathetic about being on the winning team?

Mrs. Baker teaches a self-contained class of 5 special-education students. Each of the children has unique behavior problems. One child is withdrawn and rarely talks, two children are overly active and talkative, and two children demand the teacher's constant attention by clinging and whining. Describe how Mrs. Baker could use the good-behavior game in her classroom. What behaviors do you think should earn timeout in her classroom? Which of these behaviors should she focus on first to give her more time to spend with the entire class?

∞∞∞∞

13. Ignoring and Praising

After you have mastered timeouts and the good-behavior game, begin to improve the way you use attention to strengthen children's behavior. Any behavior to which you attend (in either a positive or negative manner) will be more likely in the future. You will have reinforced this target behavior. Most people have problems with using their attention selectively. Some guidelines follow that you can use to improve your use of attention.

When inappropriate behaviors are consistently ignored, they become weaker. When inappropriate behaviors are sometimes ignored and sometimes rewarded with attention (either positive or negative), they grow stronger. If you know that a certain behavior will be impossible for you or the children to ignore, call timeout. If you know that you can consistently ignore a behavior and the children probably won't comment on the behavior, ignore it. Behaviors you may be able to ignore include: whining; complaining; personal questions; negative talk about self or others; attempts to talk out of turn; and rude, insulting, or bizarre remarks.

Ignoring involves not talking or responding to in any way a child who is engaged in inappropriate or undesirable behavior. For example, Patrick is talking out of turn. Mr. Smith says: "Patrick, I'm ignoring you because you're talking out of turn." Mr. Smith is paying attention to, not ignoring, Patrick's talking out of turn. If Mr. Smith never called on or looked at Patrick when the boy talked out of turn, Mr. Smith would, in effect, be ignoring Patrick.

It is not a good idea to switch from ignoring to timeout in midstream. If you begin ignoring quiet but rude remarks, keep ignoring them until the child engages in some other more appropriate behavior, then pay attention.

Call timeout whenever a child's inappropriate behavior will capture someone's attention. Do not ask classmates to ignore one another's inappropriate behavior; that practice merely calls attention to the undesirable behavior. It is often hard to ignore mischievous behavior, which stirs up all sorts of emotions in us—humor, anger, even fear. It is also hard to notice and praise happy and cooperative behavior, since these are quiet and cause no one any problems. Such behavior is often taken for granted. Teachers who consistently ignore good behavior train children to be unhappy and uncooperative.

Praise desirable behavior when it happens; let children know what they have done that has earned your appreciation. You could say, for example, "Rita, your smile makes me feel very good. You look very happy" or "I'm proud of you, Tim. You've been working quietly on your own for 30 minutes." Make sure your praise is descriptive of what you like, that it is honest, and that it is not exaggerated. The statement "That is a very complicated design you've drawn" said in a warm tone of voice is more effective than "That is fantastic" said in a sarcastic manner.

∞∞∞

1. Why is it that attention, positive or negative, makes the target behavior more likely in the future? What are some examples of this principle from your classroom?
2. Why is it so hard to ignore mischievous behavior and to notice and praise cooperative behavior?
3. What are some behaviors that you frequently see and believe you could consistently ignore?
4. What is a classroom situation in which it would be better to call timeout than to ignore undesirable behavior?
5. When should you praise students?

> Tom has been sitting quietly at his desk, doing his math assignment. This is unusual for Tom, since he frequently wanders around the room when given an independent math assignment. How could Tom's teacher praise Tom descriptively? What sarcastic praise should Tom's teacher avoid? Why?

∞∞∞

14. Communicating with Parents about Children's Behavior

Once you have put in place timeouts and the good-behavior game, you will have no need to contact parents about children's inappropriate behavior. The only time you will need to contact parents is to notify them about their children's good behavior, via good-news notes. When parents are only notified about their children's good behavior, children feel better about school, and the relationship between parents and children improves. Parents are frequently frustrated when teachers contact them about children's inappropriate behavior, since they rarely know how to remedy the school problem.

∞∞∞

1. How will you contact parents about children's appropriate behavior?
2. How do parents and children benefit when parents are only notified about their children's good behavior?
3. Why are parents frequently frustrated when teachers contact them about children's inappropriate behavior?

∞∞∞

15. Assertiveness, Apologies, Restitution, and Good Manners

Once timeout and the good-behavior game are working well, you can focus on finer aspects of children's school behavior. Provide a good example of assertive, well-mannered, thoughtful, and kind behavior. Provide an example of assertiveness by getting used to saying no without being angry at the person you are refusing and saying no without giving any explanation. Effective assertiveness involves knowing how to satisfy your needs in a way that considers other people. Unassertive people take care of other people's needs, not their own. Aggressive people satisfy their needs at the expense of other people. Teachers who don't know how to say no to children or who say no too often and too aggressively have social-skill deficits that should be remedied before they focus attention on the problems of their students. Teachers who are overly concerned about their students liking them and are therefore unwilling to set limits, as well as teachers who don't care about children's feelings, may need to reexamine their relationships with family, friends, and co-workers before focusing on the problems of their students. If students and adults frequently take advantage of you or if you often get your way by intimidating children, you would benefit from assertiveness training. There are a number of self-help guides to assertiveness available.

Teach children to apologize assertively by apologizing when you believe you are in error but only then. Expect children to apologize when they have hurt someone and to make restitution for damages they do to other people's property. Guide children through the process of apology and restitution. They often don't know how to go about these acts. Compliment them when they've followed through completely.

Provide an example of good manners by using the words *please* and *thank you* when you really mean these words. Do not preface routine instructions with the word *please*. Save this word for optional, nonmandatory requests.

∞∞∞

1. Why do some adults have a hard time saying no to children?
2. Do good teachers need children to like them all the time? Why is this impossible?
3. What kinds of problems could occur in classrooms of unassertive and overly aggressive teachers?
4. We all could be more effectively assertive. In what situations could your assertiveness be improved? What steps could you take to become more assertive?

∞∞∞

16. What to Do When Good Behavior and Happiness Do Not Increase

The school behavior and the mood of unhappy children usually improve from classroom management of the sort encouraged in this module. If there is a decrease in good or happy days, however, you may need to determine if this, or the previous School-Problem Module, is the source of trouble. You could establish this by briefly discontinuing the module's procedures. If the frequency of positive interactions rises again to baseline level, change in the method of using the School-Problem Module may be necessary. For example, problems may arise if the procedures are not being implemented according to instructions or if the procedures or the child's behavior is being discussed in front of the child's classmates.

A child's unhappy behavior may not decrease substantially if the source of the unhappiness is outside of the classroom environment. Stronger intervention may need to be taken by using the Home-Problem Modules 12 and 13, which deal with the problems of loneliness, unhappiness, fearfulness, self-injury, swearing, lying, cheating, stealing, fire setting, and violence. These modules could be implemented by parents at home, or, in the case of parents who will not become involved, could be modified for classroom use.

∞∞∞

1. How can you determine if intervention is decreasing a child's good behavior or happiness? What should you do if this is the case?
2. What can you do if the source of a child's unhappiness is outside of the school environment?

∞∞∞

17. Returning to the Beginning of This Module

The procedures described in this module, including maintenance of the assessment chart, are designed to be used throughout the school year. The procedures are designed to bring about short- and long-term improvements in school behavior. If the procedures are abandoned as soon as short-term progress is evident, there is no reason to expect miraculous long-term gains. If you start using the procedures described in this module and then stop, if you think you aren't using the procedures correctly, or if you aren't consistently using the procedures, return to the beginning of this module.

∞∞∞

1. When is it a good idea to begin Module 4 again?

∞∞∞

Answer these questions after you have begun using timeout
1. What behaviors will earn timeout in your classroom?
2. What area are you using in your classroom for timeout? Are there any problems with this area?
3. What area are you using for back-up timeouts? Are there any problems with this area or the back-up timeout supervisor?
4. How will you solve your problem (if any) with timeout?
5. Were there any problems when you explained timeout to your students? Looking back, how could you have simplified or improved upon your presentation?

Answer these questions after you have begun using the good-behavior game
1. How are you using the good-behavior game in your classroom?
2. What reward menu have you worked out with your students?
3. Will you use the good-behavior game to encourage specific, positive behavior? Why have you selected this positive goal? Will it benefit just one child or many? After you've succeeded with this positive goal, what will be your next goal?
4. What problems have you encountered in the use of the good-behavior game and how could you solve these problems?

Bibliography

Chapter 1

Achenbach, T. M., & Edelbrock, C. S. (1981). Behavioral problems and competencies reported by parents of normal and disturbed children aged four through sixteen. *Monographs of the Society for Research in Child Development, 46* (1, Serial No. 188).

Addison, R. M., & Homme, L. E. (1966). The reinforcing event (RE) menu. *Journal of the National Society for Programmed Instruction, 5,* 8-9.

Alexander, J. F., & Parsons, B. (1973). Short-term behavioral intervention with delinquent families: Impact on family process and recidivism. *Journal of Abnormal Psychology, 81,* 219-225.

Association for Advancement of Behavior Therapy. (1974). The domain of behavior therapy. *Association for Advancement of Behavior Therapy Newsletter, 1,* 7.

Baer, D. M., & Wolf, M. M. (1970). The entry into natural communities of reinforcement. In R. Ulrich, T. Stachnik, & J. Mabry (Eds.), *Control of human behavior* (Vol. 2, pp. 319-324). Glenview, IL: Scott, Foresman & Co.

Bandura, A. (1969). *Principles of behavior modification.* New York: Holt, Rinehart & Winston.

Bandura, A. (1976). *Social learning theory.* Englewood Cliffs, NJ: Prentice-Hall.

Bandura, A., & Walters, R. H. (1963). *Social learning and personality development.* New York: Holt, Rinehart & Winston.

Baum, C. G., & Forehand, R. (1981). Long term follow-up assessment of parent training by use of multiple outcome measures. *Behavior Therapy, 12,* 643-652.

Bernal, M. E., Duryee, J. S., Pruett, H. L., & Burns, B. (1970). Behavior modification and the brat syndrome. In R. Ulrich, T. Stachnik, & J. Mabry (Eds.), *Control of human behavior* (Vol. 2, pp. 161-170). Glenview, IL: Scott, Foresman & Co.

Bernal, M. E., Klinnert, M. D., & Schultz, L. A. (1980). Outcome evaluation of behavioral parent training and client-centered parent counseling for children with conduct problems. *Journal of Applied Behavior Analysis, 13,* 677-691.

Bijou, S. W. (1984). Parent training: Actualizing the critical conditions of early childhood development. In R. F. Dangel & R. A. Polster (Eds.), *Parent training: Foundations of research and practice* (pp. 15-26). New York: Guilford Press.

Bijou, S. W., & Baer, D. M. (1961). *Child development: Vol. 1. A systematic and empirical theory.* New York: Appleton-Century-Crofts.

Bijou, S. W., & Baer, D. M. (1965). *Child development: Vol. 2. Universal stage of infancy.* New York: Appleton-Century-Crofts.

Bijou, S. W., & Baer, D. M. (1978). *Behavior analysis of child development.* Englewood Cliffs, NJ: Prentice-Hall.

Blechman, E. A. (1977). Objectives and procedures believed necessary for the success of a contractual approach to family intervention. *Behavior Therapy, 8,* 275-277.

Blechman, E. A. (1981). Toward comprehensive behavioral family intervention: An algorithm for matching families and interventions. *Behavior Modification, 5,* 221-236.

Blechman, E. A., Budd, K. S., Christopherson, E. R., Szykula, S., Wahler, R., Embry, L. H., Kogan, K., O'Leary, K. D., & Riner, L. S. (1981). Engagement in Behavioral Family Therapy: A multi-site investigation. *Behavior Therapy, 12,* 461-472.

Bousha, D. M., & Twentyman, C. T. (1984). Mother-child interactional style in abuse, neglect and control groups: Naturalistic observations in the home. *Journal of Abnormal Psychology, 93,* 106-114.

Bronfenbrenner, U. (1977). Toward an experimental ecology of human development. *American Psychologist, 32,* 513-531.

Budd, K. S., Leibowitz, J M., Riner, L. S., Mindell, C., & Goldfarb, A. L. (1981). Home-based treatment of severe disruptive behaviors. *Behavior Modification, 5,* 273-298.

Christensen, A., Johnson, S. M., Phillips, S., & Glasgow, R. E. (1980). Cost effectiveness in behavioral family therapy. *Behavior Therapy, 11,* 208-226.

Christopherson, E. R., Barnard, J. D., Ford, D., & Wolf, M. M. (1976). The family training program: Improving parent-child interaction patterns. In E. J. Mash, L. C. Handy, & L. A. Hamerlynck (Eds.), *Behavior modification approaches to parenting* (pp. 36-56). New York: Brunner/Mazel.

Conway, J. B., & Bucher, B. D. (1976). Transfer and maintenance of behavior change in children: A review and suggestions. In E. J. Mash, L. A. Hamerlynck, & L. C. Handy (Eds.), *Behavior modification and families* (pp. 119-159). New York: Brunner/Mazel.

Cowen, R. J., Jones, F. H., & Bellack, A. S. (1979). Grandma's Rule with group contingencies: A cost-efficient means of classroom management. *Behavior Modification, 3,* 397-418.

Dangel, R. F., & Polster, R. A. (1984). *Parent training: Foundations of research and practice.* New York: Guilford Press.

D'Zurilla, T. J., & Goldfried, M. R. (1971). Problem solving and behavior modification. *Journal of Abnormal Psychology, 78,* 107-126.

Egeland, B., Breitenbucher, M., & Rosenberg, D. (1980). Prospective study of the significance of life stress in the etiology of child abuse. *Journal of Consulting and Clinical Psychology, 48,* 195-205.

Eyberg, S. M., & Johnson, S. M. (1974). Multiple assessment of behavior modification with families: Effects of contingency contracting and order of treated problems. *Journal of Consulting and Clinical Psychology, 42,* 594-606.

Eyberg, S. M., & Robinson, E. A. (1982). Parent-child interaction training: Effects on family functioning. *Journal of Clinical Child Psychology, 11,* 130-137.

Fleischman, M. J., & Szykula, S. A. (1981). A community setting replication of a social learning treatment for aggressive children. *Behavior Therapy, 12,* 115-122.

Forehand, R., & Atkeson, B. M. (1977). Generality of treatment effects with parents as therapists: A review of assessment and implementation procedures. *Behavior Therapy, 8,* 575-593.

French, J. R. P., Jr., & Raven, B. (1968). The bases of social power. In D. Cartwright & A. Zander (Eds.), *Group dynamics: Research and theory* (pp. 256-269). New York: Harper & Row.

Gardner, R. A. (1970). *The boys' and girls' book about divorce.* New York: Bantam.

Gardner, R. A. (1979). *The parents' book about divorce.* New York: Bantam.

Gelfand, D. M., & Hartmann, D. P. (1975). *Child behavior analysis and therapy.* New York: Pergamon.

Ginott, H. G. (1965). *Between parent and child: New solutions to old problems.* New York: Avon.

Griest, D. L., & Wells, K. C. (1983). Behavioral family therapy with conduct disorders in children. *Behavior Therapy, 14,* 37-53.

Harris, S. L. (1982). A family systems approach to behavioral training with parents of autistic children. *Child and Family Behavior Therapy, 4,* 21-35.

Hawkins, R. P. (1972). It's time we taught the young how to be good parents (and don't we wish we'd started a long time ago!). *Psychology Today, 6,* 28-35.

Hawkins, R. P., Peterson, R. F., Schweid, E., & Bijou, S. W. (1970). Behavior therapy in the home: Amelioration of problem parent-child relations with the parent in a therapeutic role. In R. Ulrich, T. Stachnik, & J. Mabry (Eds.), *Control of human behavior* (Vol. 2, pp. 232-236). Glenview, IL: Scott, Foresman & Co.

Homme, L. E., deBoca, P. C., Devine, J. V., Steinhorst, R., & Rickert, E. J. (1963). Use of the Premack principle in controlling the behavior of nursery school children. *Journal of the Experimental Analysis of Behavior, 6,* 544.

Horne, A. M., & Van Dyke, B. (1983). Treatment and maintenance of social learning family therapy. *Behavior Therapy, 14,* 606-613.

Kanfer, F. H., & Phillips, J. S. (1970). *The learning foundations of behavior therapy.* New York: John Wiley & Sons.

Kelly, J. A. (1983). *Treating child-abuse families: Intervention based on skills-training principles.* New York: Plenum.

O'Dell, S. (1974). Training parents in behavior modification: A review. *Psychological Bulletin, 81,* 418-433.

O'Leary, K. D. (1980). Pills or skills for hyperactive children. *Journal of Applied Behavior Analysis, 13,* 191-204.

Parsons, B. V., & Alexander, J. F. (1973). Short-term family intervention: A therapy outcome study. *Journal of Consulting and Clinical Psychology, 41,* 195-201.

Patterson, G. R. (1974). Intervention for boys with conduct problems: Multiple settings, treatments and criteria. *Journal of Consulting and Clinical Psychology, 42,* 471-481.

Patterson, G. R. (1975). *Families: Applications of social learning to family life* (rev. ed.). Champaign, IL: Research Press.

Patterson, G. R. (1976). *Living with children: New methods for parents and teachers* (rev. ed.). Champaign, IL: Research Press.

Patterson, G. R. (1982). *A social learning approach: Vol. 3. Coercive family process.* Eugene, OR: Castalia.

Premack, D. (1965). Reinforcement theory. In D. Levine (Ed.), *Nebraska Symposium on Motivation* (pp. 123-180). Lincoln: University of Nebraska Press.

Ross, A. O. (1981). *Child behavior therapy: Principles, procedures, and empirical basis.* New York: John Wiley & Sons.

Tavormina, J. B. (1974). Basic models of parent counselling: A critical review. *Psychological Bulletin, 81,* 827-835.

Tharp, R. G., & Wetzel, R. J. (1969). *Behavior modification in the natural environment.* New York: Academic Press.

Wahler, R. G., Winkel, G. H., Peterson, R. F., & Morrison, D. C. (1965). Mothers as behavior therapists for their own children. *Behaviour Research and Therapy, 3,* 113-124.

Wolfe, D. A., Sandler, J., & Kaufman, K. (1981). A competency-based parent training program for child abusers. *Journal of Consulting and Clinical Psychology, 49,* 633-640.

Chapter 2

Azrin, N. H., Sneed, T. J., & Foxx, R. M. (1974). Dry-bed training: Rapid elimination of childhood enuresis. *Behaviour Research and Therapy, 12,* 147-156.

Baldwin, A. L., Cole, R. E., & Baldwin, C. P. (Eds.). (1982). Parental pathology, family interaction, and the competence of the child in school. *Monographs of the Society for Research in Child Development, 47* (5, Serial No. 197).

Bandura, A. (1977). Self-efficacy: Toward a unifying theory of behavioral change. *Psychological Review, 84,* 191-215.

Bandura, A., Ross, D., & Ross, S. (1961). Transmission of aggression through imitation of aggressive models. *Journal of Abnormal and Social Psychology, 63,* 575-582.

Bandura, A., & Walters, R. H. (1963). *The social learning of deviant behavior: A behavioristic approach to socialization.* New York: Holt, Rinehart & Winston.

Bane, M. J. (1976). *Here to stay: American families in the twentieth century.* New York: Basic Books.

Bane, M. J. (1976). Marital disruption and the lives of children. *Journal of Social Issues, 32*, 103-117.

Baumrind, D. (1973). The development of instrumental competence through socialization. In A. Pick (Ed.), *Minnesota symposia on child psychology* (pp. 3-46). Minneapolis: University of Minnesota Press.

Baumrind, D. (1978). Parental disciplinary patterns and social competence in children. *Youth & Society, 9*, 239-276.

Blechman, E. A. (1981). Competence, depression and behavior modification with women. In M. Hersen (Ed.), *Progress in behavior modification* (Vol. 12, pp. 227-264). New York: Academic Press.

Blechman, E. A. (1982). Are children with one parent at psychological risk? A methodological review. *Journal of Marriage and the Family, 44*, 179-195.

Blechman, E. A. (1984). Competent parents, competent children: Behavioral objectives of parent training. In R. F. Dangel & R. A. Polster (Eds.), *Behavioral parent training: Issues in research and practice* (pp. 34-66). New York: Guilford Press.

Blechman, E. A., Berberian, R. M., & Thompson, W. D. (1977). How well does number of parents explain unique variance in self-reported drug use? *Journal of Consulting and Clinical Psychology, 45*, 1182-1183.

Blechman, E. A., & Manning, M. (1976). A reward-cost analysis of the single-parent family. In E. J. Mash, L. A. Hamerlynck, & L. C. Handy (Eds.), *Behavior modification and families* (pp. 61-90). New York: Brunner/Mazel.

Blechman, E. A., & McEnroe, M. J. (1985). Effective family problem solving. *Child Development, 56*, 429-437.

Blechman, E. A., & Rabin, C. (1982). Concepts and methods of explicit marital negotiation training with the Marriage Contract Game. *The American Journal of Family Therapy, 10*, 47-55.

Blechman, E. A., Rabin, C., & McEnroe, M. J. (in press). Family communication with board and computer games. In C. E. Schaefer & S. Reid (Eds.), *Game play: Therapeutic uses of childhood games.* New York: John Wiley & Sons.

Blechman, E. A., Tinsley, B., Carella, E. T., & McEnroe, M. J. (1985). Childhood competence and behavior problems. *Journal of Abnormal Psychology, 94*, 70-77.

Bond, C. R., & McMahon, R. J. (1984). Relationships between marital distress, child behavior problems, maternal personal adjustment, maternal personality, and maternal parenting behaviors. *Journal of Abnormal Psychology, 93*, 348-351.

Bott, E. (1971). *Family and social network.* New York: Free Press.

Bould, A. (1977). Female-headed families: Personal fate control and the provider role. *Journal of Marriage and the Family, 39*, 339-349.

Bradley, R. H., & Caldwell, B. M. (1980). The relation of home environments, cognitive competence, and IQ among males and females. *Child Development, 51*, 1140-1148.

Brandwein, R. A., Braun, C. A., & Fox, F. M. (1974). Women and children last: The social situation of divorced mothers and their families. *Journal of Marriage and the Family, 36*, 498-515.

Bronfenbrenner, U. (1960). Freudian theories of identification and their derivatives. *Child Development, 31,* 15-40.

Bronfenbrenner, U. (1979). Contexts of child rearing: Problems and prospects. *American Psychologist, 34,* 844-850.

Carpenter, C. J., & Huston-Stein, A. (1980). Activity structure and sex-typed behavior in preschool children. *Child Development, 51,* 862-872.

Cochran, M. M., & Brassard, J. A. (1979). Child development and personal social networks. *Child Development, 50,* 601-616.

Coopersmith, S. (1967). *The antecedents of self-esteem.* San Francisco: Freeman, Cooper & Co.

Crnic, K. A., Greenberg, M. T., Ragozin, A. J., Robinson, N. M., & Basham, R. B. (1983). Effects of stress and social support on mothers and premature and full-term infants. *Child Development, 54,* 209-217.

Dumas, J. E., & Wahler, R. G. (1983). Predictors of treatment outcome in patient training: Mother insularity and socioeconomic disadvantage. *Behavioral Assessment, 5,* 301-313.

Eiduson, B. T. (1983). Conflict and stress in nontraditional families: Impact on children. *American Journal of Orthopsychiatry, 53,* 426-435.

Emery, R. E. (1982). Interparental conflict and the children of discord and divorce. *Psychological Bulletin, 92,* 310-330.

Emery, R. E., & O'Leary, K. D. (1984). Marital discord and child behavior problems in a nonclinic sample. *Journal of Abnormal Child Psychology, 12,* 411-420.

Emery, R. E., & O'Leary, S. G. (1982). Children's perceptions of marital discord and behavior problems of boys and girls. *Journal of Abnormal Child Psychology, 10,* 11-24.

Emery, R. E., Weintraub, S., & Neale, J. J. (1982). Effects of marital discord on the school behavior of children with schizophrenic, affectively disordered, and normal parents. *Journal of Abnormal Child Psychology, 10,* 215-228.

Forehand, R., Griest, D. L., Wells, K., & McMahon, R. J. (1982). Side effects of parent counseling on marital satisfaction. *Journal of Counseling Psychology, 29,* 104-107.

Foster, S. L., & Ritchey, W. L. (1979). Issues in the assessment of social competence in children. *Journal of Applied Behavior Analysis, 81,* 827-835.

Gewirtz, J. L., & Stingle, K. G. (1968). Learning of generalized imitation as the basis for identification. *Psychological Review, 75,* 374-397.

Griest, D. L., Wells, K. D., & Forehand, R. (1979). An examination of predictors of maternal perceptions of maladjustment in clinic-referred children. *Journal of Abnormal Psychology, 88,* 277-281.

Hargis, K. R., & Blechman, E. A. (1979). Social class and training of parents as behavior change agents. *Child Behavior Therapy, 1,* 69-74.

Harter, S. (1981). A new self-report scale of intrinsic versus extrinsic orientation in the classroom: Motivational and informational components. *Developmental Psychology, 17,* 300-312.

Hetherington, E. M., Cox, M., & Cox, R. (1981). Effects of divorce on parents and children. In M. Lamb (Ed.), *Nontraditional families* (pp. 233-288). Hillsdale, NJ: Lawrence Erlbaum Associates.

Hirsch, B. J. (1980). Natural support systems and coping with life changes. *American Journal of Community Psychology, 8,* 159-172.

Hoffman, L. W. (1961). Effects of maternal employment on the child. *Child Development, 32,* 187-197.

Hoffman, L. W. (1979). Maternal employment: 1979. *American Psychologist, 34,* 859-865.

Hoffman, L. W., & Nye, F. I. (1974). *Working mothers.* San Francisco: Jossey-Bass.

Holahan, C. J., & Maas, R. H. (1981). Social support and psychological distress: A longitudinal analysis. *Journal of Abnormal Psychology, 90,* 365-370.

Holmstrom, L. L. (1972). *The two-career family.* Cambridge, MA: Schenkman.

Hops, H. (1983). Children's social competence and skill: Current research practices and future directions. *Behavior Therapy, 14,* 3-18.

Horowitz, F. D. (1976). Directions for parenting. In E. J. Mash, L. A. Hamerlynck, & L. C. Handy (Eds.), *Behavior modification and families* (pp. 7-33). New York: Brunner/Mazel.

Mash, E. J., & Johnson, C. (1983). Parental perceptions of child behavior problems, parenting self-esteem, and mothers' reported stress in younger and older hyperactive and normal children. *Journal of Consulting and Clinical Psychology, 51,* 86-99.

McLean, P. D. (1976). Parental depression: Incompatible with effective parenting. In E. J. Mash, L. C. Handy, & L. A. Hamerlynck (Eds.), *Behavior modification approaches to parenting* (pp. 209-220). New York: Brunner/Mazel.

Oltmanns, T., Broderick, J., & O'Leary, K. D. (1977). Marital adjustment and the efficacy of behavior therapy with children. *Journal of Consulting and Clinical Psychology, 45,* 724-729.

Rabin, C., Blechman, E. A., Kahn, D., & Carel, C. (1985). Refocusing from child to marital problems using the Marriage Contract Game. *Journal of Marital and Family Therapy, 11,* 75-85.

Rabin, C., Blechman, E. A., & Milton, M. C. (1984). A multiple baseline study of the Marriage Contract Game's effects on problem solving and affective behavior. *Child and Family Behavior Therapy, 6,* 45-60.

Rickard, K. M., Forehand, R., Atkeson, B. M., & Lopez, C. (1982). An examination of the relationship of marital satisfaction and divorce with parent-child interactions. *Journal of Clinical Child Psychology, 11,* 61-65.

Risley, T. R., Clark, H. B., & Cataldo, M. F. (1976). Behavioral technology for the normal middle-class family. In E. J. Mash, L. A. Hamerlynck, & L. C. Handy (Eds.), *Behavior modification and families* (pp. 34-60). New York: Brunner/Mazel.

Ross, D. M., & Ross, S. A. (1976). *Hyperactivity: Research, theory, and action.* New York: John Wiley & Sons.

Ross, H. L., & Sawhill, I. V. (1975). *Time of transition: The growth of families headed by women.* Washington, DC: The Urban Institute Press.

Sears, R. R., Maccoby, E. E., & Levin, H. (1957). *Patterns of child rearing*. New York: Harper & Row.

Stuckey, M., McGhee, P. E., & Bell, N. J. (1982). Parent-child interaction: The influence of maternal employment. *Developmental Psychology, 18*, 635-644.

Van Houten, R. (1979). Social validation: The evolution of standards of competency for target behaviors. *Journal of Applied Behavior Analysis, 12*, 581-591.

Wahler, R. G. (1980). The insular mother: Her problems in parent-child treatment. *Journal of Applied Behavior Analysis, 13*, 207-219.

Werner, E. E., & Smith, R. S. (1981). *Vulnerable but invincible: A longitudinal study of resilient children and youth*. New York: McGraw-Hill.

Chapter 3

Aldous, J., Condon, T., Hill, R., Straus, M., & Tallman, I. (Eds.). (1971). *Family problem solving: A symposium on theoretical, methodological, and substantive concerns*. Hinsdale, IL: The Dryden Press.

Alexander, J. F. (1973). Defensive and supportive communications in normal and deviant families. *Journal of Consulting and Clinical Psychology, 40*, 223-231.

Aragona, J. A., & Eyberg, S. M. (1981). Neglected children: Mothers' report of child behavior problems and observed verbal behavior. *Child Development, 52*, 596-602.

Association for Advancement of Behavior Therapy. (1977). Ethical issues for human services. In *Professional consultation and peer review services*. New York: Author.

Bizer, L. (1978). *Generality of treatment effects in single parent-child problem solving*. Unpublished doctoral dissertation, University of Massachusetts, Amherst.

Blechman, E. A. (July, 1974). The family contract game: A tool to teach interpersonal problem solving. *Family Coordinator*, pp. 269-281.

Blechman, E. A. (1974). A new way to teach contracting: The Family Contract Game. *Psychotherapy, 11*, 294.

Blechman, E. A. (1977). Objectives and procedures believed necessary for the success of a contractual approach to family intervention. *Behavior Therapy, 8*, 275-277.

Blechman, E. A. (1980). Family problem-solving training. *The American Journal of Family Therapy, 8*, 3-22.

Blechman, E. A., & Olson, D. H. L. (1976). The Family Contract Game: Description and effectiveness. In D. H. L. Olson (Ed.), *Treating relationships* (pp. 133-150). Lake Mills, IA: Graphic Publishing.

Blechman, E. A., Olson, D. H. L., & Hellman, I. D. (1976). Stimulus control over family problem-solving behavior. *Behavior Therapy, 7*, 686-692.

Blechman, E. A., Olson, D. H. L., Schornagel, C. Y., Halsdorf, M., & Turner, A. J. (1976). The Family Contract Game: Technique and case study. *Journal of Consulting and Clinical Psychology, 44*, 449-455.

Blechman, E. A., Taylor, C. J., & Schrader, S. M. (1981). Family problem solving vs. home notes as early intervention with high-risk children. *Journal of Consulting and Clinical Psychology, 49*, 919-926.

Christensen, A., Phillips, S., Glasgow, R. E., & Johnson, S. M. (1983). Parental characteristics and interactional dysfunction in families with child behavior problems: A preliminary investigation. *Journal of Abnormal Child Psychology, 11,* 153-166.

Hess, R. D., & Shipman, V. C. (1965). Early experience and the socialization of cognitive modes in children. *Child Development, 36,* 869-886.

Jurkovic, G. J., & Prentice, N. M. (1974). Dimensions of moral interaction and moral judgment in delinquent and nondelinquent families. *Journal of Consulting and Clinical Psychology, 42,* 256-262.

Kifer, R. E., Lewis, M. A., Green, D. R., & Phillips, E. L. (1974). Training pre-delinquent youths and their parents to negotiate conflict situations. *Journal of Applied Behavior Analysis, 7,* 357-364.

Patterson, G. R. (1976). The aggressive child: Victim and architect of a coercive system. In E. J. Mash, L. A. Hamerlynck, & L. C. Handy (Eds.), *Behavior modification and families* (pp. 267-316). New York: Brunner/Mazel.

Robin, A. L., Kent, R., O'Leary, K. D., Foster, S., & Prinz, R. (1977). An approach to teaching parents and adolescents problem-solving communication skills: A preliminary report. *Behavior Therapy, 8,* 639-643.

Shure, M. B., & Spivack, G. (1978). *Problem-solving techniques in childrearing.* San Francisco: Jossey-Bass.

Spivack, G., & Shure, M. B. (1974). *Social adjustment of young children: A cognitive approach to solving real-life problems.* San Francisco: Jossey-Bass.

Straus, M. A. (1983). Ordinary violence, child abuse, and wife-beating: What do they have in common? In D. Finkelhor, R. J. Gelles, G. T. Hotaling, & M. A. Straus (Eds.), *The dark side of families: Current family violence research* (pp. 213-234). Beverly Hills, CA: Sage Publications.

Tallman, I. (1970). The family as a small problem solving group. *Journal of Marriage and the Family, 32,* 94-104.

Turner, J. H. (1970). *Family interaction.* New York: John Wiley & Sons.

Urbain, E. S., & Kendall, P. C. (1980). Review of social-cognitive problem-solving interventions with children. *Psychological Bulletin, 88,* 109-143.

Weathers, L., & Liberman, R. P. (1975). The family contracting exercise. *Journal of Behavior Therapy and Experimental Psychiatry, 6,* 208-214.

Chapter 4

Achenbach, T. M., & Edelbrock, C. S. (1981). Behavioral problems and competencies reported by parents of normal and disturbed children aged four through sixteen. *Monographs of the Society for Research in Child Development, 46* (1, Serial No. 188).

Achenbach, T. M., & Edelbrock, C. S. (1983). *Manual for the Child Behavior Checklist and Revised Child Behavior Profile.* (Available from University Associates in Psychiatry, 1 South Prospect St., Burlington, VT 05401.)

Addison, R. M., & Homme, L. E. (1966). The reinforcing event (RE) menu. *Journal of the National Society for Programmed Instruction, 5,* 8-9.

278   Bibliography

Baer, D. M., Wolf, M. M., & Risley, T. R. (1968). Some current dimensions of applied behavior analysis. *Journal of Applied Behavior Analysis, 1*, 91–97.

Barlow, D. H., Hayes, S. C., Nelson, R. O. (1985). *The scientist practitioner: Research and accountability in clinical and educational settings.* New York: Pergamon.

Beneke, W. M., & Harris, M. B. (1972). Teaching self-control of study behavior. *Behavior Research and Therapy, 10*, 35–41.

Blechman, E. A. (1979). Short- and long-term results of positive home-based treatment of childhood chronic constipation and encopresis. *Child Behavior Therapy, 1*, 237–247.

Clark, H. B., Greene, B. F., Macrae, J. W., McNees, M. P., Davis, J. L., & Risley, T. R. (1977). A parent advice package for family shopping trips: Development and evaluation. *Journal of Applied Behavior Analysis, 10*, 605–624.

Corte, H. E., Wolf, M. M., & Locke, B. J. (1971). A comparison of procedures for eliminating self-injurious behavior of retarded adolescents. *Journal of Applied Behavior Analysis, 4*, 201–213.

Doles, D. M., Wells, K. C., Hobbs, S. A., Roberts, M. W., & Cartelli, L. M. (1976). The effects of social punishment on noncompliance: A comparison with timeout and positive practice. *Journal of Applied Behavior Analysis, 9*, 471–482.

Dweck, C. S., Davidson, W., Nelson, S., & Enna, B. (1978). Sex differences in learned helplessness: II. The contingencies of evaluative feedback in the classroom and III. An experimental analysis. *Developmental Psychology, 14*, 268–276.

Ericksen, J. A., Yancey, W. L., & Ericksen, E. P. (1979). The division of family roles. *Journal of Marriage and the Family, 41*, 301–313.

Flanagan, S., Adams, H. E., & Forehand, R. (1979). A comparison of four instructional techniques for teaching parents to use time out. *Behavior Therapy, 10*, 94–102.

Forehand, R. (1977). Child noncompliance to parental requests: Behavioral analysis and treatment. In M. Hersen, R. M. Eisler, & P. M. Miller (Eds.), *Progress in behavior modification* (Vol. 5, pp. 111–148). New York: Academic Press.

Foxx, R. M., & Shapiro, S. T. (1978). The timeout ribbon: A nonexclusionary timeout procedure. *Journal of Applied Behavior Analysis, 11*, 125–136.

Gelfand, D. M., & Hartmann, D. P. (1975). *Child behavior analysis and therapy.* New York: Pergamon.

Geller, E. S., Casali, J. G., & Johnson, R. P. (1980). Seat belt usage: A potential target for applied behavior analysis. *Journal of Applied Behavior Analysis, 13*, 669–675.

Giebenhain, J. E., & O'Dell, S. (1984). Evaluation of a parent-training manual for reducing children's fear of the dark. *Journal of Applied Behavior Analysis, 17*, 121–125.

Graziano, A. M., & Mooney, K. C. (1980). Family self-control instruction for children's nighttime fear reduction. *Journal of Consulting and Clinical Psychology, 48*, 206–213.

Hersen, M., & Barlow, D. H. (1976). *Single-case experimental designs: Strategies for studying experimental change.* New York: Pergamon.

Hersen, M., & Bellack, A. S. (1976). *Behavioral assessment: A practical handbook.* New York: Pergamon.

Holden, G. W. (1983). Avoiding conflict: Mothers as tacticians in the supermarket. *Child Development, 54,* 233–240.

Holland, C. J. (1969). Elimination by the parents of fire-setting behavior in a 7-year-old boy. *Behavior Research and Therapy, 1,* 135–137.

Jacobson, E. (1970). *Modern treatment of tense patients.* Springfield, IL: Charles C Thomas.

Kanfer, F. H., Karoly, P., & Newman, A. (1975). Reduction of children's fear of the dark by competence-related and situational threat-related verbal clues. *Journal of Consulting and Clinical Psychology, 43,* 251–258.

Kazdin, A. E. (1982). *Single-case research designs: Methods for clinical and applied settings.* New York: Oxford University Press.

Kendrick, C., & Dunn, J. (1983). Sibling quarrels and maternal responses. *Developmental Psychology, 19,* 62–70.

Lefkowitz, M. M., & Tesiny, E. P. (1980). Assessment of childhood depression. *Journal of Consulting and Clinical Psychology, 48,* 41–50.

Lindsley, O. R. (1966). An experiment with parents handling behavior at home. *Johnstone Bulletin, 9,* 27–36. (Available from Dr. Ogden Lindsley, University of Kansas, 9 Bailey Hall, Lawrence, Kansas, 66044.)

Lovaas, D. I., Freitag, G., Gold, V. J., & Kassorla, I. C. (1965). Experimental studies in childhood schizophrenia. I. Analysis of self-destructive behavior. *Journal of Experimental Child Psychology, 2,* 67–84.

Neville, M. H., & Jenson, W. R. (1982). The inexpensive lock: Key to the television reinforcer. *Child and Family Behavior Therapy, 4,* 205–206.

Quay, H. C., & Werry, J. S. (Eds.). (1972). *Psychopathological disorders of childhood.* New York: John Wiley & Sons.

Rosen, H. S., & Rosen, L. A. (1983). Eliminating stealing: Use of stimulus control with an elementary student. *Behavior Modification, 7,* 56–63.

Tesiny, E. P., & Lefkowitz, M. M. (1982). Childhood depression: A 6-month follow-up study. *Journal of Consulting and Clinical Psychology, 50,* 778–780.

Wahler, R. G., & Fox, J. J. (1980). Solitary toy play and time out: A family treatment package for children with aggressive and oppositional behavior. *Journal of Applied Behavior Analysis, 13,* 23–39.

Chapter 5

Atkeson, B. M., & Forehand, R. (1978). Parents as behavior change agents with school-related problems. *Education and Urban Society, 10,* 521–538.

Atkeson, B. M., & Forehand, R. (1979). Home-based reinforcement programs designed to modify classroom behavior: A review and methodological evaluation. *Psychological Bulletin, 86,* 1298–1308.

Ayllon, T., & Roberts, M. D. (1974). Eliminating discipline problems by strengthening academic performance. *Journal of Applied Behavior Analysis, 7,* 71–76.

Barrish, H. H., Saunders, M., & Wolf, M. M. (1969). Good behavior game: Effects of individual contingencies for group consequences on disruptive behavior in a classroom. *Journal of Applied Behavior Analysis, 2,* 119–124.

Blechman, E. A., Kotanchik, N. L., & Taylor, C. J. (1981). Families and schools together: Early behavioral intervention with high-risk students. *Behavior Therapy, 12,* 308–319.

Blechman, E. A., Taylor, C. J., & Schrader, S. M. (1981). Family problem solving vs. home notes as early intervention with high-risk children. *Journal of Consulting and Clinical Psychology, 49,* 919–926.

Bucher, B., & Hawkins, J. (1974). Comparison of response cost and token reinforcement systems in a class for academic underachievers. In R. D. Rubin, J. P. Brady, & J. D. Henderson (Eds.), *Advances in behavior therapy* (Vol. 4, pp. 271–278). New York: Academic Press.

Cantrell, R. P., Cantrell, M. L., Huddleston, C. M., & Wooldridge, R. L. (1969). Contingency contracting with school problems. *Journal of Applied Behavior Analysis, 2,* 215–220.

Cowen, R. J., Jones, F. H., & Bellack, A. S. (1979). Grandma's Rule with group contingencies: A cost-efficient means of classroom management. *Behavior Modification, 3,* 397–418.

Dietz, S. M., & Repp, C. A. (1973). Decreasing classroom behavior through the use of DRL schedules of reinforcement. *Journal of Applied Behavior Analysis, 6,* 457–463.

Edelbrock, C., & Achenbach, T. M. (1984). The teacher version of the child behavior profile: I. Boys aged 6–11. *Journal of Consulting and Clinical Psychology, 52,* 207–217.

Foxx, R. M., & Shapiro, S. T. (1978). The timeout ribbon: a nonexclusionary timeout procedure. *Journal of Applied Behavior Analysis, 11,* 125–136.

Gambrill, E., & Richey, C. E. (1976). *It's up to you: Developing assertive social skills.* Millbrae, CA: Les Femmes/Celestial Arts.

Gesten, E. L., Flores de Apodaca, R., Rains, M., Weissberg, R. P., & Cowen, E. L. (1979). Promoting peer-related social competence in schools. In M. W. Kent & J. E. Rolf (Eds.), *The primary prevention of psychopathology: Vol. 3. Social competence in children* (pp. 230–247). Hanover, NH: University Press of New England.

Greenwood, C. R., Hops, H., Walker, H. M., Guild, J. J., Stokes, J., Young, K. R., Keleman, K. S., & Willardson, M. (1979). Standardized classroom management program: Social validation and replication studies in Utah and Oregon. *Journal of Applied Behavior Analysis, 12,* 235–253.

Hawkins, R. P., Sluyter, D. J., & Smith, C. D. (1972). Modification of achievement by a simple technique involving parents and teacher. In M. B. Harris (Ed.), *Classroom uses of behavior modification* (pp. 101–119). Columbus, OH: Charles E. Merrill.

Hay, W. M., Hay, L. R., & Nelson, R. O. (1977). Direct and collateral changes in on-task and academic behavior resulting from on-task versus academic contingencies. *Behavior Therapy, 8,* 431–441.

Hewett, F. M., Taylor, F. D., & Artuso, A. A. (1969). The Santa Monica Project: Evaluation of an engineered classroom design with emotionally disturbed children. *Exceptional Children, 35*, 523-529.

Homme, L. (1970). *How to use contingency contracting in the classroom*. Champaign, IL: Research Press.

Johnson, M. R., Turner, P. F., & Konarski, E. (1978). The "Good Behavior Game": A systematic replication in two unruly transitional classrooms. *Education and Treatment of Children, 3*, 25-33.

Jones, F. H., & Eimers, R. C. (1975). Role playing to train elementary teachers to use a classroom management "skill package." *Journal of Applied Behavior Analysis, 8*, 421-433.

Kazdin, A. E., & Geesey, S. (1980). Enhancing classroom attentiveness by preselection of back-up reinforcers in a token economy. *Behavior Modification, 4*, 98-114.

O'Leary, K. D., & Drabman, R. S. (1971). Token reinforcement programs in the classroom: A review. *Psychological Bulletin, 75*, 379-398.

Patterson, G. R. (1976). *Living with children: New methods for parents and teachers* (rev. ed.). Champaign, IL: Research Press.

Patterson, G. R., Cobb, J. A., & Ray, R. S. (1972). Direct intervention in the classroom: A set of procedures for the aggressive child. In F. W. Clark, D. R. Evans, & L. A. Hamerlynck (Eds.), *Implementing behavioral programs for school and clinics* (pp. 151-201). Champaign, IL: Research Press.

Russo, D. C., & Koegel, R. L. (1977). A method for integrating an autistic child into a normal public-school classroom. *Journal of Applied Behavior Analysis, 10*, 579-590.

Schumaker, J. B., Hovell, M. F., & Sherman, J. A. (1977). An analysis of daily report cards and parent-managed privileges in the improvement of adolescents' classroom performance. *Journal of Applied Behavior Analysis, 10*, 449-464.

Sulzer-Azaroff, B., & Mayer, G. R. (1977). *Applying behavior-analysis procedures with children and youth*. New York: Holt, Rinehart & Winston.

Trovato, J., & Bucher, B. (1980). Peer tutoring with or without home-based reinforcement for reading remediation. *Journal of Applied Behavior Analysis, 13*, 129-142.

Van Houten, R., & Van Houten, J. (1977). The performance feedback system in the special education classroom: An analysis of public posting and peer comments. *Behavior Therapy, 8*, 366-376.

About the Author

Elaine Ann Blechman received her Ph.D. in Clinical and Social Psychology from the University of California at Los Angeles in 1971. Since then she has held faculty positions at the University of Maryland, Yale University, and Wesleyan University. She is now a Professor in the Department of Psychiatry and the Director of the Behavior Therapy Program at the Albert Einstein College of Medicine/Montefiore Medical Center, Bronx, New York.

Dr. Blechman's clinical research focuses on training one- and two-parent families in communication and problem solving and on identifying and treating socially and academically high-risk children. She is particularly concerned with distinguishing characteristics of effective families and competent children.

Dr. Blechman has written numerous articles and chapters about children and families and has edited two books, *Behavior Modification with Women* and *Behavioral Medicine for Women*.